Recreation SPORT & Park Administration

Hugh Gibson

MISSOURI STATE UNIVERSITY

Kendall Hunt
publishing company

www.kendallhunt.com
Send all inquiries to:
4050 Westmark Drive
Dubuque, IA 52004-1840

Copyright © 2018 by Kendall Hunt Publishing Company

ISBN 978-1-5249-5182-5

Published in the United States of America

CONTENTS

CHAPTER 1

Perspectives on Leisure: The Profession Dedicated to Quality Living

I always wanted a career that would legitimize my interest in people and having fun. Recreation and Leisure Studies proved to be the ideal career choice for me, and along the way I have come to understand that recreation and leisure is much more about quality living than merely having fun.

—MALCOLM WILSON, DIRECTOR, PARKS AND RECREATION

Think of this book as a doorway, an entrance that leads to a series of learning experiences that are designed to help you enrich your life through increased understanding and appreciation for the role that recreation and leisure can play in your life. As you travel through the subsequent pages, you will be presented with an array of information designed to further your understanding of what we believe is an extraordinary and important field of study.[1]

We make no apologies for our choice of words. We really mean it when we say "important field." But, as you will no doubt learn, not everyone understands the value of leisure and recreation. There may even be some people who won't understand why anyone would even want to study leisure recreation or play. All of us in the field of recreation and leisure studies have had experiences that suggest that many people really don't know how important leisure is or how much value recreation has in their lives.[2]

People often take recreation and leisure for granted. This may be the result of growing up in a world where recreation and leisure experiences abound. Because of the abundance of recreational opportunities, many people come to view recreation and leisure as commonplace, something as familiar to them as eating and sleeping. These people may view leisure as nothing special, just part of one's daily routine. To those people leisure is one aspect of life that doesn't justify a university course. Other people may look at leisure and recreation as unessential or trivial. Some even look at it as harmful or sinful. A philosophical notion referred to as the *Puritan Work Ethic*[3] has influenced many people to view leisure and recreation as detrimental. However, it is important to note that many philosophers view leisure as neither trivial nor detrimental.

Philosophers Speak Out for Leisure and Recreation

Although there are some philosophers who find little value in leisure and recreation, you will find most view leisure and recreation as possessing the potential to make an important contribution to both the individual and society. You can get an idea as to how philosophers view recreation and leisure through the following quotes:

Charles K. Brightbill (1960)

Recreation has an intriguing way of accommodating both reality and fantasy by simultaneously releasing and disciplining the imagination. It may well be the only known way of running away from and toward life at the same time. It can shore up our self-respect and dignity by animating and generating an appreciation of our own abilities to accomplish. It can help us recognize that inward satisfactions precede outward delights. While it may help us through the years, it does not neglect the past: it recaptures life, as a child knows it. Its focus is more upon living now than upon hoping to exist tomorrow. The proper use of leisure can help tighten spiritual bonds, encourage higher codes of ethics and morals, help heal and rehabilitate the ill and the handicapped, and even add to our material wealth. But these are intentions it sets and victories it claims not primarily for itself. The only threshold upon which the need for it in its best sense has ever soundly stood is the chance for everyone to live a decent, wholesome, satisfying, and creative kind of existence.[4]

Ida Craven (1933)

Leisure is not only the germinating time of art and philosophy, the time in which the seer attains glimpses of the values and the realities behind ordinary appearance; it is also the opportunity for appreciation, the time in which such values get across into common experience. The quality of a civilization depends upon the effectiveness of the transmission of such values.[5]

Robert Pirsig (1975)

The gumption-filling process occurs when one is quiet long enough to see and hear and feel the real universe, not just one's own stale opinions about it. But it's nothing exotic. That's why I like the word. You see it often in people who return from long, quiet fishing trips. Often they're a little defensive about having put so much time to 'no account' because there's no intellectual justification for what they've been doing. But the returned fisherman usually has a peculiar abundance of gumption, usually for the very same things he was sick to death of a few weeks before. He hasn't been wasting time. It's only our limited cultural viewpoint that makes it seem so."[6]

Witold Rybczynski (1991)

All this has called into question the traditional relationship between leisure and work, a relationship about which our culture has always been ambivalent. Generally speaking, there are two opposing schools of thought. On the one hand there is the ideal, held by thinkers as disparate as Karl Marx and the Catholic philosopher Josef Pieper, of a society increasingly emancipated from labor. This noting echoes the Aristotelian view that the goal of life is happiness, and that leisure, as distinguished from amusement and recreation, is the state necessary for its achievement. 'It's commonly believed that happiness depends on leisure,' Aristotle wrote in his Ethics, 'because we occupy ourselves so that we may have leisure, just as we make war in order that we may live at peace.' Or, to put it more succinctly, as did the title of Lover Boy's 1982 hit song, we are 'Working for the Weekend.[7]

J. B. Nash (1953)

Leisure provides time for many uses; to rest and relax, to daydream, to dabble with useless knowledge, to hear good music or read a book, to listen and look at the best of our many mass communication programs—the printed page, the radio, the television, and the motion pictures. Above all else, leisure time should be an opportunity of men—all men—to make some creative contribution to themselves and their group, else one be judged not to have lived in his day.

Recreation, the wholesome use of leisure, must therefore, be thought of in terms of satisfying a human need. It becomes an outlet for inner urges and drives. How men and women will use it becomes the important question. More and more in the future, civilizations will be known by the quality of recreation they choose for their leisure-time activities.[8]

C. Gilbert Wrenn and D. L. Harley (1941)

The case for encouraging and assisting the individual to develop creative and cultural leisure-time interests need not be left to rest simply on the pleasure these produce or even on the obvious value to society of having its citizens happy and contented. Human beings, whatever we may sometimes think of their actions, are the highest form of life of which we have direct knowledge. To develop their personalities, enrich their lives, and in any way to help them realize the full extent of what they are capable of being and doing must be considered one of the most commendable uses to which human endeavor can be put. This recreation can accomplish.

In our leisure time we may enter a new world, a world from which the hindrances and limitations that ordinarily surround us have largely vanished, a world in which our individuality expands and in which we feel freer and easier. Of course we must inevitably come back to our ordinary routine existence, but to be out of it for a while, to feel ourselves something like the free agents that human beings were intended to be, is an experience worth having. We have caught a glimpse of the dimly seen pattern of ideal human existence. Whether we consider that pattern divinely established or primarily of aesthetic value, or interpret it in some other way, we can probably agree that any effort which brings us closer to it is worth making.[9]

A. W. Zelmek (1959)

Concern with our use of leisure is not just awakening, although certainly it is getting more of the attention it deserves. Almost twenty-five years ago William Butterworth, formerly president of the United States Chamber of Commerce, wrote that it should be of general concern that the new spare time be used advantageously and that it should not be a cause for deterioration of workmanship or citizenship. I do not mean to imply that recreation is in any way wasteful. On the contrary, satisfying recreation is essential to individual and community health. But when a leisure activity is undertaken simply because there is nothing else to do or because every one else is doing it, then we had better take time to consider just where the new emphasis on leisure is taking us if we can regard free time as a raw material, we will come to think more in terms of its constructive use.[10]

You can see from the foregoing quotations that leisure and recreation can be viewed as having significant value to both the individual and society. Nevertheless, some people might criticize the sentiments presented above as the product of conjecture or idealistic thinking. What some people want is data, hard-evidence, to support the claims made by the recreation and leisure service profession. Fortunately, within recent years, science has produced numerous studies that lend credibility to the thinking of leisure philosophers. Many of these scientific studies clearly demonstrate the value of recreation, leisure, and play. What follows is just a sample of such scientific findings, but it does serve to give you a sense as to what science is learning about leisure and its concomitants, play and recreation.

What Science Tells Us about Recreation

It has just been within recent years that science has addressed questions pertaining to recreation and leisure. Fields such as sociology, psychology, government, economics and leisure studies have all made important contributions to our understanding of recreation and leisure. Insight into what science is discovering about the importance of recreation and leisure, and how recreation and leisure relate to other areas of human concern is developing and growing daily. We have summarized, in the following section, several studies, both historical and contemporary, that illustrate what science is learning about this important field.[11]

Recreation Helps with Marriage

Smith, Snyder, Trull and Monsma showed a strong correlation between leisure functioning and marital satisfaction.[12] People who enjoy an active recreation and leisure lifestyle seem to have happier marriages than those people who don't have satisfying leisure.

Recreation Helps with Physical Health

Roberts, Lamb, Dench and Brodie showed a direct relationship between physical health and leisure involvement (1989). People who participate in physical recreation experience a number of health benefits including enhanced immune systems, low body fat, and cardiovascular health. Other studies support this finding, including an important study done by Lemaitre and associates (1999) the results of which suggest that regular participation in moderate-intensity activities, such as walking and gardening, are associated with a reduced risk of cardiovascular disease.[13]

Recreation Can Help with Job Search Skills

Bradley demonstrated that leisure skills correlate with job search skills (1989). Presumably, people who function well in leisure also have the intelligence and social abilities to develop the skills requisite to success in the pursuit of employment.

Recreation Helps People Age Successfully

DeCarlo, in a pioneering study, showed that recreational involvement was a good predictor of aging with minimum inconvenience (1975). Successful aging is correlated with not only physical recreation, but also recreation that is intellectually stimulating. As for longevity, intellectually stimulating recreation may be just as important as physical activity. That physical activity is essential to longevity and good health in later is life is shown by Suzanne G. Leveille and her colleagues (1999) in a study that showed that living an active life without a major disability may be a function of physical activity. In this study it was shown that physically active older people were twice as likely to die without prior disability than sedentary people.[14]

Recreation Contributes to Growth and Development in Children

A number of fairly early studies demonstrated that play can contribute to learning in children (Lee, 1971; Burner, J., 1974; Feitlson and Ross, 1973; Ellis, l973). Play is common to all mammals, and is essential for successful growth and development. Children deprived of normal play can experience social, mental, emotional, and social retardation. That play has a role in education is suggested by the work of Olga Jarret (1999) whose research illustrates that play can improve learning in science and math courses.[15]

Recreation Contributes to Psychological Adjustment

Iso-Ahola, following an extensive review of leisure, concluded that leisure involvement is significantly related to psychological adjustment (1980). The term psychological adjustment relates to having a sense of balance in one's life. Leisure involvement seems essential for a balanced lifestyle.

Recreation Is Life Enhancing

Tinsley and Howard found that leisure tended to meet a person's need for life enrichment through enhancing such variables as self-actualization, companionship, power, compensation, security, social service, tension, and enhance concentration.

Recreation May Help Prevent Depression

Leisure involvement may help prevent depression. In a study of the leisure patterns of senior citizens and measures of affect, it was found that among men, low physical leisure activity was related to a probability of depression. Among women depression was linked to low levels of leisure satisfaction.[16]

Recreation Has Therapeutic Value

Leisure has therapeutic value. There are a number of studies that demonstrate the healing and therapeutic value of leisure and recreation among special populations. For example, Mactavish and Schlein discuss leisure as a beneficial catalyst for skill, interest, and self development, but potentially the most accepting and enduring social and recreation outlet for children with a developmental disability.[17]

Outdoor Recreation Promotes Important Values

Outdoor recreation offers special opportunities for people. Ulrich and Addoms[18] found that a residential park provided the following values to users: aesthetic value, environmental contact value, and social experiences.

Recreation Has a Spiritual Component

Leisure, particularly outdoor recreation, may provoke a spiritual experience.[19] When faced with wonders of nature, people often find themselves contemplating metaphysical questions of existence and purpose as well as reflecting on the nature of beauty. An awareness of a divine purpose often occurs during such moments.

This is just a sample of what science is discovering about recreation, leisure, and play. Your own experiences will no doubt support some of these findings.

TRY THIS

Take a few moments and reflect on the value that you find in recreation, leisure, or play. In your own experience, what are the benefits you experience through personal leisure or participation in organized recreation?

Throughout this book, you will note a tone of advocacy. We believe that play, recreation, and leisure makes an important contribution to the quality of one's life. In addition to being familiar with some of the research findings focusing on the value of leisure, we know from personal experience about the value of leisure in our own lives and the effect it has had on our continued growth and development. In addition, over the years, we have heard the testimony of countless students who, following their study of leisure, have told us about remarkable changes that occurred in their lives as a result of having learned to appreciate leisure more fully and apply it more effectively. As a recent student put it, "Leisure works!"

Contributions to the Economy

Recreation and leisure activities have a tremendous impact on the economy. When you consider the amount of money people spend on direct recreation and leisure services and products as well as indirect services and products, you find another reason for viewing recreation and leisure as an important field.

TRY THIS

Before reading on, take a moment and consider how much money you spend on direct and indirect recreational services and products. Take into account the cost of driving to recreational activities, clothing for such activities, incidental costs like snacks, etc. Are you surprised at how much you spend?

In the above chart, Dr. Ruth Russell gives us an indication as to the extent to which Americans invest in recreation and leisure products and experiences. Although this chart is based on figures dating back to the 1990s, it does suggest the scope of American spending on recreation and leisure.

It is difficult to get an accurate estimate of just how much money people spend on leisure and recreation. For example, do you count the cost of driving to a concert under "recreation and entertainment" or under "transportation"? What about food purchased while attending a concert? What about clothing purchased just for a concert?

What Americans Spend on Recreation in an Average Day:

$149,360	buying Spider-man Comics
$212,325	on basketballs
$973,150	on golf balls
$1,247,280	on fishing licenses
$1,780,825	for admission to Disney World and EPCOT
$13,698,630	on health-club membership fees
$17,561,644	supporting arts charities
$18,904,110	on video rentals
$33,561,644	buying lottery tickets
$272,876,712	buying products by mail order
$434,246,575	on toys
$1,600,000,000	in shopping malls[20]

The U.S. Bureau of Economic Analysis provides an accounting of personal consumption expenditures in the U.S. Recreation is listed as one category, but as you can imagine, many of the items purchased under other categories may be related to recreational activities or involvement.[21]

In the chart that follows on the next page, you see an overview of recreation related expenditures (stated as billions of dollars) in the U.S. during the years from 1991 to 1997.[22] This chart gives only a small picture of the overall spending pattern in the U.S. For a look at a comprehensive accounting of all personal expenditures for this time period, visit the appendix.

For more on economic indicators visit:
http:// almanac.webdata.com

The kind of contribution a local parks and recreation agency can make to a local economy is illustrated by the county recreation and parks department of Monterey, California. There, the county is a major provider of visitor-serving facilities and programs, and as such it plays an important role in the local tourism economy.[23] During fiscal year 1994 the economic activity generated by the Parks Department's programs and all of the lessees, concessionaires, and nonprofit corporations associated with county parks and

	1991	1992	1993[R]	1994[R]	1995[R]	1996[R]	1997
Recreation	292	310.8	340.2	370.2	402.5	432.3	462.9
Books, maps	16.9	17.7	19	20.6	22.1	24.2	25.2
Magazines, newspapers, sheet music	21.9	21.6	22.7	24.5	25.5	27.6	29.1
Nondurable toys and sport supplies	32.8	34.2	36.6	39.7	42.2	45.1	47.8
Wheel goods, sports and photographic equipment, boats, pleasure aircraft	29.5	29.9	32.6	35.6	39.1	42.3	48.1
Video and audio products, computers, musical instruments	57.3	61.2	68.1	78.5	85.2	92	96.5
Flowers, seeds, potted plants	11.3	12.3	12.7	13.4	13.9	14.8	15.9
Admissions to specified spectator amusements	15.7	16.6	18.1	19	20.2	21.9	23.3
Motion picture theaters	5.3	5	5.2	5.6	6	6.2	6.6
Legitimate theater, opera	6	6.8	7.8	8.2	8.7	9.3	10
Spectator sports	4.5	4.8	5.1	5.2	5.5	6.4	6.7
Clubs, fraternal organizations	9.6	10.3	11.2	11.8	12.7	13	13.8
Commercial participant amusements	23.8	27.2	31.5	36.2	41.5	44.7	49.1

recreation contributed $148,413,407 to the local economy. These same programs provided 291 jobs to local residents as well as generating $3,019,568 in sales taxes and $839,850 in transient occupancy taxes. In total, over $150 million was generated by the recreation.[24] Dr. Russell highlights the economic value of recreation and leisure in the following manner:

Our pastimes have tremendous economic significance, especially in the capitalist economies of services. It is common for people to spend more money on leisure than on any other single category, including housing, food, clothing, health care or education.[25] Every indication also suggests that leisure has become the primary economic base for many cities.[26] The competition for conventions, tourism, shopping, sports, entertainment, festivals and celebrations, and fine arts have become major tools for urban renewal projects. Promoting leisure makes good economic sense; the return is always greater than the outlay.

For example, the presence of leisure facilities and programs attracts businesses and industries to particular locales. These cultural and sport events have public relation value for the corporations that support them . . . They enhance the company's image and ultimately increase profits. Well-planned leisure services can also help reduce the costs of vandalism and crime, particularly in urban areas . . . In the United States, total annual expenditures for leisure pastimes are said to be higher than $259 billion or an average of about $1,000 per year for every man, woman, and child (U.S. Bureau of Economic Analysis 1991). According to many, however, this estimate is very conservative.[27]

Recreation, leisure, and play make an important contribution to both the individual and society. Through recreation, leisure, and play people are offered an opportunity to grow and develop, enjoy life more fully and live healthier lives. In addition the money generated through recreation and leisure makes an important contribution to the economy. Just as we said at the beginning, recreation and leisure studies is an important field.

More about This Book

In writing this book, we have had several goals in mind.

1. **We want to keep you interested.** Consequently, we have kept the narrative to a minimum, focused on the important points and moved quickly on. In our surveys of student readers a frequent complaint was "wordiness." We have made an effort to get to the point.

2. **We want to provide access to supportive materials.** You will note in the boxes and in the footnotes that there are frequent references to web sites. These sites contain information that complements the concepts found in the text. We encourage you use them.

3. **We want to motivate you to think about the topics presented.** Throughout the text you will find "boxed thoughts." These are either comments or questions that are designed to provoke critical thinking regarding the subject matter being treated. We view this book as not so much a definitive work, but rather a collection of ideas that might serve as a point of departure for further independent exploration as well as exciting dialogue and discussion.

4. **We want the book to be a resource.** The book contains a great deal of information. It is broad in scope and comprehensive in treatment. Although it is not intended to be a definitive work, we hope it proves a useful resource to the student interested in leisure, recreation, and play.

5. **We want the book to be an enjoyable and fun read.** There is no reason why learning can't be fun, indeed, real learning is self-rewarding. In fact, some might call real learning "leisure." Just look at the excitement a child experiences when s/he gains a new skill. Further, we have written this book in a conversational tone, made an effort to be clear and concise and tried to include as much humor as seemed appropriate. Some of the chapters are written in first person, some might seem a little more formal, but all of them are designed to be "reader friendly."

6. **We want the book to serve as a workbook.** At the back of the book you will find exercises suitable for homework and self-study. For convenience, these sheets are designed to permit easy removal.

NOTES

1. The internet has a wealth of information relating to this field. We will suggest some links as we go along.

2. Everyone seems to think they are experts in leisure, even if their only direct experience with leisure comes in the form of their refrigerators and televisions. And, of course, this limited scope of experience will be reflected in their preconceptions and stereotypical notions of leisure and the field of leisure studies.

3. The Puritan Work Ethic or Protestant Work Ethic, as it is sometimes called, was a philosophical belief that viewed work as inherently good and leisure as potentially sinful (the work of the devil).

4. Brightbill, Charles K. *The Challenge of Leisure.* (Englewood Cliffs, N.J.: Prentice-Hall, Inc. 1960) 12.

5. Craven, Ida. "Leisure," *Encyclopedia of the Social Sciences.* (New York: The Macmillan Company, 1933).

6. Pirsig, Robert M. *Zen and the Art of Motorcycle Maintenance.* (New York: A Bantam Book. 1975): 279.

7. Rybczynski, Witold. *Waiting for the Weekend.* (New York: Penguin Books, 1991): 86.

8. Nash, Jay B. *Philosophy of Recreation and Leisure.* (St. Louis: C. V. Mosby Co., 1953): 125.

9. Wrenn, C. Gilbert and D. L. Harley. *Time on Their Hands.* (Washington, D.C.: America Council on Education, 1941): xix.

10. Zelmek, A. W. *A Changing America: at Work and Play.* (New York: John Wiley & Sons, Inc., 1959): 103–104.

11. Want to know more about the science of recreation? Visit http://www.NRDAnet.com

12. Smith, G. T., Douglas K., Synder, T. J. Trull, and B. R. Monsma. "Predicting Relationship Satisfaction from Couples' Use of Leisure Time." (*American Journal of Family Therapy 16.1. 1988*): 1–13

13. Lemaitre, David S. et al. Leisure-"Time Physical Activity and the Risk of Primary Cardiac Arrest," *Archives of Internal Medicine* 159.7 (1999): 686.

14. Leveille, Suzanna *et al.* "Aging Successfully Until Death in Old Age: Opportunities for Increasing Active Life Expectancy," *American Journal of Epidemiology* 149.7 (1999): 654.

15. Jarret, Olga. "Playfulness: A Motivator in Math and Science Teacher Preparation," *School Science and Mathematics* 98.4 (1998): 181.

16. Lomraz, J., S. Bergman, E. Simon, and N. & S. Dov. "Indoor and Outdoor Activities of Aged Women and Men as Related to Depression and Well-Being." *International Journal of Aging and Human Development* 26.4 (1988): 303–314.

17. Mactavish, Jennifer B. and Stuart J. Schlein, "Playing together growing together: Parents' perspectives on the benefits of family recreation in families that include children with a developmental disability." *Therapeutic Recreation Journal*, 32.3 (1998): 207–230.

18. Ulrich, Roger S., and David L. "Psychological and Recreational Benefits of a Residential Park." *Journal of Leisure Research* 13 (1981): 43–65.

19. McDonald, Barbara L., and Richard Schreyer. AFFILIATION: National Oceanic & Atmospheric Administration, Strategic Assessment Branch, Forestry Sciences Lab, Athens, GA, "Spiritual benefits of leisure participation and leisure settings." 1991 p. 179–94, IN: Driver, B. L.

20. Russell, Ruth V. *Pastimes: The Context of Contemporary Leisure.* (Chicago: Brown & Benchmark, 1996) 304.

21. "The World Almanac and Book of Facts Year: 1998." http://firstsearch (4 Oct. 1999).

22. "Selected Personal Consumption Expenditures in the U.S., 1991–97." *Bureau of Economic Analysis, U.S. Dept. of Commerce:* almanac.webdata.com/ economics/ economic58.htm (April 10, 2001).

23. For more examples of recreation department's impact on local economy, visit the Internet.

24. Soderberg, Pete. "The Wheel of Service-Parks and the Public: A Powerful Partnership." Monterey County Parks Department, Monterey County, California, 1994.

25. Chubb, M., and H. R. Chubb. *One Third of Our Time? An Introduction to Recreation Behavior and Resources.* (New York: John Wiley & Sons, Inc., 1981).

26. Godbey, G. *The Future of Leisure Services: Thriving on Change.* (State College, PA: Venture, 1989).

27. Russell, Ruth V. *Pastimes: The Context of Contemporary Leisure.* (Chicago: Brown &Benchmark, 1996)

REFERENCES

Brightbill, Charles K. *The Challenge of Leisure.* Englewood Cliffs, N.J.: Prentice-Hall, Inc., 1960.

Chubb, M. and H. R. Chubb. *"One Third of Our Time?"* An Introduction to Recreation Behavior and Resources. New York: John Wiley & Sons, Inc., 1981.

Craven, Ida. "Leisure." Encyclopedia of the Social Sciences. New York: The Macmillan Company, 1933.

DeCarlo, T. J. "Recreation Patterns and Successful Aging." *Gerontology.* No. 29, 1974, pp. 416–422. 1975.

D'Antonio, I. J. "The Use of Humor with Children in Hospital Settings. *"Journal of Children in Contemporary Society."* 1988, Vol 20(1–2): 157–169.

Ellis, G. D. and P. A. Witt. *The Leisure Diagnostic Battery: Background, Conceptualization, and Structure.* Division of Recreation and Leisure Studies, North Texas State University, Denton, 1982.

Ellis, M. J. *Why People Play.* Englewood Cliffs, New Jersey: Prentice-Hall, 1973.

Feitelson, D. and G. S. Ross, "The Neglected Factor." *Play and Human Development.* 1973, 16, 202–223.

Glazier, S. *Word Menu.* New York: Random House, 1994.

Godbey, G. *The Future of Leisure Services: Thriving on Change.* State College, PA: Venture, 1989.

Iso-Ahola, Seppo. *The Social Psychology of Leisure and Recreation.* Dubuque, Iowa: Wm. C. Brown, 1980.

Krain, M. A. "Policy Implications for Aging Well: Employment, Retirement, Education, and Leisure Policies for the 21st Century." *American Behavioral Scientist.* 1995, Nov–Dec Vol 39(2): 131–151.

Lomraz, J., S. Bergman, E. Simon, and N. & S. Dov. "Indoor and Outdoor Activities of Aged Women and Men as Related to Depression and Well-Being." *International Journal of Aging and Human Development.* 26.4, 1988.

McDonald, Barbara L. and Schreyer, Richard. "Spiritual Benefits of Leisure Participation and Leisure Settings." pp. 179–194, in Driver, B. L. (Ed); Brown, Perry J. (Ed); et al; *Benefits of Leisure.* State College, PA: Venture Publishing, Inc, 1991.

Nash, Jay B. *Philosophy of Recreation and Leisure.* St. Louis: C. V. Mosby Co., 1953.

Pirsig, Robert M. *Zen and the Art of Motorcycle Maintenance.* New York: A Bantam Book. 1975.

Russell, Ruth V. *Pastimes: The Context of Contemporary Leisure.* Chicago: Brown & Benchmark, 1996.

Rybczynski, Witold. *Waiting for the Weekend.* New York: Penguin Books, 1991.

Smith, G. T., Douglas K., Snyder, T. J. Trull, and B. R. Monsma. "Predicting Relationship Satisfaction from Couples' Use of Leisure Time." *American Journal of Family Therapy.* 16.1. 1988.

Ulrich, Roger S., David L., Addoms. Psychological and Recreational Benefits of a Residential Park. *Journal of Leisure Research.* v13 n1 pp. 43–65 1981.

Wrenn, C. Gilbert and D. L. Harley. *Time on Their Hands.* Washington, D.C.: American Council on Education, 1941.

Zelmek, A. W. *A Changing America: At Work and Play.* New York: John Wiley & Sons, Inc., 1959.

Leisure Definition and Theories: What We Believe and Why We Do It

CHAPTER 2

Definition of Leisure

Leisure could be defined as activities, behaviors, and experiences that people engage in voluntarily for internal or self-reward (Peterson & Stumbo, 2000). Leisure behavior is used to explain a variety of human experiences that are voluntary in nature, allow free choice and intrinsic motivation, and are meaningful and pleasurable to the participants involved. The benefits of leisure identified by Bammel and Burrus-Bammel (1996) are the following areas: physiological, social, relaxation, educational, psychological, and aesthetic. Other benefits include but are not limited to learning, peace, stress release, freedom, fellowship, and family time (Edginton, Hanson, Edginton, & Hudson, 1998). Leisure is viewed in many different ways as being beneficial to an individual's development. Leisure could be seen as a time to "re-create" oneself, mentally, physically, emotionally, and spiritually. It is a time to grow personally and socially. Recreational activities assist in the formation and development of a person's perceived identity. Leisure often serves as a buffer to the stressors of life and allows time to collect the resources needed to cope with our problems. A change must not always occur in a person to count as a benefit of leisure. Maintaining the homeostasis of one's life is often the desired outcome of leisure. The most basic concept of leisure may be that it is fun and makes us feel "good" about ourselves. Godbey (1994) best described the importance of leisure this way,

During the journey from birth to death, the activities which we find pleasurable, what we do voluntarily and economic and social constraints on our free time, *health, and work roles are in a state of change, and these changes affect our . . . behaviors (p. 171).*

Leisure and recreation are critical components of a healthy person's growth and development.

What We Know about Leisure

The beginnings of leisure can be traced back to each of the great ancient civilizations such as The Greeks, Egyptians, Romans, Aztecs, Sumerians, Persians, and so on (Edginton, Jordan, DeGraaf, & Edginton, 2002). The dimension of leisure experiences has been greatly hypothesized by a variety of theorists and researchers. A vast amount of characteristics has been attributed to leisure experiences. The following definitions will give us a vast array of key components.

Pieper viewed leisure through psychological perspective (1963). Pieper viewed the process of leisure as a mental and spiritual way of believing; not just the result of external factors or free time. Kaplan (1974) attempted to further this social psychological concept with the following definition of leisure:

leisure is not an activity, but a construct of elements which are emphasized with roles that are pertinent to the individual rather than to economic, political, educational, religious, or marital life. These elements may, in modified form, be found in other institutions as well. Leisure, then, can be said to consist of relatively self-determined activities and experiences that fall one' economically free-time roles, that are seen as leisure by the participants, that are psychologically pleasant in anticipation and recollection, that potentially cover the whole range of commitment and intensely, that contain characteristic norms and restraints, and provide opportunities for recreation, personal growth and service to others (p. 232).

Mannell (1980) went on to define leisure as a psychological state of mind that may be easily interrupted. Mannell's research found that participants experienced positive affect, a decreased awareness of time and physical environment. He used an experimental setting to discover that these three dimensions of leisure (positive affect, a decreased awareness of time, and physical environment) were experienced diversely by the participants according to experimental conditions.

de Grazia's (1962) definition of leisure refers to it being a personal state of mind. He raised the question about the manner in which the term leisure is perceived. de Grazia believed the whole concept of leisure was changed when researchers started evaluating leisure in the amount of a person's free time. He felt that free time could be more easily measured than leisure, but had changed the qualitative qualities of leisure to a quantitative concept of free time.

Kleiber (1999) used a social psychological approach to view a leisure experience. He incorporated the nurture information of Erikson and Piaget with the nature beliefs of the definitions of leisure to view leisure as being affected by biology with what people are born with as well as the taking into account their socialization process and development.

Gunter's (1987) research with self-reported essays established a variety of leisure dimensions. The eight most identified aspects of a leisure experience are the following: "a sense of separation from the everyday world, freedom of choice in one's actions, a feeling of pleasure or pleasurable involvement in the event, spontaneity, timelessness, fantasy, a sense of adventure and exploration, and self-relaxation" (p. 119).

Shaw (1984, 1985) examined the essential dimensions of leisure through the use of time diaries. In these diaries, the participants categorized activities as leisure, work, mixed work and leisure, or neither work nor leisure. Shaw also conducted interviews to further examine and explain certain events from the diaries. The dimensions associated with her research were the following: "enjoyment, freedom of choice, relaxation, motivation and the lack of evaluation."

Tinsley and Tinsley (1986) also used a psychological lens in which to view leisure. They believed that there are two different components of a leisure experience: an evaluative aspect and potency aspect. The evaluative aspect refers to the qualitative evaluation of leisure and the value an individual may assign to that experience. The potency aspect of a leisure experience refers to the quantitative elements of a leisure experience. They viewed leisure experiences as having cognitive and affective attributes. Some of the dimensions of leisure identified included absorption in the experience, loss of self, feeling free, heightened perceptions, more emotion, increased physical sensitivity, and loss of time.

Sullivan (1990), in her work and leisure research, categorized many dimensions of a leisure experience. She found there were six critical aspects that made leisure essentially different than work. Those dimensions are the following: focus, evaluation by others, creativity, distractibility, choice, and intrinsic motivation or positive affect.

Kaplan (1974) noted his own seven essential dimensions of a leisure experience. Leisure must be different than work. The experience must be pleasant or be viewed as pleasant in its recollection. Leisure experiences tend to have elements of a social role within it. A perception of freedom must exist in a leisure activity. Leisure experiences tend to have a level of importance and be close to the participants' values. Play is also viewed as an essential dimension of a leisure experience.

Huizinga (1955) viewed play as directly related to leisure. The characteristics of play he identified were as follows: fun, opposite of serious, voluntary, stepping out of the usual, elements of tension, limited in time and place, awareness of pretending.

Dumazedier's (1974) concept of leisure "allows for recovery from daily stresses and strains, freedom from daily boredom or entertainment, and escape from routine and stereotypes." He stated that there are characteristics or properties of leisure. They are as following: liberating (freedom), disinterested (intrinsic motivation), hedonistic (pleasure), and personal (self-actualization).

Hood (1992) identified nine dimensions of leisure in her study of family functioning. The nine dimensions she examined are the following: intrinsic motivation, pleasure or enjoyment during the experience, focus on the activity and reduced distractibility, loss of self, a sense of timeless when evolved in the experience, absence of others evaluating or other constraints, creativity, sense of control over one's actions in the experience, choice or perceived freedom in selection of continuation of a leisure experience.

Furthermore, most of the benefits for leisure which have been identified have been for individuals during the use of leisure. The following is a short list of examples of the benefits of leisure: psychophysiological, personal and social, spiritual, relaxation, relational, educational, psychological, personal learning, peace, stress release, freedom, fellowship, communication, cohesion, and family time (Bammel & Burrus-Bammel, 1996; Csikszentmilhalyi & Kleiber, 1991; Edginton et al., 1998; Orthner & Mancini, 1990; Ulrich, Dimberg, & Driver, 1991; Wankel & Berger, 1991). The mere definition of leisure is individualistic in nature.

There are three constant reoccurring themes when discussing leisure; they are perceived freedom, intrinsic motivation, and pleasure. As noted above, many leisure theorists have incorporated these three basic dimensions of leisure, while most of the other theorists may use only one or two of the dimensions. A comprehensive understanding of the theorized dimensions will help explain the phenomenon of a leisure experience; it is helpful to identify the key components of recreation and play to better explain leisure as well.

The following definitions led the following key critical elements being identified by Gibson in 2005 for Leisure, Recreation, and Play.

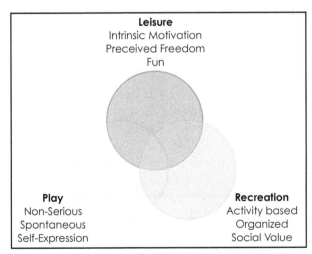

Leisure, Recreation, and Play
Source: Hugh Gibson

There are a number of positive outcomes of leisure participation. Leisure could be seen as a time to re-create oneself mentally, physically, emotionally, and spiritually. It is a time to grow personally and socially. Leisure activities assist in the formation and development of a person's perceived identity. Leisure often serves as a buffer to the stressors of life and allows time to collect the resources needed to cope with our problems. A change need not always occur in a person to count as a benefit of leisure. Maintaining the homeostasis of one's life is often the desired outcome of leisure. Leisure and recreation could be considered critical components of a healthy person's growth and development (Kleiber, 1999).

Leisure behavior is used to explain a variety of human experiences that are voluntary in nature, allow free choice and intrinsic motivation, and are meaningful and pleasurable to the participants involved. The three most important aspects of leisure are generally categorized as perceived freedom, intrinsic motivation, and pleasure. First, a necessary characteristic of leisure experiences is the perception the person is choosing this experience for himself or herself freely. This perception of choice allows the person to fully engage in the leisure experience. Second, the main reward for this experience must come from within the person or people engaging in the experience. Finally, the participant engaging in the leisure activity must view the leisure experience as enjoyable. The leisure experience may not be viewed as pleasurable at the time of the event, but may be looked back upon fondly. The person involved in the leisure subjectively assigns the concept of pleasure for the leisure experience. The order is irrelevant as long as all three components are present.

The main components for recreation are activity based, organized, and social value. Most of what recreation and leisure professionals program for in their professional career would fall under this category. As a profession, we aspire to have leisure occur but as a practical issue we program and determine success in the recreation area. Activity based are all the programs in which we can *do* something. That *doing* something has become a main part of who we are as a profession. The organized portion of recreation becomes critical because the activity starts to have rules and regulations that are accepted by all involved. The third critical area is social value. Social value in recreation is interesting because it will change from one subculture to another. As a recreation professional we must observe what participants value, not dictate our values to them. What is valued in one part of the country may be totally unacceptable in another part of the country as a recreational activity. We are the providers of those activities, not the ones who should judge whether activities are acceptable or not. Recreation should be done for the participants' consumption not our own.

Play is the most devalued out of all three components. It goes back hundreds of years to the Puritan work ethic, when play was viewed as detrimental to the existence of society. Play to this day is most often associated with children or childlike behavior. However, play is vital to understanding leisure and recreation. The critical components of non-serious, spontaneous, and self-expression are essential to human development. It is during the non-serious times of play when we are children that we learn the majority of what society says we need to learn to be decent human beings. The non-serious play of a child teaches him/her how to interact with their environment for the rest of their lives. It is also during this time that spontaneous thought, change, and responses are rewarded as a whole. Spontaneity is seen as positive because we are being creative, while in a few short years this trait will be viewed as a negative trait and seen as indecisive by most. Which brings us to the last critical element for play, self-expression. Self-expression is especially very prominent in children. It allows them to try out different elements of their personalities before they are fully developed. Self-expression allows people to find him/herself during play. Self-expression in play would be strongly related to creativity.

Theories to Explain Leisure

Maslow

The motivation for participating in leisure has been researched from many different views. Maslow's Hierarchy of Needs identified five major types in the following ascending order: physiological, safety, love, esteem, and self-actualization. Motivation is considered to be an important aspect of leisure. Motivation in leisure has been categorized into two main areas: intrinsic and extrinsic. Intrinsic motivations are behaviors in which people participate for no apparent external reward. Extrinsic motivation is when one participates in an activity for rewards outside themselves (Kleiber, 1999). Maslow's Hierarchy of Needs is also an established theory used often by leisure and recreation professionals. It is

based on a pyramid of human needs. At the bottom of the needs is physiological needs. If they do not have their basic needs of food, water, shelter, and air met it is impossible for them to think about recreation or leisure. The next level of basic human need is safety. That would be physical, psychological, and emotional safety. Once again interest in recreation and leisure is not really going to exist if one is concerned about one or more element of their safety. The next level is belonging. This level is a huge component of recreation and leisure services. Being part of a community and/or a teammate is an essential part of what we do in recreation. Most of our recreation programs are built on the notion that an individual is becoming part of something bigger than themselves, which belong to others is a basic human need. The next level is self-esteem. For many in our society their self-esteem is something that we have talked about for decades, especially for the millennial generation. Self-esteem is basically how one feels about themself. In the past how people felt about themselves was an issue; however, for millennials, this is not a problem. What we should be focusing on is the last and highest level: self-actualization. Self-actualization is being the best person you can be, which is different than how you feel about yourself. Many people feel good about themselves even though they may not be reaching their own full potential.

Flow Theory

Csikszentmihalyi (1975) developed the concept of *flow* which is the complete involvement of the actor within their activity. The characteristics of flow consists of the following: merging of action and awareness, centering the attention on the stimulus, loss of self-consciousness, coherent unambiguous feedback, feelings of control, momentary loss of anxiety and constraint, and enjoyment. The concept of flow has been well accepted by leisure professionals and researchers. Flow has been embraced as sharing many of the same dimensions as leisure. Flow Theory by Dr. Csikszentmihalyi has been used by the field of recreation and leisure studies to explain leisure. It comes from psychology and he actually did his initial research with pianists, brain surgeons, and rock climbers. Often in sports flow is called being in the "zone." It is viewed as a transient psychological state where people get into and out of it very easily. One really cannot tell they are in it, but once they realize they are they can pop right out of it. Many view this as very comparable to a leisure moment.

Maslow's Hierarchy of Needs
© Pyty/Shutterstock.com

Flow Theory
© Kendall Hunt Publishing Company

EXCHANGE THEORY

Exchange Theory is built on the premises that people are constantly reconfiguring or renegotiating their relationship and place with life. Exchange Theory believes that all people search for gratification for their behaviors or activities and do so with the hope of the cost to them being very minimal. Each individual seeks to maximize their rewards and minimalize their costs. When seeking leisure, they will participate in things that give the greatest reward and smallest cost. However, since leisure is defined by the individual these rewards and cost may all be internal. Exchange Theory believes that this process is a continual process of ebbs and flows, the same should be true for leisure (Orthner & Mancini, 1990). Therefore, as long as a person is getting rewards from a certain leisure activity they will continue to participate in that leisure activity. They can also bank up these rewards from doing them over a number of years or a lifetime. So, they could have a large number of rewards in the bank. But as soon as the costs outweigh the rewards a person will quit that activity.

COMPENSATORY THEORY

Compensatory Theory is seen as free time to balance out the agony we go through while earning a living. It is based on the concept that we are compensating for what we don't have in life. Therefore, if you are working outdoors you will recreate indoors to make up for the type of work you have to do. If you travel a lot with work, you will stay around the house during your leisure time. An individual will look for the opposite of the type of activities or mental and physical requirements in their work day in their leisure pursuits to reach homeostasis.

Spillover Theory

Spillover Theory suggests your work and leisure parallels each other. If one works as a computer programmer this theory suggests that their leisure interests will involve computers as well.

If you're a gardener by trade, odds are you probably are going to garden at home sometimes for leisure interest as well.

JB Nash

JB Nash's pyramid of leisure starts off at the bottom with acts against society. Within the level of acts against society, some of the main actions are vandalism, destroying public property, and graffiti. The reason we participate in these activities are not really known to ourselves at the time. The next level is called detrimental or injury to self. An example of this would be alcohol use, cutting oneself, or drug use. Once again we are hurting ourselves but no one else. The next level after that is called Entertainment. Examples for this level could be media entertainment and cell phone and computer use within American society. Our society has become much more of a spectator society than active society. The following level after that is called emotional participation. Emotional participation can be found in a variety of activities whether from books, multimedia, or storytelling. As long as a person has an emotional connection, it can be emotional participation. Fans with their favorite sports teams are a good example.

The next level is active participation. Active participation is where we would like for a lot of people to be in our parks and recreation profession. Being part of our active programs this is where most of our recreation programs head toward and try to get people participating in our programs; this is the crux of the parks and recreation profession. The last level is creative participation. With creative

participation we tend to think of the arts whether it is a dance, music, or other creative things such as that. Creativity means so much more than just those activities. Creativity can be the way we approach DIY projects, it can be the way we plan our vacations, the way we approach fashion and style. Therefore, that creative participation we tend to just put in a box throughout the years, means much more than we ever thought. There are some very interesting links between creativity and leisure that should be explored by our profession.

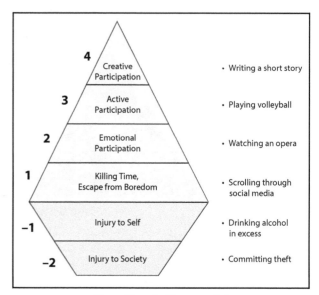

The Nash Pyramid
Source: Hugh Gibson

Aristotle's Pyramid of Leisure

At the bottom of Aristotle's pyramid is amusement. Things that provide us with just simple enjoyment. The next level would be entertainment. Plays, dramas, good discussions would fit nicely in this level. The last level is contemplation. Contemplation was the highest level for Aristotle because he believed leisure in its highest form was learning and being allowed to think. Still to this day one of the leisure field's main journals is called *Scholes*. This is directly from the Greeks and is the root of our word school. To Aristotle, leisure came in no better form than being able to think and ponder things, during a time in history when most people had to put in long hours each day just to get their food, water, and shelter.

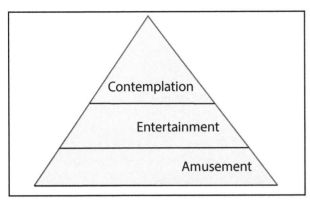

Aristotle's Leisure Pyramid
Source: Hugh Gibson

Why Are Leisure Theories Important to Practioners?

When I was a young Parks and Recreation professional in Bowling Green, Kentucky, I worked at a community center park. During the summer we had over 100 people at one time and one very small facility but we had a program that was always our number one program with the ages of five through 15. I never could figure out why it was the number one program and it was not until years after I did the program, can you guess what the program was?

It was cooking and the reason it was cooking was because the people at the program were not getting enough food and enough substance and nutrition in their daily diet. It took me years to understand why this one program was so popular. I just thought it was interesting at the time. It was not until years later when I was teaching that I finally understood that theory would have helped me realize that my participants were hungry. If I was a better professional at the time I would have realized this earlier and I would replicate that program at least once a week; instead I did not. Because I did not know any theories I did not provide my participants with the basic need they had. What are you missing and how can theories help you better provide for your participants?

Which Theory Is the Best?

Which theory is the best is a trick question. There is not one theory that is the best, that is why I teach so many theories. The hope is that you can at least get two or three theories in your tool belt that you understand. There is never going to be one theory that works in every situation. That is why you need a vast multitude of theories in your arsenal so that you can fully understand what is going on in different settings with different people. A wide array of theories from a variety of fields can help one fully understand and explain every type of leisure and recreation participation one comes in contact with in the future.

Does Work Define Leisure or Does Leisure Define Work?

Most of these theories still see leisure as a consequence of work. However, the other view being proposed is the opposite. Work is a consequence of leisure. Gone are the times of having one job for 30 years, retiring, getting the gold watch, and playing golf. During that time people asked, "Where do you work?" That was a good way of understanding who you were, where you lived, what religion you were, and so forth. Those days are gone! In our current working situation where you will have at least 5–7 jobs in 50 years, leisure will be the item in our life that defines us more. Work will become the thing we do to be able to enjoy our weekends and purchase the needs for our leisure interests. Leisure will define us more than our work, especially for the millennial generation and subsequent generations.

References

Bammel, G., and L. L. Burrus-Bammel. *Leisure & Human Behavior*. Dubuque, IA: Times Mirror Higher Education Group, 1996.

Csikszentmihalyi, M. *Beyond Boredom and Anxiety*. San Francisco: Jossey-Bass, 1975.

Csikszentmilhalyi, M., and D. A. Kleiber. "Leisure and Self-Actualization." In *Benefits of Leisure* edited by B. L. Driver, P. J. Brown, and G. L. Peterson, 91–102. State College, PA: Venture Publishing, 1991.

de Grazia, S. *Of Time, Work, and Leisure*. Hartford, CT: Twentieth Century Fund, 1962.

Dumazedier, J. *Sociology of Leisure*. Amsterdam: Elsevier Publishing, 1974.

Edginton, C. R., C. J. Hanson, S. R. Edginton, and S. D. Hudson. *Leisure Programming: A Service Centered and Benefits Approach*. 3rd ed. Boston, MA: McGraw-Hill, 1998.

Edginton, C. R., D. J. Jordan, D. G. DeGraaf, and S. R. Edginton. *Leisure and Life Satisfaction: Foundational Perspectives.* 3rd ed. New York: McGraw-Hill, 2002.

Gibson, H. (2005). A Q-study of the perceptions of leisure shared by young married individuals with no children Doctoral Dissertation). Oklahoma State University.

Godbey, G. *Leisure in Your Life: An Exploration.* 4th ed. Philadelphia, PA: Venture, 1994.

Gunter, B. G. (1987). "The Leisure Experience: Selected Properties." *Journal of Leisure Research, 19*(2) (1987): 115–130.

Hood, C. D. "*Family Functioning and Adolescent Leisure Patterns.*" Unpublished dissertation, University of Illinois at Urbana-Champaign, Urbana, IL, 1992.

Huizinga, J. *Homo Ludens: A Study of the Play Element in Culture.* Boston, MA: Beacon Press, 1955.

Kaplan, M. "New Concepts of Leisure Today." In *Concepts of Leisure: Philosophical Implications, edited by J. F. Murphy.* Englewood Cliffs, NJ: Prentice-Hall, 1974.

Kleiber, D. *Leisure Experience and Human Development: A Dialectical Interpretation.* New York: Basic Books, 1999.

Mannell, R. "Social Psychological Techniques and Strategies for Studying Leisure Experiences." In *Social Psychological Perspectives on Leisure and Recreation,* edited by Se. E. Iso-Ahola. Springfield, IL: Charles C. Thomas, Publisher, 1980.

Orthner, D. K., and J. A. Mancini. "Leisure Impacts on Family Interaction and Cohesion." *Journal of Leisure Research, 22*(2) (1990): 125–137.

Peterson, C., Stumbo, N.J. (2000.) Theerapeutic Recreation Program Design: Principles and Procedures. Allyn & Bacon. Needham Heights: MA. Pieper, J. *Leisure: The Basis of Culture.* New York: Random House, 1963.

Shaw, S. "The Measurement of Leisure: A Quality of Life Issue." *Society and Leisure, 7 (1984):* 91–107.

Shaw, S. "The Meaning of Leisure in Everyday Life." *Life Sciences, 7 (1985):* 1–24.

Sullivan, K. *An Exploratory Investigation of the Relationship between Work and Leisure.* Unpublished doctoral dissertation, University of Illinois, Urbana-Champaign, 1990.

Tinsley, H., and D. A. Tinsley. "Theory of Attributes, Benefits, and Causes of Leisure Experience." *Leisure Sciences, 8 (1986):* 1–45.

Ulrich, R. S., Dimberg, U. and Driver, B. L. (19910) Psychophysiological indicators of leisure benefits. In Driver, B. L., Brown, L. R. and Peterson, G. L. (eds) *Benefits of Leisure.* Venture Publishing, State College, Pennsylvania, pp. 73–89.

Wankel, L. M., & Berger, B. G. (1991). The personal and social benefits of sport and physical activity. In B. L. Driver, P. J. Brown, & G. L. Peterson (Eds.), *Benefits of leisure.* Venture Publishing, State College, Pennsylvania, pp. 121–144.

CHAPTER 3

PERSPECTIVES ON ADVENTURE: LIVE LIFE AS AN EXCLAMATION—NOT AS AN EXPLANATION

William J. Finch

"Nothing compares to the intoxicating joy of taking great risks and surviving on the strength of your own skill and courage" (Coonts, xiv).

INTRODUCTION TO ADVENTURE

"Adventure" is not just limited to the realm of recreation and leisure. It is as broad as life itself. It is found everywhere. It is in our daily vocabulary. We see a constant dosage of it in the media and our senses are challenged by the countless possibilities available to all of us just for the asking. We are invited to engage in adventure daily. Some invitations are for vicarious adventure offered by movies and books. Other invitations offer real-life adventure activities. Most of us have entertained the idea of accepting such an invitation, most of us have dreamed of scaling great heights, taking great risks, and experiencing the exhilaration offered by adventure. Yet for most of us, these ideas are the stuff of dreams, not reality.

In this chapter you are invited to learn how to facilitate a life of adventure. This is a serious invitation. By accepting it, you open the door to a life of excitement, discovery, and personal growth. You become an adventurer. Some people choose to live their lives as an *explanation,* others choose to live life as an *exclamation.* Which do you prefer?

The information to help you live life as an exclamation is found in this chapter. The decision is yours.

In this chapter we will examine the meaning of adventure, the role of risk in adventure activities, mental and attitudinal aspects of adventure, optimal arousal and flow as a basis of adventure, and offer "tools" for adventuring.

ADVENTURE CAN BE FOR EVERYONE

In days past, authors have focused on adventuring as those difficult and sometime monumental activities undertaken only by those with presumed superhuman ability and in possession of the vast sums of money seemingly necessary to engage in such activities. This is no longer the case. Today, people have available to them literally hundreds of adventures as well as greater ability to access natural areas in which many of these activities are performed. Three factors have influenced the upsurge of interest and involvement in adventure activities during the past decade.

- The first is due to the pioneers whose vision and dedicated interest in breaking new ground have been instrumental in the advance of adventuring as a means to making optimal experiences available to all of us.

- The second relates to the advances in technological innovation that have allowed more and more people to have increased mobility and performance through a variety of new equipment designs intended to allow one to function more successfully and in greater safety than in the past.

- The third is due to the people who have become adventure providers, thus offering easier avenues of ingress to the arena of adventure experiencing heretofore unavailable to the once "ordinary common man."

Together, these factors not only have opened new frontiers, they have stimulated the appetite and the interest of we mortal humans so that all of us may expand our horizons by becoming the participant rather than remaining the spectator.

Adventure Is Opportunity to Live

While adventure experiences are perceived as challenges and risky, they are, above all else, opportunities for the participant to *live the experience.* They are experiences that will stimulate the senses and put people in touch with their inner feelings and emotions which, when peaked[1], provide them with the exhilarating sense of being fully alive and connected to their surroundings in ways not experienced in the usual course of daily living. Adventure experiences extend beyond "normal life" as they allow people to discover themselves by presenting opportunities to go beyond their self-imposed boundaries and self-perceived limits. An element common to all adventure experiences is immersion, which is that total sense of commitment and involvement to the point of being totally absorbed in the process of the experience itself. Some refer to this quality as "becoming one with" the experience. These experiences will give the individual a significantly heightened sense of accomplishment, fulfillment, and personal growth. Further, these experiences have innate within them the potential of presenting people with the opportunity to experience the leisure state of "flow."[2]

Activities that possess the potential to be adventure experiences for the participant where they will not merely *have* the experience but *live the experience* include but are not limited to:

Flying	Skydiving
Ballooning	Downhill skiing
Rodeoing	Scuba diving
Racing	Ropes course
Windsurfing	Spelunking
Snowmobiling	Fishing
Paragliding	Snow skiing
Flying Ultralights	Surfing
Kayaking	Orienteering
Trail Drives	Survival School
Sailing	River Boarding
Whitewater rafting	Martial arts
Hang gliding	Snorkeling
Water skiing	Wilderness camping
Rock climbing (with aids)	Mountain climbing
Rock climbing (top roping)	Mountain Bike Touring
and others . . .	

Adventure experiences may be personal or shared experiences. Generally speaking, adventure experiences involve a high degree of physical, mental, and emotional participation. However, there are exceptions where events that are not physical can still demand all of one's mental and emotional energy and result in achieving and deriving a full measure of satisfaction and fulfillment as well.

Everyone deserves to live their adventure as fully and completely as they are able. But some people are more able than others. These are the people who possess the power produced by knowledge and the ability to apply it. They know and understand the meaning of leisure. They possess a broad overview of the differing views of leisure presented by authors from diverse perspectives. Following are areas of discussion which will serve to empower the reader with the knowledge and tools to begin what will be a successful journey reaching levels of optimal experience in their adventure pursuits. **Enjoy the knowledge. Enjoy your adventure.**

Adventure Defined

In 1930, Robert Marshall stated that adventure "implies breaking into unpenetrated ground, venturing beyond the boundary of normal aptitude, extending oneself to the limit of capacity, courageously facing peril."[3]

For an endeavor to qualify as an adventure experience, it must meet three criteria: first, it must be entered into voluntarily and of free choice; second, it must be intrinsically motivating in and of its own merit; and, third, the outcome must be uncertain. Paul McMenamin corroborates this point of view in his *The Ultimate Adventure Sourcebook* where he states "adventure by definition involves the unexpected."[4]

Hill also distinguishes between two types of adventure: *hard adventure* and *soft adventure*. He defines "hard adventure" as activities with high levels of risk that require intense commitment and advanced skills. He defines "soft adventure" as those activities with a perceived risk but in actuality possess low levels of real risk requiring minimal commitment and beginning skills.[5] Whereas most of hard adventure activities involve direct personal participation and involvement, experienced guides lead most of the soft adventure activities.

"Adventure is a human need. We recognize it as the daring thing that makes us bigger than our usual selves. Adventure is the curiosity of man to see the other side of the mountain, the impulse in him that makes him break his bonds with lesser things and frees him for greater possibility." Walt Burnett—The Spirit of Adventure

Risk as a Component of Adventure

Simply stated, risk is the potential for the loss of something valuable. Risk may be physical, mental, social, and financial.[6] It might be simply viewed as the potential for an accident.[7] There are aspects of risk that we can attempt to mitigate by applying risk management practices and procedures. Examples would be acquiring skills where they are lacking and using safer equipment rather than the opposite. There are also uncontrollable factors of risk such as the weather and its unpredictable affect such as flooding and other hazards over which mere mortals exert little if any influence. And there is an undeniable truism that cannot be avoided no matter how well we are prepared and that is: accidents happen.

However, it is that very "exposure to a variety of risks in an outdoor context which produces an uncertainty of outcome which is central to the

adventure experience."[8] Brown goes on to explain that such uncertainty sets the stage for personal challenge, commitment, cooperation with your fellows, goal setting with very clear unambiguous feedback, and transformation. Engaging risk in the adventure setting allows the participant to experience exhilaration, personal growth, and come away from the experience with increased self-esteem and self-confidence.

For decades psychologists have sought answers to questions seeking to discover why we human beings actively pursue risk when we don't have to. Our civilized lives are quite comfortable, so why would we intentionally want to make life dangerous and difficult for ourselves?

Research has revealed vast amounts of valuable information from which we can draw some very significant conclusions about such things as ultimate or extreme sports and those who participate in them as well as the risk-oriented urges we all have to varying degrees. Personalities have been examined and traits have been identified that seem to separate thrill-seeking types from those who are not. Polar personalities are often distinguished from one another with labels such as the Big "T" personality and the little "t" personality. Other researchers such as Marvin Zuckerman, who identified the high-sensation seeking (HSS) personality profile, examined risk taking from the biological as well as the psychological perspective. There are studies which reveal that people will return to repeat adventure experiences so they can re-visit and re-experience the pleasure states that arise from the natural release of adrenalin and endorphins into one's system.

Other psychologists have theorized that we humans still possess ancient survival (physiological) needs that are now today no longer fulfilled as they were thousands of years ago when our cave dwelling ancestors did their best to avoid the feared saber-toothed tiger. Our ancestors were not only hunters, they were also the hunted. Survival and the confrontation of danger when hunting and gathering were the activities of the day. Today our lives are no longer filled with daily survival concerns and the accompanying risk and danger that our ancestors encountered every time they ventured out from the security of their dwelling. However, it is argued that even though these particular physiological needs have been suppressed through the civilizing processes through which we have traveled, these needs still yearn to be fulfilled. So, the theory continues, it is in the recognition of these needs and their overlooked fulfillment that we intentionally introduce elements of danger and risk into our lives so that we can once again experience the fulfillment of overcoming, conquering, achieving, and surviving to tell the tale.

If you are interested in pursuing this topic of risk and thrill seeking, you will find an abundance of information on the Internet. Significant to our focus on adventure and optimal experiencing, though, is understanding our own personal reasons that cause us to generate motivations for pursuing adventure experiences.

Intrinsic Motivation as a Component of Adventure

Leisure behavior is undertaken for the purpose of achieving satisfaction or fulfillment for all leisure motivations that provide the urge to action in our lives. As already stated, adventure is a subset of leisure. Through adventure we seek to elevate the level of intensity of our involvement in order to optimize our "experiencing" of life. But, what are the motivations underlying such experiences?

First, we need to address the difference between intrinsic motivation and extrinsic motivation. Simply stated, intrinsic motivation refers to those motivations whose fulfillment will be derived within the experience itself, during the ongoing process of "experiencing" the activity as it evolves. Extrinsic motivation refers to an external reward such as a prize for winning an event—or as a monetary payoff received after the fact, after the experience has been concluded (such as in the case of work).

With respect to leisure and adventure pursuits, intrinsic motivation is the key ingredient because we are interested in achieving fulfilling and satisfying feelings during the "experiencing" of the activity. The sole pursuit of extrinsic motivations through some activity does not constitute a leisure experience because extrinsic motivations alone offer no opportunity to feel fulfilled during the experience as it unfolds. However, an experience can be an intrinsically motivated leisure experience and also have extrinsic motivations associated with it. A good example is that of exercising. Many people enjoy the "experiencing" of their body in motion and the movement of their muscles, and they are treated to the after-the-fact improvement of personal fitness and health.

As to where our motivations originate, author Richard Kraus states that many factors intrinsically motivate individuals to pursue leisure. These factors vary from person to person, depending upon their unique personalities, lifestyles, goals, and needs. To explore the many aspects that contribute to the making of motivations, let us establish a category heading we will label "Urges." Under this heading, we may list all of our personal wants, dreams, aspirations, hopes, wishes, longings, yearnings, fantasies, ambitions, as well as the list of basic human needs addressed by Abraham Maslow. These urges play an important role in shaping our behavior. As the intensity of these urges increases, intrinsic motivations are generated. By shaping and focusing the intrinsic motivations into well-formed goals, the probability of engaging in related behaviors is increased. Thus, when one's motivations point to action, risk, and excitement, you begin to seek leisure-adventures. In other words, your behavior is purposefully directed at fulfilling or satisfying the collection of motivations tending you toward the adventure experience. The fundamental drive to participate is the expectation that you will find fulfillment for all of these motivations during the progression of the experience.

Motivations are also generated from expectations that we form when we approach an event or activity. If we think an activity has the potential for imparting enjoyment, satisfaction, and fulfillment, such thinking shapes our expectations. But are these expectations based on the personality, lifestyle, goals, and needs? Or, do people establish their own set of expectations (innate to) based upon how they subjectively relate to the event or activity? Is it possible that each innate event or activity has innate is a recognizable set of motivations that we can apply to everyone equally? Student exercises with the Leisure Motivations Assessment (LMA) will introduce the student to the vocabulary of specific leisure motivations and will enable them to pursue them to there fullest satisfaction in a wide variety of leisure and adventure undertakings.

Attitude as a Component of Adventure

Attitude is one of the strongest "mental state" processes known to man. It is powerful when positive and can propel their owners to great heights of accomplishment and success. When negative, it can be destructive, and in the worst case scenario promote dysfunctional behavior.

In its positive sense, attitude is a condition of thinking and acting that embodies optimism and enthusiasm and is responsible for maintaining high states of mental and emotional health. Attitude is how you feel about something. It is revealed as emotion or in one's mood; it is apparent in how one carries and projects themselves. Not only do we have personal attitudes concerning different subjects, we also have what authors refer to as a lifestyle attitude. "Lifestyle attitude is not only just in your head, it is embodied in the way you stand and move, dream and perceive, and interact with your surroundings. Your personal lifestyle attitude is the true expression of how you live and consequently of who you are."[9] Attitude is responsible for, and at the same time, a product of raising consciousness through the increased focus on and attention toward an idea of growing interest in which people will eventually involve themselves—such as the idea of participating in an adventure activity. Part of the thinking process, attitude is responsible for shaping the choices in the activities in which people will experience leisure and adventure.

Attitude is a strong contributor to a person's capacity to conquer mountains, run marathons, become an accomplished tennis player, or enjoy a personal accomplishment while savoring the view from Cloud's Rest in Yosemite. We all have seen adventure attitudes portrayed by those involved in adventure activity. Most of us have seen people in adventure settings. They dress for the role and exhibit the mannerisms. They talk the talk and walk the walk. Many of us have seen people commit to and immerse themselves so completely in the experience that we no longer can separate the person from the activity. These people have become the experience itself. This was well expressed by Geba, "You are your attitude."[10]

Understanding Leisure So We Can Understand Adventure as a Leisure Experience

In order to enhance our ability to experience adventure to its fullest potential, we need to re-engage our discussion on the meaning of "leisure." Focus on understanding leisure will provide the knowledge necessary to actualize your experiences; whereas, lacking understanding or having an incorrect perception of leisure in your life will prevent you from realizing the full reward any experience has to offer. In truth and from my personal experience of teaching leisure, I am completely aware of the confusion that can and does occur when students come into contact with the challenge to understand the meaning of the concept of leisure for the first time of their lives. Most students view leisure as "free time" or an "activity" to do in their free time. Not only are these perceptions limiting, they can act as a strong impediment to an important alternative view. The first thing the student holding such beliefs must do is set aside perceptions and proceed with an open mind to learn a more expensive definition of leisure. This definition will allow you to not only fully experience adventure but also live life more effectively.

Life Is a Mental Process and So Is Leisure

One of the most important things to remember and focus on is that our lives are not lived because of time, or as a result of time, or because of the work or other activities in which we engage. The mind is the key factor here. In all of its glorious wonder, the mind transforms impressions and thoughts into appropriate action that establishes meaningful realities. Just how meaningful is dependent upon one's ability to control the mind in accurately shaping and directing one's course of action in the pursuit of goals. These goals are pursued through the process of intrinsically (and extrinsically) motivated behaviors. Such behaviors are selected for their capacity to yield fulfillment and satisfaction, and more specifically in the context of this chapter, their capacity to motivate one to experience adventure.

Please recognize that everything about our life process that we have experienced, are experiencing, and will experience is occurring, and will occur in the mind in the form of thoughts, dreams, expectations, motivations, and goals. Thoughts are antecedent to experience, and they are the basis of reflection once the activity is passed. Both one's motivation to engage in the activity, and one's evaluation of a past activity occurs in the neurons of the mind. Hence, it is impossible to separate the anticipatory ideas and the reflective assessment from the adventure activity itself.

One quick qualification before we continue. I thoroughly understand that there exists a multitude of unforeseen events and happenings that can descend upon us and force the alteration of any course we may have mapped out or may be proceeding upon. While such occurrences may be disastrous to some people, for those who have mentally taken control of their lives, these unexpected and perhaps uncontrollable events will seem as minor detours in the overall course of our lives as we have chosen to live them. Through the careful process of establishing goals and gaining empowering information about the functioning of life, we are equipped to deal with the unexpected.

Leisure Defined as a State of Mind

Introductory texts present a number of perspectives that define leisure across a broad spectrum from quantitative (objective time and activity) orientations on one side to the qualitative (subjective mentally engaging experiential) orientation on the other side. I will state that each is valid in its own particular esoteric context for which it was developed. However, in my opinion, only a select few, and one concept in particular, are appropriate to best prepare a person to enjoy the adventure experience as a fully engaged participant.

That definitional approach is that *leisure is defined as a state of mind with its attendant qualities of attitude, intrinsic motivation, perceived freedom, and flow.* Bammel states ". . . leisure is a state of being, an attitude, a mental condition; it has nothing to do with time and little to do with space and activity.[11] Neulinger defines leisure as a "state of mind" rather than activity or time. Leisure is neither the environment nor the behavior but the attitude

accompanying the behavior.[12] Each of the preceding authors has made a specific effort to declare that leisure should not be defined in association with time. Leisure is not "time out" from life, nor is it something with an activity name to indicate how we spent some of our time. It is best thought of as a state of mind.

When leisure is perceived as a "state of mind," leisure is seen as essentially interior: "it is what goes on within the person which can be expressed in many different external ways."[13] This "state of mind quality" is examined in terms of the psychological perceptions of "leisure behavior." That is to say it is examined in terms of leisure-oriented values, attitudes, feelings, and emotions within the participants as they are involved in the process of "experiencing" leisure activities. Unless these aforementioned qualities are in tune with the experience, leisure may not occur for the participant. For example, McDowell states categorically that the attitude you foster toward any experience often decides whether it is leisure or not (#1, p. 5). Again, and as a testament to the mental power of one's attitude, McDowell tells us that leisure must flow from you as a positive set of attitudes and values in your lifestyle (#1, p. 5).

Leisure then, from this point of view, is mental in its origin, in its process, and its product. It is attitude, it is thought, it is motivation, and it is emotion; it is an urge to action, it is experiencing, it is fulfilling, it leads to individual complexity and personal growth. Leisure first presents itself as a state of mind, merging itself with our thoughts and emotions. Only then does leisure emerge within an activity or experience (McDowell, #1, p. 5). Kelly states that leisure defined as a state of mind refers to an attitude characterizing an activity that is done largely for its own sake.[14]

In this mental approach to defining leisure, the "experience" perspective looks at the quality of the leisure experience in terms of the participant's mental, emotional, and physical involvement, the process or the "ongoingness" of the continuing, evolving course of experiencing all the event has to offer as well as the interplay with those whom we share or are sharing the experience process.

The participants (actors) are important of course with respect to what they bring to the event for processing. Their personal needs, intrinsic motivations, and their goal-focused behavior in the experience are mentally orienting. Of interest is the interplay between the participant and the "focal object" causing and allowing the experience to proceed to conclusion. And proceeding all the while the experience is building, evolving, and growing, we observe the mental evaluation of feedback about how one is relating to the developing experience process. Ongoing mental judgments about the fulfillment and satisfaction levels being derived during the processing of the experience are constantly being compared with and against the established motivational expectations going into the experience. "Leisure is in part individual experience, a state of consciousness; leisure is also in part decision that inaugurates action which has a beginning, development, and end. Leisure is more than action; leisure is meaning. As situated action, leisure is the freedom to be and become."[15]

Many of my students have gained a solid grasp of leisure. I've included a few examples here for the reader's benefit. These examples of their discoveries show the marked change over the course of a semester where they progressed from thinking leisure was just so much free-time to something much more meaningful.

A Listing of Student Definitions—Students Discoveries

A student states: "Leisure is expressed as well as experienced. . . . It is learned and cultivated. It is a gift of the mind. It is a celebration of the heart and soul."

A student states: "Leisure is a state of mind. It is an inner harmony that I possess. It is the self-reflection of what makes me happy, relaxes me and challenges me. My mind-set brings me happiness—it brings me leisure."

A student states: "Leisure is essential in my life because it is in my passionate pursuit of leisure that I realize the rich reward of flow which occurs when intense enjoyment is achieved due to a connected, flowing state of mind."

A student states: "All of our lives we have been taught that leisure is just an extracurricular activity we perform sometimes for 'fun' and that we must set aside a block of time in which to perform this activity. I now believe leisure is an internal phenomenon which manifests feelings of well-being and is the product of a positive attitude."

And now, I would like to add that leisure is life itself being lived at its most satisfying (gratifying) best.

And, inasmuch as this relies upon clear thinking, evaluation, and reflection, it is fair to say that leisure is clearly a mental process. Two thousand four hundred years ago, Aristotle defined leisure as the goal of all human behavior, the end toward which all action is directed.[16] Now as we enter the twenty-first century, we pause and reflect upon the significance of this idea and proceed to refine and build upon this early concept.

Optimal Experience and Flow

For over 50 years, psychologists and leisure scientists have focused on gaining an increased understanding of how people involve themselves wholly and completely in behaviors with for the seemingly single purpose of enjoying the rewards of the experience process itself—the experience is done for its own sake. Ideas advanced as self-actualization, optimal arousal, peak experiencing, optimal experience, and flow have been examined. The purpose of these investigations has been to identify situations in which people seek to maximize and extend their duration of heightened meaning within the experience as it develops.

Salient to this discussion is the aspect of "flow" advanced by Mihaly Csikszentmihalyi. He has studied this concept for over 30 years. With the publication of his landmark book on the subject, *Flow: The Psychology of the Optimal Experience,* the conditions of the flow experience were presented for everyone to study and apply to their own human functioning to enhance their abilities to experience life optimally. We in the field of leisure studies are excited with this information due to its innate relevance and direct application to leisure in general and specifically to adventuring where optimal experiencing is the goal.

The characteristic dimensions of the "flow experience" are:

1. A **challenging** activity that requires the participant abilities to be up to the challenge.

2. The **merging** of awareness and action.

3. The task undertaken has clear **goals.**

4. The task undertaken provides immediate and unambiguous **feedback** as to performance.

5. There is complete **concentration** on the task at hand.

6. There is a strong sense of personal **control** and the exercising of control during the task.

7. There is the **loss of self-consciousness** or concern for the self during the activity.

8. The sense of the duration of **time is altered.** Time is made irrelevant.

Here is some amplifying discussion to help you see the relevance of each of these characteristics and to begin to see how this knowledge can be applied to your own experiencing process.

1. **When an activity's challenges and the participant's necessary abilities are in the proximity of balance, then the experience can become optimal (flow) as we confront demanding tasks that we have a chance of completing.**[17] In flow, the challenges need to be *high* enough so as to require and absorb *all* of a person's skills.[18] There is a sense that one's skills are commensurate (adequate to cope) with the challenges at hand.[19] Any activity has a "bundle" of opportunities for action, or "challenges," that require appropriate skills to realize success. For those without the skills and the perception that they cannot acquire the necessary skills, the activity is not challenging, it is meaningless.[20]

   Enjoyment arrives at a very specific point: whenever the opportunities for action perceived by the individual are equal to his or her capabilities. Enjoyment appears at the boundary between boredom and anxiety, when the challenges are just balanced with the person's capacity to act.[21] Please see the discussion regarding control in paragraph 6 below regarding balance of challenges and skills.

2. **In the merging of awareness and action, one becomes so focused and involved in the experience that the usual dualism between actor and action disappears.** This "unified consciousness" is perhaps the most telling aspect of the flow experience. When one is immersed in flow, the actor is at one with the action.[22] As a result of total concentration (the merging of awareness and action), one of the most universal and distinctive features of "optimal experience" takes place: People become so involved in what they are doing that the activity becomes spontaneous, almost automatic; they stop being

aware of themselves as separate from the actions they are performing.[23] The participants become one with the experience; being totally absorbed by, thoroughly engrossed, or immersed in the experience and totally unaware of anything else. It is for this reasoning that we call optimal experience "flow."[24]

3. **The task undertaken has clear goals.** The goals are "autotelic." *Auto* means "self," and *telos* means "goal." The experience is an end in itself; it is done for its own sake. The goals are unambiguous, intrinsically motivated, and provide a sense of guidance as the experience builds and unfolds. In some creative situations where goals are not clearly set in advance, a person must develop a strong personal sense of what he or she "intends" to do.[25] The true optimal experience is a goal-directed, rule-bound action system that provides clear clues as to how well one is performing.[26]

4. **The task undertaken provides immediate and unambiguous feedback as to how one is performing.** The experiencing does not stop so that feedback can be evaluated. Incoming information is continually weighed and compared with one's intrinsically motivated goals in terms of: "How am I doing?" Unless the participant learns to set goals and recognize and gauge feedback in such activities, the participant will not enjoy them.[27] That is why setting clear goals based on intrinsic motivations is so important. The weighing and gauging the feedback against your goals is a process of "self communication"[28] to determine if and to what degree you are enjoying the ongoing experience (i.e., flowing).

5. **There is complete concentration on the task at hand.** Deep concentration results in a focusing on the present so that the worries and frustrations of everyday life that are a drain on psychic energy tend to disappear.[29] Concentration, the focusing of "attention," is so intense that there is no "attention" left over to focus on anything irrelevant or to worry about problems.[30] When *all* of a person's relevant skills are needed to cope with the challenges of an activity, that person's total "attention" is completely absorbed by the activity.[31] There simply is no excess psychic energy (attention) left over to process any information but what the activity offers. *All* of

one's "attention" is concentrated (focused on/merging with) on the relevant stimuli. The *challenges* of the activity are what force us to concentrate.[32]

6. **There is a strong sense of personal control and the exercising of control during the task.** One is allowed to exercise a *sense* of control or "potential" control over their actions. What people enjoy is not the sense of *being* in control, but the sense of *exercising* control in difficult situations.[33] If challenges and skills are in balance, it *is possible* for a person to experience a sense of control, but in a [high] flow state, one is not, in fact, in complete control. If one were, the balance between challenges and skills would tilt in the favor of skill and the intensity of the experience would decrease.[34] In this state, the individual is in control of his or her actions and of the environment. A person has no active awareness of control, but is simply not worried by the possibility of the lack of control or failure. In this situation, one feels a sense of personal control or power.[35]

7. **There is the loss of self-consciousness.** The concern for the self disappears. The loss of self-consciousness does not involve a loss of self, and certainly not a loss of consciousness, but rather, only a loss of consciousness *of* the self (i.e., the *concept of self).*[36] In "flow" there is simply no room for self-scrutiny.[37] While the concern for the self disappears, the *sense of self* immerges stronger after the flow experience is over.[38] The loss of the *sense* of a self (separate from the world around it) is sometimes accompanied by a feeling of union with the environment.[39] The loss of self-consciousness can lead to self-transcendence, a feeling that the boundaries of our being have been pushed aside.[40] This generates a feeling that is referred to as "being at on with . . . ."

8. **The sense of the duration of time is altered.** One of the most common descriptions of optimal experience is that time no longer seems to pass the way it ordinarily does. Being totally absorbed by, thoroughly engrossed, or immersed in the experience leads to the total disregard for time in a mechanical (quantitative) sense because it (time) is rendered completely irrelevant by the rhythms of the experience.[41] Although it seems likely that losing track of the clock is not one of the major elements of enjoyment, freedom from the tyranny of time does add to the exhilaration we feel during a state of complete involvement.[42]

When one is in flow, the sense of time becomes a natural feature of one's total experience, rather than an arbitrary restraint that ignores what we do and how we think about it.

The information shared and discussed in this section has revealed the observed and felt characteristics of the flow experience. In examining them, we see many that can be used effectively as tools to engage the flow process. Other characteristics reflect observable and felt outcomes from experiencing the flow process such as transcendence of self and time.

Adventure and the Flow Experience

Dr. Csikszentmihalyi and Isabell Selega, in their article "Adventure and the Flow Experience," state that to understand why adventure is so attractive, it is important to understand what happens to people when they experience flow.[43] An underlying assumption of flow producing activities is that there are ways for people to test the limits of their being, to transcend their former conception of self by expanding skills and undergoing new experience. Even though in an ideal state, pure involvement would result in flow there are some who need extra incentive to get into flow such as the risk and physical danger found in many adventure activities.

When the adventure activity becomes the goal in and of itself, when it becomes a flow producing experience, it generates clearly observable characteristics within the participant. These are discussed by Csikszentmihalyi and Csikszentmihalyi in "Adventure and the Flow Experience." What follows is a summary of these characteristics as presented in this article.

1. **Regarding Goals and Feedback:** "A person in flow knows clearly what must be done and gets quick feedback about how he or she is doing. Action and reaction have become so well synchronized that the resulting behavior is automatic. Knowing that he or she is doing well allows the enjoyment of the flow experience to be felt."

2. **Regarding Merging of Awareness and Action:** "Because goals and feedback are so clear, the flow experience involves a merging of awareness and action. A person in flow has awareness of the action, but not an awareness of the self. One stops being aware of oneself as separate from the adventure being engaged in."

3. **Regarding Concentration and Focus:** "The merging of awareness and action is made possible by a third characteristic of flow experience: concentration and focus of attention on a limited stimulus field. Through strong concentration, one's consciousness is narrowed so that irrelevant stimuli are excluded. Irrelevant information is weeded out. The adventure experience becomes a world unto itself, significant only to itself."

4. **Regarding Loss of Self-Consciousness:** "A consequence of intense concentration is the next characteristic of the adventure flow experience which is often described as a 'loss of ego' and 'self-forgetfulness.'" . . . or the loss of the self-construct 'I', which as the actor, stands between the actor and the action. Once gone, the door is open for becoming one with the experience. "The loss of the sense of self is sometimes accompanied by the feeling of union with the environment—the physical aspect of the adventure such as the water or the granite, or with one's team, or the universe." Also during this period, transcendence of time may occur, also transcendence of place where the participant can feel as though their personal boundaries have been expanded. "This expansion of one's being accompanied by a successful matching of skills to challenges is deeply enjoyable (fulfilling)" and at the same time, it produces a participant enriched by new complexity and stronger self-confidence.

5. **Regarding Control:** "People in flow feel potentially in control of their actions and of their environment. Rather an active awareness of control, one ceases to worry about losing control—as one might in real life." With respect to adventuring, the authors state "risk takers often claim that their enjoyment comes not from the danger itself, but from their ability to minimize it because they possess the 'feeling' that they are able to control potentially dangerous forces."

Adventure participants are searching for a particular state of experience, an experience that is rarely accessible in everyday life. The authors conclude by stating "the flow model suggests that to derive enjoyment from life (adventure included) reliably requires the ability to get into flow, stay in it, and make the process evolve."

The Tools for Adventure

And just how do we get into flow, stay in it, and make the process evolve? From the information previously discussed, you can easily discover the elements of flow and leisure definition that can be shaped into mental tools, over which you have control, that can be applied to the experience process to establish flow and gain optimal experiencing—optimal adventuring!

One tool of adventure is "awareness." Being aware as to when one is in flow is an imnportant aspect of understanding both flow and its antecedents. David Farmer, reviewed Czikszentmihalyi's discussion of flow and concluded the following:

Flow is characterized by the following:

1. You are completely involved and focused in the activity at hand.

2. There is a transcendent sense of well-being, some might even say ecstasy.

3. Inner clarity . . . you know what needs to be done and how to do it.

4. A sense of capability . . . you know that you have the skills to do what needs to be done.

5. A sense of serenity . . . present oriented, no ego concerns.

6. Timeliness . . . you don't notice the passing of time.

7. Intrinsic motivation . . . the activity, driven by flow, produces its own reward.

When the above characteristics are present, you have found a good match between your sensory needs and the opportunity at hand. If these characteristics are not present, then the experience lacks adventure or presents too many challenges.

Take charge of the experience. By using your combined knowledge of your skills and basic nature along with your knowledge of specific leisure activities, you can make reasonable decisions as how to approach the adventure experience. Here are some suggestions for taking charge of the adventure experience.

1. Take control of exercising freedom of choice and voluntarily engaging in the adventure process.

2. Learn what your set of intrinsic motivations are for any given choice of adventure experience and let them guide the way in setting goals for your adventure.

3. Become an autotelic adventurer. Give yourself permission to exercise the decision making process and set goals that will allow you adventure optimally and flow successfully.

4. Choose an adventure experience that will be highly challenging.

5. Make the effort to acquire the necessary skills to meet the challenge.

6. Learn to focus your attention on the task at hand. Develop the skills of concentration.

7. Learn to recognize and gauge feedback so you can evaluate your performance against the established goals.

8. Exercise personal control in shaping the dimensions of the adventure experience as well as exercising control during the tasks undertaken during the experience of your adventure.

Manktelow, the creator of MindTools.com states that finding flow is easy if you follow several simple principles.[44] As you embark on adventure activities, it is wise to keep in mind the following:

1. You perceive that your skills are good enough to match the perceived difficulty of the task. In other words, don't overestimate your abilities. Match your ability to the challenge.

2. If you select an unchallenging task, you risk boredom and inattention. This can be dangerous.

3. Flow challenges your attention. This can be lifesaving.

4. An appropriate level of arousal is critical to success. Some activities require a relaxed state of mind and body; other activities require physical arousal and mental alertness.

5. Flow must develop naturally, it cannot be forced. If you are not at flow, modify or change your activity. Add complexity where there is too much simplicity, or add novelty.

On to Adventure

In the beginning of this chapter, I extended to you a serious invitation to consider and accept the idea of living an adventurous lifestyle. Now I am inviting you to RSVP in the affirmative and begin today to a lifestyle of characterized by flow.

Put the ideas of this chapter to work. Become an effective life adventurer with the capacity to experience leisure fully, to get into the flow and stay in it. Make this process the driving force for a personal evolution of growth and development from now and throughout the whole of your life.

Notes

1. Ellis would perhaps use the term "optimal arousal" here. Olson might use the term "percephially fread."

2. Flow is discussed later in this chapter.

3. Hill, Brian J. "A Guide to Adventure Travel." *Park and Recreation*, Vol. 30, No. 9, September 1995, pp. 56–65.

4. Miles, John C., and Simon Priest (eds). *Adventure Programming.* State College, PA: Venture Publishing, Inc., 1999.

5. Miles, 7.

6. Miles, 113.

7. Miles, 274.

8. Mile,s 273.

9. Geba, Hans Bruno. *Being at Leisure, Playing at Life.* La Mesa, CA: Leisure Science Systems International, 1985.

10. Geba, p. 28.

11. Geba, 199.

12. Kelly, John R. *Leisure Identities and Interactions.* Boston: George Allen & Unwin, 1983.

13. Bammel, Gene, and Lei Lane Burrus-Bammel. *Leisure and Human Behavior.* Third Edition. Dubuque, IA: Wm. C. Brown Publishers, 1995.

14. *Freedom to Be.* New York: MacMillan Publishing Company, 1987.

15. Kelly, 238, Freedom, 119.

16. Bammel, 187.

17. *Creativity: Flow and Psychology of Discovery and Invention.* New York: Harper Collins Publishers, Inc.,1996.

18. *The Evolving Self: A Psychology for the Third Millennium.* New York: Harper Collins Publishers, Inc., 1993.

19. Flow, 71.

20. Flow, 50.

21. Flow, 52.

22. Evolving, 183.

23. Flow, 53.

24. Flow, 54.

25. Flow, 55.

26. Flow, 71.

27. Flow, 55.

28. Evolving, 180.

29. Evolving, 184.

30. Flow, 71.

31. Flow, 53.

32. Flow, 97.

33. Flow, 61.

34. Evolving, 181–182.

35. Edginton, Christopher R. and others. *Leisure and Life Satisfaction.* Dubuque, IA: Brown and Benchmark Publishers, 1995.

36. Flow, 64.

37. Flow, 63.

38. Flow, 49.

39. Flow, 63.

40. Flow, 64.

41. Flow, 66.

42. Flow, 67.

43. Flow, 153.

44. Manktelow, Mind Tools.com.

REFERENCES

Bammel, Gene, and Lei Lane Burrus-Bammel. *Leisure and Human Behavior,* Third Edition. Dubuque, IA: Wm. C. Brown Publishers, 1995.

Bang, Richard. (ed.). *Adventure Vacations.* Santa Fe, NM: John Muir Publications, 1990.

Coonts, Stephen. *War in the Air.* New York: Pocket Books, 1996.

Csikszentmihalyi, Mihaly. *Finding Flow.* New York: Basic Books, A Division of HarperCollins Publishers, Inc., 1997.

———. *Creativity: Flow and Psychology of Discovery and Invention.* New York: Harper Collins Publishers, Inc., 1996.

———. *The Evolving Self: A Psychology for the Third Millennium.* New York: Harper Collins Publishers, Inc., 1993.

———. *Flow: The Psychology of the Optimal Experience.* New York: Harper & Row, Publishers, 1990.

Csikszentmihalyi, Mihaly, and Isabell Selega Csikszentmihalyi. "Adventure and the Flow Experience" in Miles, John C., and Simon Priest (eds). *Adventure Programming.* State College, PA: Venture Publishing, Inc., 1999, pp. 153–158.

———. *Optimal Experience: Psychological Studies of Flow in Consciousness.* New York: Cambridge University Press, 1988.

Darst, Paul W., and George P. Armstrong. *Outdoor Adventure Activities for School and Recreation Programs.* Prospect Hgts, IL: Waveland Press, Inc., 1991.

Dickerman, Pat. *Adventure Travel.* New York: Adventure Guides, Inc., 1983.

Edginton, Christopher R., and others. *Leisure and Life Satisfaction.* Dubuque, IA: Brown and Benchmark Publishers, 1995.

Ewert, Alan W. *Outdoor Adventure Pursuits: Foundations, Models and Theories.* Columbus, OH: Publishing Horizons, Inc., 1989.

Fair, Erik. *California Thrill Sports.* San Francisco: Foghorn Press, 1992.

Ford, Phyllis, and James Blanchard. *Leadership and Administration of Outdoor Pursuits,* second edition. State College, PA: Venture Publishing, 1993.

Geba, Hans Bruno. *Being at Leisure, Playing at Life.* La Mesa, CA: Leisure Science Systems International, 1985.

Hattingh, Garth. *The Climbers Handbook.* Mechanicsburg, PA: Stackpole Books, 1998.

Hill, Brian J. "A Guide to Adventure Travel" *Park and Recreation,* Vol. 30, No. 9, September 1995, pp. 56–65.

Kelly, John R. *Leisure Identities and Interactions.* Boston: George Allen & Unwin, 1983.

———. *Freedom to Be.* New York: MacMillan Publishing Company, 1987.

———. *Leisure,* second edition. New York: Prentice-Hall, Inc., 1990.

Kraus, Richard. *Recreation and Leisure in Modern Society,* fifth edition. New York: Addison-Wesley Educational Publishers, Inc., 1997.

Leitner, Michael J., and Sara F. Leitner. *Leisure Enhancement.* New York: The Haworth Press, 1989.

McMenamin, Paul. *The Ultimate Adventure Sourcebook.* Turner Pub., Inc., 1992.

Manketelow, MindTools.com (2007).

Mannell, Roger C., and Douglas A. Kleiber. *A Social Psychology of Leisure.* State College, PA: Venture Publishing, Inc., 1997.

Meier, Joel F., Talmadge, W. Morash, and George E. Welton. *High Adventure Outdoor Pursuits: Organization and Leadership.* Columbus, OH: Publishing Horizons, Inc., 1989.

Miles, John C. and Simon Priest, eds. *Adventure Programming.* State College, PA: Venture Publishing, Inc., 1999.

Myers, David G. *The Pursuit of Happiness.* New York: Avon Books, 1993.

Rossman, J. Robert. *Recreation Programming: Designing Leisure Experiences,* 2nd ed. Champaign, IL: Sagamore Publishing Inc., 1995.

Russell, Ruth V. *Pastimes: The Context of Contemporary Leisure.* Dubuque, IA: Brown & Benchmark Publishers, 1996.

Zuckerman, Marvin. *Behavioral Expressions and Biosocial Bases of Sensation Seeking.* Cambridge University Press, 1994.

CHAPTER 4

PERSPECTIVES ON THE HISTORY OF RECREATION AND LEISURE

IN THE BEGINNING

Historians have a unique problem: they never know where to start. In this book, we solved that problem. We decided to start at the beginning—the very beginning. We start our discussion on the history of recreation and leisure with the birth of the universe, the beginning of time.1

Astronomers tell us that the universe was born in an immense explosion spewing hot gases into previously empty space. As the gases cooled, some of the resultant matter took the form of planets—one which came to be known as planet Earth. For billions of years, Earth was inhospitable to life. But eventually it cooled, took its present form, and provided a fertile environment for the simple life forms that began to develop. The life forms gradually, and over millions of years, became increasingly complex, and eventually the planet was dominated by giant lizard-like reptiles. Today we call them dinosaurs.[2]

Complex reptilian life forms had come to dominate planet Earth, but in spite of their size and complexity, it appears that their evolution did not include cognitive development. While in many instances their bodies grew to great proportions, their brains remained disproportionably small. For example, it is estimated that the modern-day rabbit had more brainpower than a giant brontosaurus. With such limited intelligence, and lacking the capacity to learn, dinosaurs functioned on an instinctive level. As creatures of instinct, they lacked the capacity to engage in even the simplest forms of problem solving. It is equally unlikely that dinosaurs had the capacity to engage in anything resembling play. Their lives were characterized by eating, sleeping, and avoiding preditors. Play was beyond their capacity and absent from their behavior. However, their lack of intelligence did not seem to adversely affect them, for they thundered across the planet for millions of years. Then, about 65,000,000 years ago, something went terribly wrong for Earth's giant reptiles. Almost overnight, most of them became extinct.

With the demise of dinosaurs, mammals emerged. Evolving both intellectually and physically, mammals became "smart" animals, and over millions of years evolved into the upright standing, creatively thinking, and emotionally feeling species known as *Homo sapien*. Humans, unlike their reptilian predecessors, had all of the tools to engage in **playful behavior,** and to organize that behavior into increasingly complex forms of structured play that came to be known as **recreation.** In addition, humans also had the intellectual capability to conceptualize and ponder abstract ideas, including the phenomenon now referred to as **leisure.**[3]

TRY THIS

Test the notion that play is characteristic of mammals, but not generally found in reptiles (the descendants of dinosaurs). You can do this by going to the zoo. Compare the behavior of mammals to reptiles.

Primitive Peoples

A few years back, there was a movie out by the name of *Caveman*. It gave the impression that primitive people spent most of their time pursuing food and recreation. But then, what else could you expect from a band of Cro-Magnons led by Ringo Starr? Set in the Paleolithic Period (Stone Age), this movie suggested that early *Homo sapiens* essentially enjoyed the same kind of recreational pleasures that we enjoy today. In actuality, however, it is quite unlikely that primitive people had nearly the fun of Ringo's band. In fact, it is quite unlikely that recreation or leisure, as we conceive it today, existed at all.[4]

To primitive people, magic and religion were powerful forces. All aspects of their lives were influenced by mysterious forces that instilled awe and wonderment, and often fear and anger as well. To modern people, lightning and thunder, the changing seasons, rain and snow, and other natural phenomena are easily explained through the application of scientific principles. But to primitive folks, these same phenomena were only understandable when explained in religious or magical terms. Consequently, the mindset of early humans must have largely been directed at bringing some degree of order to what no doubt appeared a frightening and chaotic world. In order to do this, primitive people resorted to prayer and supplication, which often took the form of dancing, chanting, and singing. Storytelling played an important role among primitive peoples, as did crude drawings and symbols. Even though one may look at these activities as being recreational, among primitive peoples these activities were primarily engaged in to influence the mysterious forces that constantly appeared intent on disrupting their lives.

One can see this in operation among certain contemporary indigenous peoples. For example, the Hopi Indians of Northern Arizona have lived an isolated existence for centuries. Their villages are generally built on high mesas with access limited by narrow roads and precipitous trails. Up until the early 1970s, many of these villages did not have modern conveniences such as indoor plumbing, television, or telephones. The lifestyle of Hopi Indians revolved around their need to influence the weather to treat them favorably, to protect tribal members from outside dangers, and to ensure that tribal traditions were passed on to subsequent generations. Consequently, tribal members gather together at prescribed times to dance and sing to the gods, to supplicate for rain and fertile soil. Children still learn tribal traditions through games, songs, and through playing with Kachina dolls.[5,6]

THINK ABOUT THIS

Compare your understanding of weather when you were young to what you know now. Clouds were cotton candy and the sun came up in the morning and went down at night. Now as an adult you have a different view of these phenomena.

Should you be fortunate enough to visit one of the Hopi mesas, you will see how recreational activities are used for socialization purposes. Although diluted by modern influences such as television, education, movies, tourists, etc., the good people of Shongopovi, Arizona, each year practice the ancient rituals of their ancestors. In their rain dances, night dances, and harvest dances, they attempt to persuade capricious gods to look kindly upon them. Children still play with Kachina dolls, not merely for fun, but to learn the magic of sacred colors, symbols, and the nature of Hopi gods.[7]

Early humans traveled in small bands, hunting and foraging, often passing whole lifetimes without crossing the path of other groups; but as the planet became more populated and as people became more learned in ways to manipulate their environment, play and recreation became an increasingly important part of tribal life. Play became a primary means of education and socialization, and provided a way of practicing important survival and battle skills. Even in recent time in New Guinea, the

Welligman-Wallaua and the Wittaia tribes engage weekly on traditional fighting grounds in a deadly war game.[8] The games of Arctic Eskimos reflect the danger and harshness of their environment and are described by Kraus as games of "self-torture."[9]

Nearly 10,000 years ago in what later became known as Mesopotamia, a major transition in the lifestyle of *Homo sapiens* began to occur. People settled in fixed villages and cities, a written language was developed, an aristocracy was created, and an economic interdependence between social and vocational classes emerged. Civilization had come to planet Earth.

Now that the wheel is invented, I've got so much time that . . . I invented something I call—BOREDOM.

Pre-Christian Civilization

Human beings have been described as "animals that like to figure things out."[10] The productivity, complexity, and advances of early civilizations attest to that notion. Ancient Egyptians were masters of astronomy, engineering, agriculture, and construction. They appeared equally adept at entertaining themselves. Modern nightclubs find their roots in ancient Egypt; the bullfight, music, drama, and dance were important sources of recreation and worship. During the latter part of its history, many of these activities lost their religious significance and were participated in primarily for their recreation value. Even prostitution became a licensed leisure occupation.[11]

It was the Ancient Greeks, however, who placed the greatest value on leisure, particularly those living in the period known as the "Golden Age of Pericles" (500–400 B.C.). Because of the value accorded organized leisure activities, this period is referred to by some scholars as the "First Recreation Revolution."[12] Competitive sports were a frequent form of entertainment; even such formal events as weddings featured sports for the amusement of the guests. The modern Olympics find their origin during this period. Music and drama played an important role. Although the relationship between leisure and other social values was recognized, leisure was viewed as having value in and of itself. To the ancient Greeks, leisure was an end to which all free people aspired. As Aristotle said:

"Nature requires that we should not only work well, but to use leisure well; . . . for the first principle of all action is leisure."[13]

Regrettably—and this is an important point—not all of Greece was free to enjoy the benefits of a leisure-oriented society. The leisure enjoyed by the free citizens of Greece came at the expense of those who were enslaved. It is often stated that in Athens there were four slaves to every free male. It was this underclass that did the chores that liberated a minority of free citizens from obligations that would have otherwise interfered with their recreational pursuits. Ironically, the very people who made leisure possible for the free citizen were unable to engage in leisure themselves. Leisure was unavailable to slaves and members of the lower class, and was, to a very large extent, available only to the male members of upper-class society. Even free women were considered second-class citizens whose function was primarily to tend to the home and attend to family matters.[14]

The Roman view of leisure was not nearly as idealistic as the Greeks. The Roman hierarchy viewed recreation in pragmatic and utilitarian terms. Initially, leisure was looked upon as being essential to good health, useful in teaching correct values, and of economic value. But as the empire began to sag with its own political burdens and excesses, and as free Roman citizens found themselves with increasing free time, the prevailing leisure philosophy was one of entertainment and distraction. By the first century A.D., sports and games had become commercialized and professionalized. By the year 93 A.D., there were 159 public holidays. The famous Roman baths provided endless amusement and recreational opportunities. By the end of the fourth century it is estimated that there were approximately 856 such facilities, capable of accommodating over 60,000 people at one time. And, of course, there were the arenas, the largest of which (the Circus Maximus) could accommodate 350,000 people. Arenas throughout the empire became known as the sites of increasingly bloody entertainment. During the reign of Caligula and Nero, recreation took monstrous forms, and the glory which had been Rome descended into the depths of human deprivation and prepared the way for the Mongolian hordes that ultimately crushed the greatest of empires.[15]

The Roman empire spanned nearly 1,110 years. Its recreation and leisure evolved from simple pastimes to orgies of blood and sensation.[16] Early in its history,

Roman recreation was similar to that of the Greeks, but increased unemployment, free-time, and social unrest led to increasingly colorful and extreme forms of leisure entertainment. This, the "de-evolution" of leisure among the Romans was in part the result of a political and philosophical system that failed to recognize that the human spirit needs not be fed a diet of escalating entertainment, but rather needs to be nourished on opportunities to grow and develop. History might have taken a different course had the prevailing philosophy of Ancient Rome been more akin to that of Ancient Athens.[17]

EXPLORE

To what extent has our contemporary society come to embody some of the values that led to the destruction of the Roman Empire? Watch television for 30 minutes, changing channels every 60 seconds. Count the number of times you see violence, sex, or sensational images. What can you infer from your findings?

THE MIDDLE AND DARK AGES

With the **fall of the Roman Empire,** a period of great social stagnation and decline emerged. Warring tribes and unreliable coalitions shattered the central authority once held by Rome, leaving Europe in chaos. With time the Catholic Church arose as the dominant and unifying force throughout Europe, and with its ascendance to power came a decline in the values that had characterized the Roman lifestyle. Many of the commonly accepted leisure activities of ancient Rome were viewed by Catholicism as sinful. In addition, it is well to remember that under the Romans, Christians had been severely persecuted. Consequently, culture and Roman developments were generally despised by Catholic Church leaders.

The antagonism felt by the Church for things Roman resulted in a severe backlash against anything reflective of Roman culture. Consequently, many of the advancements made by the Romans (and Greeks as well) were lost. For example, the art of soap production was lost, making the Dark Ages

not only dark but dirty. It is believed that much of the disease associated with this period could have been prevented had the knowledge of soap-making not become a forgotten art. Critical thinking generally suffered during this time as well. Music, arts, sciences, and philosophy were inhibited during this time. It is fair to assess this period as a time characterized by limited opportunity and strong religious and political sanctions against play and entertainment.[18]

To characterize the **Dark** and **Middle Ages** as a period of time devoid of recreation and leisure would be an unfortunate overstatement. One of the defining characteristics of humanity is a universal need for play and relaxation. Certainly, this need was not eliminated by the circumstances of this period. Rather, the form that recreation and play took was influenced by the social circumstances of the time. Society during the Middle Ages was stratified along social-economic lines. At the top of the order were the nobility and the clergy, then came the peasants who were further ranked as freemen, villains, serfs, and slaves. Men dominated all levels, and women were generally viewed as inferior to men. Play and recreational opportunities were influenced as much by rank as by the inhibiting influence of the Church.

The nobility had more opportunities for leisure than the lower classes. The peasant classes were extremely poor and relatively defenseless against the demands of the nobility. The nobility had more free time for leisure pursuits than the downtrodden lower classes. Not only did the nobility have more time for leisure, they engaged in more sophisticated forms of recreation than those of lower rank. For example, hunting was a favored sport among the nobility; whereas, among the peasant classes, hunting was an essential means of procuring food. Music, dance, and sports were popular among the nobility; whereas among the peasants cockfighting, bull-baiting, and wrestling were popular.

During the Dark Ages, the Church even orchestrated leisure opportunities through religious celebrations and festivals.

With the passage of time, the backlash of the Church against the depravity of Rome lessened, and for that matter, the controlling influence of the Church diminished as well. With these changes, the people of Europe began to experience a rebirth in their interest in recreation and leisure.

The Renaissance Period

There is no magic date on which one can say the Renaissance began, but historians indicate that the Renaissance began in Italy sometime during the fourteenth century. Unlike the Dark and Middle Ages, this period was marked by a renewed interest in secular things as opposed to the religious obsession that characterized the preceding 1,000 years. Although the Catholic Church remained a powerful influence throughout Europe, its political influence had diminished and its increasingly liberal stance permitted a new sense of freedom among populations that had once been seriously oppressed by the Church. Consequently, people began to explore science, art, and philosophy. Music and dance became important forms of creative expression. A philosophy celebrating the unity of the mind and body developed and thus championed a holistic perspective toward life and learning. It was in this new environment of freedom that many great thinkers, scholars, and artists emerged. Perhaps the spirit of the Renaissance is best typified by Leonardo Da Vinci, who during his life of 67 years became known for his expertise and accomplishments in art, anatomy, engineering, architecture, music, and science. Many of his inventions were remarkable for their creativity melding imagination and reason.

Recreation during the Renaissance became increasingly specialized. Musicians, visual artists, thespians, and actors slowly acquired professional status. Sports and athletic competitions became popular. Leisure and recreation assumed proportions somewhat similar to that of the Ancient Greeks, but the forces opposed to human freedom and expression were not to be denied.[19]

The Reformation

During the **Renaissance,** Catholicism lost a great deal of its political power. Furthermore, doctrinal shifts representing an increasingly liberal religious philosophy occurred as well as growing corruption in church ranks. These two factors combined to stimulate criticism of the church and a call for reformation among Catholic conservatives. Chief among these critics were Martin Luther, John Knox, and John Calvin. The protestations of these and others led to the formation of several apostate religious organizations referred to collectively as **Protestants.** Not known for their tolerance, these religions made attempts to curtail public amusements, sports, arts, and other pleasurable pastimes. The emphasis clearly was on work—indeed a grim dedication to work. Where Protestant religions became dominant, dissenters were ruthlessly suppressed and some, in the name of Jesus, were even burned at the stake. In England, Protestants themselves were repressed by the State Church, thus encouraging many "Puritans" to emigrate to the New World. Consequently, recreation in Colonial America was greatly influenced by Protestant philosophy. For example, early laws in most of the colonies legislated against any form of idleness, which was viewed as the source of all vices. Dancing, public entertainment, and other amusements were condemned as the tools of Satan.

The Reformation was not a bright chapter in the history of recreation and leisure, but the human need for play and recreation could not be repressed for long. By the beginning of the nineteenth century, prohibitions against play and recreation had been somewhat relaxed, a trend which continued until the early stages of the Industrial Revolution.[20]

Think About This

Recreation and leisure services always occur within a social context, part of which is the religious orientation of the community. Reflect on what you know about your community. Can you see how religion might have influenced the form or nature of the services provided in the community? Do different cultures reflect religion in their recreation more than others?

The Industrial Revolution

Industrialization in Europe increased the average work day from 12 hours in the early 1700s to 14 to 18 hours by the mid 1800s.[21] During this period, the Protestant ideals were reinforced, producing the **Protestant (Puritan) Work Ethic.** Work was viewed as man's self-justification, the purpose of life. By the

1850s, laws were passed protecting workers and the escalation of the average work day was reversed. But, it was, as Kraus points out, the Civil War that had the greatest impact on the increase of recreation and leisure throughout the United States. Of this he states:

*It was, however, the **Civil War** that had the greatest positive impact on recreation during this period. Army camps provided young men with an opportunity to meet men from other parts of the country and to share with them ideas and activities regarding leisure and recreation. In an effort to escape the horror of war and boredom of camp life, many soldiers sought relief through recreation, free from the puritanical influence of home and family. Consequently, following the war, soldiers returned home with a broader view of leisure and recreation and tended to promote recreation in their home communities.*[22]

During the late 1800s, commercial amusements prospered, including the development of amusement parks. Professional baseball was established in 1869. Tourism increased. Basketball was invented in 1891. Several volunteer youth-serving agencies were founded, which provided opportunities for children and teenagers, and in 1896, the Olympic Games were reopened.[23]

Basketball is the only popular American game that is not based on pre-existing sports in other parts of the world. The game was invented by James A. Naismith while working at the YMCA in Springfield, Massachusetts. In 1981, while looking for a good winter game to substitute for baseball and football, he came up with the basic idea for the new sport of basketball. It is true that early native Americans played a game that involved throwing a ball through a ring, but it is unlikely that Naismith would have had any knowledge of this game.

It was in 1864 that Congress set aside Yosemite Valley and eight years later declared Yellowstone a National Park.[24] Conservation of recreation resources became an issue during this time.[25]

An important leader in the Recreation Movement during the late 1800s was Frederick Law Olmstead, Sr. (1822–1903). Olmstead was a visionary, artist, and technician. He was one of the principle designers of New York's Central Park. His commitment to providing quality leisure environments for the public led him to design and develop many urban, regional, state, and national parks. In addition, his work influenced the direction taken by other designers and park planners.

ADDITIONAL IMPORTANT DEVELOPMENTS REGARDING MUNICIPAL PARKS DURING THIS PERIOD INCLUDE:

- Place D'armes Square, Canada's first major public park, founded in Montreal, Quebec, Canada, in 1821.
- Central Park founded in New York City in 1850.
- Enabling legislation enacted in New Jersey to permit communities to establish municipal parks in 1885. This was the first of such legislation in the United States.
- The Boston Sand Gardens are established in 1885.
- Metropolitan Park Commission founded in Boston, Massachusetts, in 1892.
- John Muir established the Sierra Club in 1892.
- Resource Driveway and Park District Act passed in Illinois in 1893. It permitted unincorporated areas the authority to establish park systems.

John Muir was a naturalist who devoted his life to the preservation of Yosemite Valley in California, and other valuable natural resources.

It was also during the 1800s that various Christian religions began to take an enlightened perspective of recreation and leisure. The Muscular Christian Movement and the YMCA set the church stamp of approval on sports. During the late 1800s intercollegiate sports became popular. The recreation movement in the United States was clearly underway.

Take a moment and look in the "Yellow Pages" for youth organizations. What did you learn?[26]

In Other Parts of the World . . .

- While Europe was going through the Dark and Middle Ages, **India** was experiencing a lifestyle filled with leisure and recreation. The wealthy created ornate gardens and lakes. Those who had leisure time—mainly the rich—spent it attending literary parties, writing poetry, and engaging in amorous adventures.[27] Sports were also widely played. This included marbles, swimming, wrestling, boxing, javelin, and various ball games.

- Like India, **Japan** did not have a "Dark Age" like that going on in Europe at the time. Public bathhouses became very popular in Japan during the sixth century C.E. Dancers and singers entertained the people who frequented these places. Japanese society enjoyed listening to music and having poetry readings in their homes. In the seventh century, Japanese drama emerged. Their plays brought together dance, music, and drama. Comedy was also very popular for the Japanese. During the sixteenth and seventeenth centuries, puppet shows, or **kabuki,** developed.[28]

- Between 500 and 1500 B.C.E., the **Muslim World** intertwined leisure with their religion. The works of the Greeks, Romans, Persians, and Eastern Indians heavily influenced their culture.[29] During the holy month of Ramadan, where they fasted from sunrise to sunset, the evenings were spent playing card and table games like chess and backgammon. Women, who had to stay in separate quarters, were entertained by female belly dancers.

- **China** has a rich cultural history and recreation has always been a part of it. Competitive archery appeared around 110 B.C.E. and soccer was developed in China during the Han Dynasty (206 B.C.E–25 C.E.). According to Ruth Russell, professor at Indiana University, the Tang Dynasty (618–907) marked "the beginning of leisure in Chinese society."[30]

Chinese estates had many buildings devoted to leisure activities such as listening to music, entertaining with writers, painters, storytellers, and admiring the moon. When Europe was going through the Renaissance, so were the Chinese in some respects. Many novels as well as plays were written in the fourteenth century. Since the 1800s, China has had to deal with Western influences on their culture although the old ways were much preferred. Men still enjoy going to teahouses. Drama is also popular. Peking Operas are favored as well as old Chinese plays. Old Chinese books are still read in leisure time and painting in the old style (flowers, birds, trees, landscapes) is preferred. The Internet is now popular in China, and Western sports like baseball and tennis are now played by Chinese youth.[31]

The Recreation Movement

Recreation and leisure scholars often speak of the "**recreation movement.**" What are they talking about? Social movements are said to involve a number of steps or stages. Movements begin in respect to some compelling social need. This need is initially addressed by an organization or groups of organizations that then set out to create fundamental changes in the way that government and society address the need. So, in reference to the **recreation movement,** *we are talking about a series of events that grew out of a perceived need relating to organized recreation and which taken together resulted in significant growth and development in the way that recreation was viewed by society and the manner in which recreational services were delivered.*

The recreation movement in the United States began in response to conditions associated with urban growth and industrial development.[32] Children had few places to play; they were increasingly at risk as they tried to find play opportunities in busy streets and industrial areas. Progressive thinkers took note of this and began to provide limited play areas for city children. One of the most notable developments occurred in Boston. Most historians give credit to the **Sand Gardens of Boston** as the inception of the recreation movement. The Sand Gardens were really nothing more than large piles of sand made available to Boston's urban children for supervised play. Developed in 1885 for the children of Boston, similar play areas soon appeared in other cities. In 1892, Jane Adams established the first model playground at the Hull House, one of the nation's first settlement houses. Park systems soon began to appear across the United States, many modeled after **Central Park** of New York City which was dedicated in 1853.

Of particular prominence during these formative times was a man by the name of Joseph Lee. Known as the "father of the playground movement," Lee was a lawyer and philanthropist who came to view recreation and play as having great value to society. He wrote extensively on the subject and was a popular orator. He was the president of the American Playground Association from 1910 until his death in 1937.

The recreation movement was not limited to urban areas. In many respects it became a national phenomenon. There were factors at work across the fabric of the nation that had far-reaching consequences. Industrialization, urbanization, commercialization of recreation, increasing crime, and concern about the environment are examples of these factors. Carlson, Deppe, Maclean, and Peterson identified nine such points that they believe led to the first formal efforts to initiate professional recreation and leisure services on a national scale.[33]

1. By the early 1900s, it was clear our national resources would eventually be depleted unless protected.

2. The Industrial Revolution had led to unpredicted free time and also had a dehumanizing effect.

3. People began moving to the cities.

4. Crime was steadily increasing.

5. Population was steadily increasing.

6. Mental health problems were steadily increasing.

7. "Unwholesome" recreation was increasing.

8. People were increasingly mobile.

9. Many cities and special interest groups began to demonstrate the need for a resource network.

Several organizations serving the recreation field were started at the turn of the century. People began to move into the cities and the demand for leisure services increased. Many men and women were concerned about "the provision of proper environments for play and the wise use of leisure."[34] This meant having regulations that would ensure the parks and playgrounds that people used would be safe. Many cities and special interest groups began to demonstrate the need for a resource network. The first playground commission was established in 1904 by the city of Los Angeles. In 1906, a group of socially conscious leaders met in Washington, DC, to resolve some of the recreation and leisure problems of the day. This led to the founding of the American Playground Association. In 1911 it was changed to the Playground and Recreation Association to reflect a broader area of interest (now it is called the National Recreation and Park Association). They advocated for increased opportunities in music, drama, and the arts in school. Laws were passed in many states mandating physical training classes and areas for recreation in school systems.[35] The purpose of this group remains to be the "promotion and development of leisure services that will bring a better quality of life not only for children but for all people."[36] As a result of this **playground movement** at the turn of the century, the National Education Association recognized the importance of recreation by including "education for leisure" as one of the Seven Cardinal Principles of Education in 1918.

Another important organization that was started at the beginning of the twentieth century was the National Park Service. In 1906, Congress passed the Antiquities Act, giving the President the power to designate national monuments and protect them from being destroyed. In 1916, Congress decided that a federal agency needed to be formed to regulate this and the Bureau of National Parks; thus the National Park Service was formed.[37]

World War I and the Roaring 20s

U.S. involvement in the "War to End All Wars" lasted from October 17, 1917 to November 11, 1918. The war itself lasted only four years. Ten million people died during this time and another 20 million were wounded. This was, however, not the last war . . .

As a result of the recreation resources made available for the military, World War I brought an upsurge in public appreciation for public recreation, and set the stage for a period of unprecedented license, "the period of emotional and social stress." In answer to both the financial needs and the emotional/social needs of this period, the federal government instituted several emergency efforts. The result was a dramatic increase in public recreational facilities and leadership training. It is interesting to note that it was during the Depression that the 18th Amendment (Prohibition) was repealed. Federal programs which contributed to the recreation movement included the Federal Emergency Relief Administration (FERA), the National Youth Administration (NYA), the Works Progress Administration (WPA), and the Civilian Conservation Corps (CCC). These agencies administered and funded many outdoor recreation developments. The arts received a boost from the Federal Arts Program. It was during this time that college training first became available for recreation workers (1937).

World War II

In spite of its carnage, World War II, just as with World War I, in the long term had a positive impact on the recreation movement. The Special Services Division of the U.S. Army, the Welfare and Recreation Bureau of the Navy, and the Recreation Service of the Marines provided organized recreation for thousands of men and women serving in the Armed Services. The Red Cross, USO, the National Recreation Association, and countless community recreation programs contributed to meeting the leisure needs of military personnel, their families, and those working in war industries. Following the war they brought their interest in organized recreation back to their communities. Just as servicemen and women had been exposed to organized recreation in the military, home-front recreation increased to provide recreational support to those working in the war industries. As a consequence of this dramatic increase in recreational opportunities, by the time the war ended, millions of Americans had become accustomed to enjoying government-sponsored recreational activities and programs. Naturally, many of these people wanted to continue to enjoy organized recreation and encouraged their communities to further develop such programs.

People with recreational training found employment opportunities serving those who had come to value organized recreation and leisure. In addition, many cities erected "living monuments" in the form of parks, stadiums, and other recreational facilities.[38]

THINK ABOUT THIS

Why do you suppose the government found it valuable to provide recreational services for military personnel?

The 1950s to the 1970s

Upon conclusion of the World War II, a healthy economy brought an increase in leisure activity. Transportation and entertainment flourished. The 1950s became appropriately, "The Fabulous 50s." Bill Haley and the Comets and Elvis Presley started a revolution that "rocks on" even today. Then came the Beetles, long hair, hippies, and the birth control pill. The 1960s were a decade of social conscience, experimentation, and conflict. From a recreational standpoint, people experienced more freedom and variety; social programs sponsored by the government provided services for the disabled and minority groups. The Civil Rights Movement touched the social conscience of the United States and great strides were made toward racial and gender equality, but Vietnam and racial strife made for shaky times and conflict.[39]

During the early 1950s international travel expanded dramatically, and with that expansion came an awareness among recreation and leisure professionals that leisure and recreation issues had global implications. In 1956, the first international association for recreation professionals was established. Initially known as the **International Recreation Association,** it later changed its name to the **World Recreation and Leisure Association.**[39] In 2006, the organization changed its name to the **World Leisure Organization.** This better reflected the organizational structure of the association as well as better related to its association with the United Nations.

In 1966, five separate professional recreation and leisure organizations—the American Association of Zoological Parks and Aquariums, American

Institute of Park Executives, American Recreation Society, National Conference on State Parks, and the National Recreation Association—merged to form the **National Recreation and Park Association.**[40] The Outdoor Recreation Review Commission (ORRC) and the Bureau of Outdoor Recreation (BOR) was established during this time in the Department of the Interior. The BOR was established by executive order in 1962. The Bureau of Outdoor Recreation was given the mission of unifying and promoting federal programs concerned with open space, natural resources, and outdoor recreation. It was responsible for managing the **Land and Water Conservation Fund** established in 1965. It also served to coordinate the services of the **National Wild and Scenic Rivers System** and the **National Trails System.** The bureau also worked closely with state and local agencies that provided recreation services. It is known for developing the first Nationwide Outdoor Recreation Plan. Renamed the Heritage Conservation and Recreation Service in 1978, this bureau was dismantled and its functions absorbed by the National Park Service three years later as a cost-cutting measure.[41]

The "Stressful 60s" were replaced by the "Sane 70s." With the end of the Vietnam conflict came a period of relative calm. The social unrest of the 1960s was replaced by an urgent need to heal the scars of the previous decade and resolve the economic problems created by the energy crisis and runaway inflation. In addition, the sexual freedom of the 1960s appeared to have spawned genital herpes, a venereal precursor of things to come. The sexual license of the flower children was suddenly challenged.[42]

One notable advancement during the 1960s and 1970s was the increase in the number of universities offering professional preparation for careers in leisure services. This was, in part, a function of society's increasing acceptance of recreation and leisure service as a legitimate and important governmental function.[43]

A Period of Austerity: The 1970s and 1980s

But the picture was not all positive. During the latter part of the 1970s, the economy took a down turn. By the early 1980s, park districts and municipal recreation agencies began cutting back on services. Several cities took severe hits in terms of programs and facilities. Some have never fully recovered. This period had a profound impact on recreation and leisure service management. The public service model of recreation service gave way to a more business, "pragmatic" approach to recreation programming. Programs became more entrepreneurial with fees and charges becoming an important part of their funding schemes. Furthermore, many agencies found value in subcontracting programs and services to private businesses. Some of the gains made on the university level for recreation and leisure study programs were lost during the late 1980s. Usually in the name of economizing, several university programs were severely reduced and in some cases completely eliminated.

In the 1980s, the natural environment became a concern for a large number of Americans. Many people saw that the land set aside for parks was dwindling, that wildlife was being endangered, and that the environment was threatened on various fronts. The public increasingly called upon government to take steps to protect our natural resources and environment. In a poll conducted in 1988, 70 percent of those questioned wanted better environmental protection even if it was at taxpayer cost or personal sacrifice.[44] There was a corresponding movement among the public to simplify. Their lifestyles supported a more conservation-oriented ethic. This was in startling contrast to the Reagan-Bush administration, which not only cut back money for recreational programs, but also sold thousands of acres of wildlife for business interests. President Reagan said in 1981 ". . . when you've seen one redwood, you've seen them all."[45] Hundreds of thousands of Americans joined environmental groups, such as the Sierra Club and Greenpeace, in opposition to the government's position toward wildlife areas. The National Recreation and Park Association published pamphlets and magazines to educate the public about the tenuous state of park facilities during this time. The National Park Service, as well as many park districts, had to struggle to maintain the land under their control. The National Parks and Conservation Association fought on behalf of the National Parks against a government that placed industry above preserving wilderness areas. Ironically, in a time where most Americans knew the importance of having land for recreational use, the government had an agenda that seemed ignorant of the social, spiritual, and recreational value of the nation's natural wildlands and open spaces.

What's going on in your community? Do you recall hearing anything about cutbacks, downsizing, or layoffs in any of the agencies offering recreational services in your community? Do you remember hearing about cutbacks happening during the late 1980s? Is there someone you can talk to who might remember how their personal recreation and leisure were affected?

While tax-funded programs were being reduced, there was a more positive picture emerging in the field of commercial recreation. Generally speaking, the past three decades have been favorable to the commercial recreation industry. Travel, tourism, theme parks, hobbies, entertainment, and professional sports have continued to grow and innovate.

On other fronts, it was in the 1980s that Halley's Comet came back for a visit, but was so faint that it was barely visible. Terrorism continued to expand, making no corner of the world safe from its evil reach; religion experienced a revival; arcades gave way to home video; and physical fitness, and the fitness industry boomed. AIDS became an international problem, making sex a scary proposition. Movies remained as popular as ever with a new emphasis on machismo and patriotism.

Although the 1980s made huge strides in technological development, it was the 1990s that showed just how remarkable technology was becoming.

The 1990s to the Present

The 1990s can be described as a kaleidoscope of events and issues passing by at seemingly warp speed. Some of these events and issues were a continuation of those that characterized the previous decade; some were quite dramatic and unexpected. Among the least anticipated were the collapse of the Soviet bloc, the fall of communism, and the rise of globalization. Other issues, such as the influence of the media, air quality, crime, multiculturalism, and the erosion of the middle class continued to be issues throughout the 1990s. Many of these concerns and issues continued into the first decade of the 2000s with concerns about energy, the economy, and global violence leading the way.

There is some confusion as to what the first decade should be called. Some suggest that it be called the "naughts." Others suggest following the already established pattern and call it the 2000s. That is the preference shown in this chapter.

The Internet, Computers, and Digital Media

Although the 1980s made huge strides in technological development, it was the 1990s that showed just how remarkable technology was becoming. During the 1990s, more and more people acquired computers. This, coupled with the rise of the Internet, set the stage for a cultural revolution driven almost exclusively by technology. Home computers became indispensable and the Internet made access to information and communication unbelievably convenient. Entertainment took an interesting turn, making home entertainment more attractive than ever before. Sitting in front of the computer no longer was equated with work. These incredible technological strides gave rise to a new set of concerns. Some observers of contemporary society began to fear that the combination of the social isolation imposed by technology coupled with ever-increasing violent and sexually explicit media content would make society a less friendly and more hostile place.[46] There was a concern that as people became more dependent upon computers and technology for their entertainment and communication, human interaction would suffer.

Think of the many ways your life is influenced by technology. How would your life be impacted if just one technology was missing . . . for example, cell phone technology?

Pop-culture during the 1990s tended toward entertainment that focused on common social themes. Comedic sitcoms proved to be particularly popular: *Seinfeld, Friends, Frasier, Full House, The Simpson's,* and *South Park* are examples of popular television shows during the 1990s. Many of these are still seen today, for example, *The Simpson's* and *South*

Park are still in production. Science fiction emerged as a popular favorite often combing social issues with fanciful storylines.

On the music scene, grunge and punk music were popular, and hip-hop gained in popularity along with rap. By the end of the decade "boy bands" had become popular.

The New Millennium brought a new emphasis on sensation. Television programs became more prone to show violence and sex. "Reality television" seemed to reflect a "winning is all that matters" philosophy. Manipulation and interpersonal deceit came to be valued on series that voted people from off the island, or from off the stage. The Internet also became more "reality based." Websites such as *MySpace* and *Match.Com* made it easy for people to maintain a social network without ever meeting face to face. Some authorities became concerned that sensation seeking through the Internet will lead to an increase in social misfits whose view of the world is based on the lens afforded them through the computer.

Once I got online with the Internet, I became an urban hermit.

—Derek Jones

In the early 1990s, child psychologists, recreation professionals, and educators began to fear that computers (and television) might have a harmful effect on children. They were concerned that the manner in which children process information would be impaired by spending too much time in front of the computer or television. They were concerned that children would begin to model their behavior on that which they watch on TV or were exposed to on the computer. These fears are still being echoed by today's social scientists.

In addition, the compelling nature of television and computers has been shown to pull children away from active outdoor recreation. It is easier to sit and be entertained than engage in physically active recreation. As a consequence, childhood obesity began to emerge as a potentially serious problem in the 1990s and continues today.

Professional recreation turned its attention to wellness issues and began to develop programs to attract children away from the television screen and to the activity field.

The Environment and Energy Issues

Some issues that plagued the recreation field in the 1980s were addressed in the 1990s while new ones emerged. In the late 1980s, it had become clear that our public parklands had both dwindled and degraded. In response to this, in the 1990s the government set aside huge amounts of land for recreational use. As an example, in 1996, President Bill Clinton set aside $6.4 million to create the Grand Staircase-Escalante National Monument in Utah. Thousands of acres were conserved from any kind of development.[47] The importance of having parks and open areas for public use was being reinforced. The environment became a hot topic as many people found out the effects that pollution and toxic waste had on recreational areas. In addition, there was increasing concern among some environmental groups, that off-road vehicles, snowmobiles, and power boats were doing serious harm to wilderness areas and federal and state parklands.

An example of the environmental conscience that developed in the 1980s and grew throughout the 1990s is Julia "Butterfly" Hill. Starting in 1997, Hill took up residence in a giant redwood tree in the Headlands Forest of Stafford, California. She lives 180 feet above ground on a platform to protect an ancient redwood tree from being cut down by a lumber company. She does her cooking on a propane stove and communicates with others via a cellular phone. Hill has said that love is her motivation for living in a tree.[48] She is truly dedicated to the protection of the ancient forest. Because of her efforts, the Department of Forestry withdrew the logging permit pending a review of their logging practices.

Global warming became one of the themes of the 1990s. Often falling along political lines, debate raged over the validity of scientific claims that the world's climate was heating up. Democrats tended to support efforts to curb "hot house" gases; Republicans tended to scoff at the science behind global warming, and argued that to institute the curbs called for by Democrats would hurt the economy. During the first half of the 2000s, the Republican Party essentially owned the government, and as such, efforts to curb pollution in the United States were stalled.

One of the landmark political agreements relating to global warming was the Kyoto Treaty. Open to signatories on March 16, 1998, a total of 169 countries had signed it by December 2006. One of the notable exceptions is the United States. The Bush Administration stands firm in its opposition to the Kyoto Treaty. Republicans argue that there is insufficient evidence to believe that Kyoto would accomplish anything significant. Opponents to the Bush Administration argue that the Republicans put corporate profit ahead of clean air and water.

It was during the 1990s that several important steps were taken to improve the condition of our national parks. New user-fees were instituted to provide a stream of revenue to be used in upgrading the national park system; steps were taken, such as reducing automobile traffic on parklands, to minimize pollution. In 1998 the government announced a moratorium on the construction of new logging roads. However, from 2000 to 2007, the government has generally sided with the logging industry and has failed to follow the trend that characterized the late 1990s.

Although California may lead the world in auto emissions, in 1997 smoking in public buildings was made illegal. The rational was that by so doing, smoking-related diseases would decrease. This suggests another important aspect of pollution. The relationship to disease and air and water pollution is widely known, yet the government refuses to take the big steps necessary to ensure the public (and the environment) is protected from the harmful effects of toxic substances associated with manufacturing and toxic emissions.

POINT TO PONDER

Are you doing anything personally to minimize pollution? If not, can you think of one thing you might do?

Globalization and Global Capitalism

Beginning with the collapse of the Soviet Union and the end of the Cold War, multinational corporations emerged as the new economic powerbrokers leading the push for a convergence of patterns of production and consumption worldwide. Referred to as globalization, this became one of the principle themes of the 1990s. Globalization set to work economic and market forces that slowly began generating *homogeneity* between once very diverse cultures. Former communist countries rushed to embrace "global capitalism." Led by China, American and European companies were welcomed behind the "bamboo curtain," creating an economic boom for China and a new market for Western manufacturers. As the new millennium approached, not only did China became increasingly wealthy, the proliferation of Western companies in China's major cities began to give China a post-industrial Western look.

Globalization was not well received in some quarters. As foreign countries became increasingly receptive to the overtures of Western companies, many American jobs were shifted to foreign workers. American workers who were displaced by job "outsourcing" found themselves unemployed and angry. Similarly, controversy arose over the North American Free Trade Agreement (NAFTA), which went into effect on January 1, 1994. This agreement lowered many of the restrictions that governed trade between Mexico, Canada, and the United States.

The debate over globalization and global capitalism did not slow down in the 2000s. A 2004 Zogby International poll reports that 71 percent of American voters believe that "outsourcing jobs overseas" hurts the economy, and another 62 percent believe that the U.S. government should impose some legislative action against companies that transfer domestic jobs overseas, possibly in the form of increased taxes on companies that outsource.[49] The government does not appear interested in taking such steps.

The effect of globalization on leisure is found primarily in the form of consumer products, travel, and entertainment. During the 1990s, more and more entertainment and communication products were produced in Asian countries, exported to the United States, and sold (often in big box stores) at affordable prices. Thus, many people were able to afford high-tech electronic tools and toys for the first time. Fashion and textiles production was dramatically increased with the acceptance of China into the World Trade Organization, thus making clothing more affordable. Travel opportunities to Asia and Eastern Europe brought new destinations to the world traveler. On the other hand, those individuals whose income potential was diminished through outsourcing found themselves unable to enjoy the vast array of products being imported from overseas, and excluded from the new opportunities to travel.

Privatization of Public Services

Recreation, security, garbage, penal institutions, and similar functions generally viewed as governmental are being increasingly operated by private enterprise. As a consequence, traditional recreation and leisure services are shifting to a more business-like model—more programs are on a pay-as-you-go basis, fewer leisure services for the poor. The business model allows for great variance in services, whereas the traditional model tended to offer more equal services.

An Increase in Violence

When the Soviet Union fell, only the United States was left as a viable military super-force. Thus, as the calendar turned to the 1990s, it seemed that there was no serious threat to Western Europe or the United States. The end of the Cold War brought a feeling of hope that peace was here to stay. Unfortunately, this hope was short-lived.

In August of 1990, Iraq, following a dispute over oil rights, invaded Kuwait. The UN levied severe sanctions on Iraq, and authorized an armed intervention which began in January of 1991. Led by the United States, a coalition of 30 nations rapidly defeated the Iraqi army. But this was only the beginning. It seemed there was always a new problem to deal with and the U.S. military had become the world's police force. In 1993, the United States became involved in the war in Somalia, and then in 1994 sent troops to overthrow the oppressive Haitian government. In 1996 troops were sent to Bosnia as part of a NATO peacekeeping force. In late March 1999, the United States joined NATO in air strikes against Yugoslavia in an effort to halt the Yugoslavian government's policy of ethnic cleansing in its province of Kosovo. The decade was to end much as it began with U.S. forces deployed in many countries, and the United States playing arbitrator, enforcer, and peace keeper throughout the world, and the worst was just ahead.

Violence was not limited to foreign fields of battle. Violence in the United States became almost commonplace during the 1990s. In 1992 riots broke out in South Central Los Angeles following the arrest and beating of Rodney King. A year later, on the East Coast, Islamic extremists attempted to bring down the World Trade Center by detonating a large bomb in the underground parking garage. It was in the same year that four federal agents were killed while raiding the Branch Davidian cult's compound in Waco, Texas. It was in 1995 that OJ Simpson was tried for the murder of his former wife, Nicole, and her friend, Ron Goldman. The trial which was watched by millions highlighted the entertainment value of real life drama, as well as the schism between black and white America. The same year, home-grown terrorists brought down the Alfred P. Murrah Federal Building in Oklahoma City.

Concerns about gun violence in the United States and the untiring efforts of Sara Brady, the wife of James Brady, who was shot during the assassination attempt on President Reagan in 1981, led to the passing of the "Brady Bill." This bill required a five-day waiting period before a person could purchase a gun. During this period, the buyer's background would be checked for use of a gun in a crime. About a decade later, the five-day waiting period was replaced by a mandatory computer check.

Even though the overall murder rate in the United States diminished during the second-half of the 1990s, unprecedented violence, in the form of classroom shootings, emerged during this period. In the months between February 1996 and April 1999 there were numerous reports of school shootings.[50] The most extreme occurred in Littleton, Colorado, at Columbine High School.

It was during the 1990s that the term "paranoid society"[51] began to appear in literature. Between the twin threats of domestic crime and international terrorism, the people of the United States began to show the symptoms of increased anxiety and concern about personal safety. Gun sales soared as people began to feel the need for a firearm for personal protection.

Perhaps the people of the United States had good reason to be paranoid. The violence seen in the 1990s continued into the "New Millennium." On September 11, 2001, Islamic Extremists finally succeeded in bringing down the World Trade Center's "Twin Towers," damage the Pentagon, and murder over 3000 innocent people. Feeling pressure to respond, the administration claimed that there was link between Iraq and Al-Queda, the extremist group behind the attack. This presumed link became the pretext for the American invasion of Iraq. Later information, revealed in a report from the National Commission on Terrorist Attacks upon the United States, concluded that there was no "credible evidence of a link between Iraq and Al-Queda in attacks against the United States,"[52] but by then the U.S. government had poured thousands of American troops into Iraq, at a huge cost in life and money. By the late 2000s, public opinion turned against the "war," but President Bush refused to alter his course. As of this writing, the fighting goes on.

The first decade of the 2000s saw the trend toward school violence continue and eclipse that of the 1990s, with the most lethal occurring on the Virginia Tech campus in April of 2007 where 39 students were killed by a single heavily armed gunman. Most schools now have a security staff, and some of have installed metal detectors to check for firearms and knives.

Unfortunately, the decline in murders overall that was reported during the latter part of the 1990s was replaced with a dramatic rise in murders in most American metropolitan areas. Today violence continues to be a part of the American way of life, with no end in sight.

The effect of violence in society on leisure and recreation is difficult to assess. However, it is clear that during the 1990s, more and more recreation providers hired private security firms and coordinated with law enforcement agencies to afford recreation users a modicum of protection from acts of violence. Practices instituted to ensure safe travel following "9-11," along with a public concern about the possibility of future terrorist plots to use airlines, has had an adverse effect on the airline and travel industries. There are concerns that violence in society is contributing to the decline of civility and neighborliness. People are less congenial and less trusting than in earlier times. Gun control remains a big issue. The gun-lobby argues that control could adversely affect recreational hunting, while gun control advocates argue that an armed society is dangerous and ultimately makes it difficult for individuals to enjoy "the pursuit of happiness" for fear of being shot.[53]

Public and non-profit agencies providing services to inner-city youth have an important role to play in reducing violence in society, as well as providing safe environments in which children can play. Kraus states that "children living in economically disadvantaged households—predominantly urban ghettos or rural slums—tend to have few resources

for constructive play." He goes on to say, "In the early 1990s the National Commission on Children reported that there was ample evidence that the poverty rates for children had increased sharply over the past three decades.[54] Kraus goes on to point out that poor children often are left to their own resources in communities that are dominated by drug dealers or youth gangs. If society is to stem the tide of violence among the young people of America, it is going to have to begin by ensuring that children have a safe environment in which to grow and develop. Recreation and leisure services can play an important role here.

POINT TO PONDER

Reflect back on your own personal history. Has violence impacted your recreation and leisure patterns in any way?

Immigration and Multiculturism

"Illegal immigration" became a hot button topic during the 1990s and continues to grow in intensity today. The *Pew Hispanic Center* reports that even though the number of legal immigrants has not changed significantly since the 1980s, the number of illegal immigrants, primarily from Mexico and Latin America, have increased significantly. During the latter part of the 1990s, nearly 75 percent of all illegal immigrants were from Mexico and Latin America.[55] Almost without exception, these "undocumented" aliens enter the United States seeking work, and many of them are able to find it. Illustrating the significance of this issue is the 1994 Proposition 187 which would have prevented illegal immigrants from receiving services funded by tax dollars. The proposition passed, but was overturned by the federal court.

Immigration, be it legal or illegal, has literally changed the face of America. Heretofore, both public recreational services and private leisure ventures have operated on the assumption that the "public" was essentially a homogeneous culture. This is no longer the case. The 1990s saw a rapid increase of non-European populations. In many major cities, non-whites outnumber Euro-Americans. Some writers refer to this phenomenon as the "browning of America." Regardless of what you call it, the face of America is clearly changing, and with it, the recreational patterns and interests of her citizens are also changing. The implication for recreation and leisure services is clear, the programming and marketing of recreational products, programs, and services will begin to reflect more and more the values and interests of different cultural groupings.

Diversity, Stratification, and Division

The United States is becoming more stratified and divided. The first major division is along economic lines. The middle class has been shrinking, while the number of people living in poverty has increased dramatically. The term "conspicuous consumption" is more applicable now than ever before. The haves not only have more, but they like to flaunt their excessive wealth. CEO's are often making more money in a year than the sum total of their workers. As the old adage goes, "The wealthy get wealthier and the poor get poorer." In part, uncontrolled immigration has played a role in this, particularly along the Mexican border. Mexican workers are willing to work for very low wages, allowing for greater profits for those who employ them.

Battle lines are also drawn along political lines, with conservatives and liberals often taking opposite points of view on social issues such as gender equity, gay rights, gun control, and the environment. Political correctness also makes "proper speak," a dividing point among many people. The leisure implications are many and varied, but one thing is certain: future recreation and leisure will reflect the increased diversity of the society.

Sports and Recreation Activities

In the 1990s rollerblading became popular. By the late 1990s snowboarding started to replace skiing as a favored winter activity. Kite surfing, bouldering, and bungee cord jumping reflect an increase in sensation seeking. The implication for leisure is not clear, but it is quite likely that sensation seeking will become increasingly popular.

Family Values

The phrase "family values" was popularized during the presidential campaign of 2000. The Republican Party promised a return to more conservative times and promised to "restore the family." It proved to be mere campaign rhetoric. What is not mere rhetoric is the fact that the structure of the American household is changing. More single moms are raising children, and many of those moms are working. Divorce is holding steady, but there are more unmarried couples. In some states, gays and lesbians have been given the opportunity enjoy a legal marriage. The educated are having fewer children, the poorly educated and poor are having larger families. The "latchkey" problem identified during the 1980s persists as more and more parents must work away from the home.

The implications for leisure are apparent. After-school programs are essential to provide activities for children who would otherwise have no adult supervision until their parents return from work. In 2002, California voters overwhelmingly supported Proposition 49, a proposition that mandated after-school programming. Unfortunately, no funding mechanism was built into the proposal. It remains unfunded to this day.

At this time in history, one thing remains clear: the role of professional recreation and leisure service is as important and vital as ever before. There is an increasing awareness that leisure and recreation services can play an important role in meeting the needs of the future. Among these are the developmental needs of children, the social needs of the aged, the conservation of our national resources, and improving the environment, as well as helping society achieve greater racial and gender equity.[57]

WHERE TO FROM HERE?

Your personal history will determine your future. Where do you want to be in five years, ten years, and twenty years? Spend a few minutes contemplating the future you would like. Write down some of the steps you think you should take to achieve your goals.

We have come along way since the beginning—since the Big Boom. But, in spite of our intelligence and ability to solve problems, the problems persist, and one of the great challenges of the future will be to develop social and personal strategies and values that ensure all people a quality life. Recreation and leisure services can play an important part in that process.

NOTES

1. Scientists can't be certain, but best estimates are that the Big Boom occurred about 18 billion years ago.

2. For more on the disappearance of the dinosaurs read Carl Sagan's *The Dragons of Eden.*

3. Want to know more? See Carl Sagan's book *The Dragon's of Eden.*

4. *Homo Sapien* refers to the genus to which human's belong. Sapien refers to "having the capacity to think."

5. To ancient peoples religion was the ultimate source of knowledge.

6. Some religious functions took a form that can be viewed as very similar to recreation—even play.

7. Primitive people use play to teach important social and metaphysical lessons. Do we do the same today?

8. Kraus, R. *Recreation and Leisure in Modern Society.* (Santa Monica: Goodyear Publishing Co., Inc., 1978): 129.

9. Ibid.

10. Carl Sagan on *The Johnny Carson Show,* (January 20, 1986).

11. Many recreational activities lost their religious significance, and became solely recreational.

12. Chubb, Michael, and R. Holly, *One-Third of Our Time? And Introduction to Recreation and Behavior and Resources.* (New York: John Wiley & Sons, 1988) p. 20.

13. Kraus, R. *Recreation and Leisure in Modern Society.* (Santa Monica: Goodyear Publishing Co., Inc., 1978): 134.

14. The Ancient Greeks viewed leisure and recreation as having great value.

15. The Ancient Romans sensationalized leisure much like contemporary Americans.

16. This can be considered a macro example of the human need to continually add complexity and novelty to daily life.

17. Is there a lesson here?

18. Renaissance essentially means "rebirth."

19. Reformation means to *reform.*

20. Religious leaders who protested against the liberal thinking of the Church were called *Protestants.* Recreation was viewed by Protestants as sin.

21. Kraus, R. *Recreation and Leisure in Modern Society.* (Santa Monica: Goodyear Publishing Co., Inc., 1978): 159.

22. The Civil War affected society's view of recreation.

23. There was a flurry of athleticism during the late 1800's: in 1869 professional baseball was begun, in 1891 basketball was invented, and in 1896 the Olympic Games were reintroduced.

24. Yellowstone National Park has to be one of the true wonders of the world. Its geysers, hot springs, raging rivers, giant gorges, and enchanting waterfalls make it a truly national treasure. It was first seen by explorers in 1870, whose first inclination was to lay claim on the area and use it for commercial purposes. Ultimately, their sense of perspective won over their greed, and they petitioned Congress to set aside this area as a public trust and protect it from commercial schemes, such as the kind they themselves, had first entertained upon discovering this wondrous land (Carlson, Deppe, Maclean, 1979, p. 123).

25. The movement toward the establishment of national parks began in the late 1800s: in 1864 Yosemite was established, and in 1872 Yellowstone National Park was established.

26. The Young Men's Christian Association was founded in Great Britain in 1844. The YWCA followed in 1866. The Boys Club was established in 1860, the Girls Club in 1864. The Boy Scouts was founded 1910; the Girls Scouts in 1912: and Camp Fire in 1912.

27. Cordes, Kathleen, and Hilmi Ibrahim. *Applications in Recreation & Leisure.* (Boston: WCB McGraw-Hill, 1999): 26.

28. "Japanese Drama." *Microsoft Encarta 98 Encyclopedia.* (CD-ROM)(1998).

29. Russell, Ruth. *Pastimes.* (Madison, WI: Brown & Benchmark, 1996): 26.

30. Ibid, 25.

31. Lang, Olga. *Chinese Family and Society.* (New Haven, CT: Yale University Press, 1950).

32. Kelly, John R. *Leisure.* (Englewood Cliffs: Prentice Hall, 1992): p. 148.

33. Carlson, R. E., J. Maclean, and T. R. Deppe, and J. Petereson. *Recreation and the Changing Scene.* (Belmont: Wadsworth Publishing Company, 1979): 42–44.

34. Sessons, Douglas. *Leisure Services.* (Englewood Cliffs, NJ: Prentice-Hall, 1984): 45.

35. Carlson, Reyold, Theodore Deppe, and Janet Maclean. *Recreation in American Life.* (Belmont, CA: Wadsworth, 1963): 43.

36. Ball, Edith, and Robert Cipriano. *Leisure Services Preparation.* (Englewood Cliffs, NJ: Prentice-Hall, 1978): 13.

37. In 1906, the American Playground Association of America was founded.

38. As ironic as it seems, times of turmoil have often given rise to important advances in the field of recreation and leisure.

39. Want to know more? Visit the WLRA home page at http://www.worldleisure.org/.

40. For more on NRPA visit their website: http://www. nrpa. org/.

41. The BOR was short-lived. It was phased out of existence in 1978. See Executive Order 11017 authorizing the formation of the BOR by visiting the CD-ROM. Bureau of Outdoor Recreation founded in 1962.

42. Educational Amendment Act of 1974 (Community Schools Act) encouraged use of schools for after-hours recreational use.

43. The 1970s and 1980s were marked by austerity, but they set the stage for the great boom that was ushered in by the high technology of the early 1990s.

44. Opie, John. *Nature's Nation: An Environmental History of the United States.* (New York: Harcourt Brace, 1998): 417.

45. Ibid, 420.

46. In 1998 John Glenn goes into space at the age of 77.

47. www.doi.gov (October 7, 1999).

48. Environment News Service, "Julia 'Butterfly' Hill's Year Atop Giant Redwood," (http://ens.lycos.com/ens/ dec98/1998L-12-10-02.html), 2.

49. Zogby, *Outsourcing,* 2004.

50. Environment News Service, "Julia 'Butterfly' Hill's Year Atop Giant Redwood", (http://ens.lycos.com/ens/ dec98/1998L-12-10-02.html), 2.

    For a time line of school shootings during the 90s go to http://www.infoplease.com/ipa/A0777958.html

51. A term sometimes used is "societal paranoia." For an interesting discussion on this concept visit http:// shrinkwrapped.blogs.com/blog/2006/09/terror_ and_soci.html

52. "Senate Report: No Saddam, Al-Queda Link" http:// www.msnbc.msn.com/id/14728447/

53. Mildred Williams, crime reporter, personal interview March 15, 2004.

54. Kraus. p. 141.

55. For the full Pew Hispanic Center Report see http:// pewhispanic.org/.

REFERENCES

Ball, Edith, and Robert Cipriano. *Leisure Services Preparation.* Englewood Cliffs, NJ: Prentice-Hall, 1963.

Brewster, Todd. "How TV Shaped America." *LIFE,* April 1999.

Butler, George D. *Introduction to Community Recreation.* New York: McGraw-Hill Book Company, 1976.

Carl Sagan on "The Johnny Carson Show," (January 20, 1986).

Carlson, R. E., J. Maclean, T. R. Deppe, and James Peterson. *Recreation and the Changing Scene.* Belmont: Wadsworth Publishing Company, 1979.

Carlson, Reyold, Theodore Deppe, and Janet Maclean. *Recreation in American Life.* Belmont: Wadsworth, 1963.

Chubb, Michael, and R. Holly. *One-Third of Our Time? An Introduction to Recreation and Behavior and Resources.* New York: John Wiley & Sons, 1988, p. 20.

Cordes, Kathleen, and Hilmi Ibrahim. *Applications in Recreation and Leisure.* New York: McGraw-Hill, 1999.

Environment News Service. "Julia 'Butterfly' Hill's Year Atop Giant Redwood." (http://ens.lycos.com/ens/ dec98/1998L-12-10-02.html) (December 10, 1999).

Foster, Rhea Dulles. *A History of Recreation: America Learns to Play.* New York: Appleton-Century-Crofts, 1965.

"Japanese Drama." *Microsoft Encarta 98 Encyclopedia.* (CD-ROM)(1998).

Kelly, John R. *Leisure.* Englewood Cliffs: Prentice Hall, 1992, p. 148.

Kraus, R. *Recreation and Leisure in Modern Society.* Santa Monica: Goodyear Publishing Co., Inc., 1978.

Lang, Olga. *Chinese Family and Society.* New Haven, CT: Yale University Press, 1950.

Lee, Robert. *Religion and Leisure in America.* New York: Abingdon Press, 1964.

Moris, D. *The Human Zoo.* New York: Dell, 1969.

Opie, John. *Nature's Nation: An Environmental History of the United States.* New York: Harcourt Brace, 1998.

Roberts, J. M. *History of the World.* New York: Alfred A. Knopf, 1976.

Russell, Ruth. *Pastimes.* Madison, WI: Brown and Benchmark, 1996.

Sessons, Douglas. *Leisure Services.* Englewood Cliffs, NJ: Prentice-Hall, 1984.

Weiskopf, Donald C. *Recreation and Leisure: Improving the Quality of Life.* Boston: Allyn and Bacon, 1982.

www.doi.gov (October 7, 1999).

www.mpaa.org (September 19, 1999).

CHAPTER 5

Perspectives on Human Development and Leisure

As the twig is bent the tree inclines.

—VIRGIL (70–19 B.C.)

In spite of the apparent simplicity and ease with which human development occurs, in reality it is a very complex process. Human growth and development is the result of the unique unfolding of human potential arising from a complex of factors too numerous to fully comprehend. Each aspect of development interacts with each other aspect in such a manner as to yield a seamless pattern of growth. In an attempt to gain insight into this complex and dynamic process, scientists have arbitrarily divided the development process into logical and reasonably manageable categories. These categories have been created for the convenience of researchers to provide a structure or framework to facilitate scientific investigation. By using a classification system based on different aspects of human development, science can examine relationships between some of the major constituents in the development process. Perhaps the most common way of examining human development is to examine it from the perspective of the following four subdivisions: (1) physical development, (2) cognitive development, (3) personality development, and (4) social development. One of the problems associated with looking at human development from this perspective is that it fails to account for the mutual interdependence of each of these areas. It must always be kept in mind that none of the areas included can be considered independent of the others.

1. **Physical Development.** Here, the emphasis is on quantitative measures that indicate physical change. Physical development is essential to cognitive and personality development because it is through the physical senses that we acquire the information necessary to function within the various contexts that our bodies carry us. Much of one's early knowledge is a result of early exploratory behavior. This type of behavior may appear of insignificant value, but in reality be the source of large amounts of information critical to the child's successful development. In later life, the aging process affects the body adversely by imposing physical limitations foreign to younger years. This, in turn, is reflected in one's feelings about self and in the type of leisure activities one chooses. Furthermore, the physical body is the repository of one's genetic potential which has a profound effect on all aspects of one's growth and development.

2. **Cognitive Development.** Here, we are concerned about the various mental abilities that a person brings to bear in his/her attempts to solve problems. In the formulation presented here, cognitive development specifically refers to learning, memory, reasoning, and creativity. In other words, cognitive development refers to the process of acquiring and applying information. It is believed that leisure experiences make an important contribution to one's understanding of self, knowledge about other people, and, of course, about the nature of leisure and its concomitants. This suggests a kind of synergism where leisure influences cognitive development, which, in turn, influences leisure choices and involvement, which, in turn, contributes to additional learning, memories, reasoning ability, and creative growth.

3. **Personality Development.** Most people have a fairly good "intuitive" idea as to the meaning of the word "personality," but among social scientists there seems to be a lack of agreement as to its definition. As a consequence, the literature regarding personality is filled with discussions on its definition and meaning. Trait theory takes a position different from phenomenological theory, both of which disagree with the psychodynamic theories, etc. One definition frequently found in psychology texts is typified by the definition found in the *Dictionary of Psychology*[1] which basically states that personality is the sum total of one's beliefs, attributes, behaviors, and values. *Webster's Unabridged Dictionary* defines personality as "an individual's emotional and behavioral tendencies."

4. **Social Development.** Much of what we call personality is a reflection of the quality of one's interactions with significant others. The formal and informal learning that accrues as one interacts with such important others as parents, siblings, peers, and teachers is believed to be a major factor in personality and cognitive development. The socialization values of leisure experiences can have positive or negative consequences depending upon the nature of the event.

STAGE THEORIES OF DEVELOPMENT

One of the early contributions to our understanding of the nature of human development is the concept of *epigenesis.* Underlying this idea is the notion that human beings, indeed, all living creatures, must develop sequentially. From this perspective, in effect, the development process involves moving from one stage of development to another. This theory is illustrated in various theories named after the phenomenon they are designed to explain. These, *stage theories,* view development as occurring in a series of steps; each step provides a developmental platform for the next. Freud viewed development as passing through five steps or stages: oral, anal, phallic, latency, and genital periods. Erik Erikson theorized eight major stages in the life cycle. Piaget believed child development occurred through four different stages.

FREUD

This theory[2] is based on the premise that all human beings pass through a series of psychosexual developmental stages. Each must be successfully completed before an individual can move on to the next phase. If an individual fails to move on to the next stage, it is said that the individual experiences *fixation.* The individual then tends to manifest personality traits related to the developmental stage of the fixation. The following is a simplified summary of Freud's psychosexual stages of development.[3]

ERIKSON

Whereas Freud tended to focus on the relationship of sexual development to psychological development, Erikson focused on the relationship of social influences to psychological development.[4] Erikson theorized that human development follows the *epigenetic principle,* i.e., everything that grows has a life plan, and if a capacity fails to develop on schedule, the rest of the development is hampered.

PIAGET

According to Piaget, development is basically a process of adaptation. Children, on the basis of their interaction with their environment, develop cognitive structures or *schemas*. Piaget viewed adaptation as involving *assimilation* and *accommodation*. Assimilation involves taking in new information and interpreting it by current schemas. Accommodation refers to changing schemas to fit new information.

The balance of accommodation and assimilation is *equilibrium,* and is the basis for new assimilations.[5]

The stages through which a child passes, according to Piaget, is summarized in the following table:

Freud's Five Stages of Development

Age	Name	Physical Zone	Characteristic	Outcome
0–18 Mos.	Oral	Mouth	Demanding, need for mothering, interest in oral behaviors.	Passive, sarcastic, talkative, obsessive eating, smoking.
8 Mos. to 3 Yrs.	Anal Expulsion Retention	Rectum Bladder	Hostile, super conformist, stingy, miserly.	Destructive, cruel, stingy, miserly.
3 to 7 Yrs.	Phallic	Genitals	Oedipal Complex, Electra Complex, so-called "penis envy."	Emotional disorders, homosexuality behavior.
7 to 12 Yrs.	Latency	Suppression	Interest in nonsexual activity.	Unable to form sexual relations.
Puberty	Genitals	Genitals	Romantic infatuation and emotional upheaval.	Unable to make commitments, infatuation.

Erikson's Eight Stages of Development
The Epigenetic Principle

Stage	Function	Outcome
1. Infancy	Basic trust vs. mistrust	Trust in self/others
2. Early Childhood	Autonomy vs. shame, guilt	Self-control
3. 4th–5th year	Initiative vs. guilt	Self-direction
4. 6th–12th year	Industry vs. inferiority	Mastery
5. Adolescence	Identity vs. role confusion	Sense of self
6. Young adult	Intimacy vs. isolation	Extended intimate relationship; capacity to work toward career
7. Adulthood	Generativity vs. stagnation	Concerned beyond family
8. Old age	Integrity vs. despair	Sense of satisfaction

Age	Name	Characteristics
0 to 2 years	Sensorimotor stage	Preoccupation with the relationship between sensations and motor behaviors
2 to 7 years	Preoperational stage	Development of the ability to use symbols; egocentric
7 to 11 years	Concrete operations	Rational thinking
11 years on	Formal operations	Ability to deal with abstract concepts and constructs

The extent to which any of these models is an accurate portrayal of child development is subject to debate. However, as suggested by all three theories, it is generally agreed that early development consists of several critical periods, which if missed have long-term consequences. Also, it seems generally agreed upon that childhood, and to less extent, the experiences of infancy, correlate with adult behavior. In short, the years of infancy and childhood are very important. And inasmuch as play is the preoccupation of infancy and childhood, it can be inferred that it serves an important role in the development process.

NOTES ON FREUD

Sigmund Freud (1856–1939) was a Viennese physician. Trained in neurology and with a keen interest in the psyche, Freud received his medical degree in 1881. After studying with Jean Martin Charcot in Paris, who was investigating the usefulness of hypnosis as a treatment for hysteria, Freud returned to Vienna. The work being done by Charcot inspired Freud to look further into solving problems associated with the mind. This led to a collaboration with Josef Breuer, a Viennese physician, who had received notoriety through his use of hypnosis in treating hysteria. Later Freud rejected hypnosis in lieu of **free association**, a process he believed permitted unrecognized ideas to emerge from the subconscious. By this time, Freud had theorized that the symptoms of

neurosis were directly traceable to a traumatic experience earlier on one's life, experiences which led to unresolved conflicts which were being struggled with on an unconscious level. Because of Freud's belief that such conflicts were largely a function of an individual's sexuality, he fell in to disrepute with such prominent men as Jung and Adler. Even though criticized for basing his conclusions from observations of his patients, a rather biased sample, Freud is considered the Father of Psychotherapy. He died in England in 1939. Freud's concept of the unconscious mind helps us understand why people often make what seems inexplicable decisions regarding their choice of leisure activities. According to Freud, the unconscious mind has a powerful influence on all aspects of our behavior.

NOTES ON ERIK ERIKSON

Erik H. Erikson was born in Frankfurt, Germany in 1902. After studying psychoanalysis at the Vienna Psychoanalytic Institute, he moved to the United States in 1933. He taught at Yale, Berkeley, and Harvard. He retired in 1968. He rejected Freud's psychological determinism and advocated a much broader approach to psychoanalysis. His model of human development places greater emphasis on social influences than did Freud.

NOTES ON PIAGET

Considered the most influential student of cognitive development of this century (Carlson 132), Jean Piaget was born in 1896 and died in 1980. Although trained in biology, he is principally known for his contributions to child psychology. He argued that development follows a genetically determined sequence of events. His conclusions were based on his observations of his own children at home and then later children at his Center for Epistemology in Geneva.

Types of Play Behavior and Development

During the first few months of childhood, amazing developmental changes occur. Born with few motor capabilities, the infant is soon capable of sitting erect, grasping, holding, crawling, and often within the first year, walking. Similarly during the first few months, important strides are taken in cognitive, personality, and social development. There is a certain irony in that among the various factors facilitating these important developments is a behavior often looked upon as trivial and unessential—this behavior is play.

Inasmuch as developmental behaviors vary by age, it might be well to view leisure behavior from the theoretical framework most appropriate to a given developmental phase. Dr. William Staso, an expert in neurodevelopment, suggests that different kinds of interaction and stimulation should be emphasized at different stages of development. Early in development, it is important that a child be spoken to frequently and that the child be held and touched often.

At 3–5 months the child's vision has developed to the point where most of his/her information about the world is through sight. Play at this stage should involve visual stimulation linked to animated conversation. At about 6 months a child begins to understand the functions of objects. Play should involve manipulation, and, once again, related conversation. At 12 months the child is now able to actually manipulate objects, but this should be done under supervision, and, yes, more conversation. Speaking of the period from 12–18 months,

Staso states, "The brain establishes accelerated and more complex associations, especially if the toddler experiments directly with objects. A rich environment will help the toddler make such associations, understand sequences, differentiate between objects and reason about them."[6] Clearly, this is a very important time in the developing child's life, and parental supervision is very important. The play that occurs during this time has profound developmental value, and even though it may appear trivial from an adult's perspective, it is a critical kind of work for the child.

In examining the relationship between play and development, it is important to recognize that just as there are different types of human development there are also different types of play, some of which are more suited for development in one area of human growth than in others. Naturally, play during early infancy is rooted in the child's exploration of his sensory and motor abilities. As these are mastered, they then provide the basis for subsequent exploration in the cognitive and social areas. In examining and classifying these different play forms, there are several alternatives available to us. One, we could categorize them by developmental stages and discuss them in sequential order. Another approach would be to classify and analyze them by developmental functions (cognitive, physical, personality, social). A third approach would be to categorize them by interaction patterns.

An example of this third approach is found in the now classic study of Mildred B. Parten[7] who observed the play of school children in nursery school settings. She identified six types of play. Each of these types of play behavior have developmental implications, and provide us with a sort of taxonomy for examining the relationship of play to development. Parten's six types of play are summarized below:

1. **Unoccupied play:** Children spend their time watching others, idly glancing about, or engaging in aimless activities (standing around, tugging clothing, etc.).

2. **Solitary play:** Children play with toys by themselves and make no effort to get close to or speak with other children.

3. **Onlooker behavior:** Children watch other children at play, occasionally talking to themselves or asking questions. However, they do not themselves join in the play.

4. **Parallel play:** Children play independently beside other children but not with them. Although they play close together and with similar toys, they do not interact.

5. **Associative play:** Children interact with one another, borrowing or lending play material, following one another with carts, cars, or trains and attempting to influence each other's behavior. Each child does as he or she sees fit; no division of labor or integration of activities take place.

6. **Cooperative play:** Children integrate their play activities. In this kind of play, the members usually take on different role responsibilities, and they often think of themselves as belonging to a group from which other children are excluded.

In 1968, building upon the theoretical work of Piaget, Smilansky suggested that play falls into four stages of development: (1) functional play (corresponds to Piaget's Sensorimotor stage), (2) constructive play (refers to play which involves the manipulation of the environment and objects within the environment to produce something new), (3) dramatic play (based on a child's ability to use language and symbols in the thought process), and (4) play involving rules and set procedures (related to Piaget's formal operations stage).[8]

Gunn and Peterson, in their text, *Therapeutic Recreation Program Design: Practices and Principles*,[9] argue that leisure activities (including play) can be examined from three developmental perspectives: (1) psychomotor, (2) cognitive, and (3) affective. They suggest that each of these dimensions can further be analyzed by the interaction patterns in the activity. Borrowing from Avedon, they identify eight interaction patterns: (1) intraindividual (action taking place within the individual), (2) extraindividual (action directed toward an object, not a person), (3) aggregate (action done in the presence of others directed at some object), (4) interindividual (action of a competitive nature), (5) unilateral (action of one against many), (6) multilateral (every player is against every other player), (7) intragroup (action of a cooperative nature), and (8) intergroup (team against team).[10]

For example, Smilansky's model is particularly applicable to the play of childhood and early adolescence, but is relatively limited in application for adult years. Gunn and Peterson present a model particularly attractive for use in therapeutic settings and perhaps for adults, but place too much emphasis on social interaction to effectively accommodate early sensorimotor play. Callois fails to place adequate emphasis on cognitive play to be useful in a broad application. The point should be clear. No one model of play is equally effective across all age groups and in all situations. In discussions of play, one may have to refer to a number of models to describe the behavior under discussion.

Regardless of the perspective one brings to the discussion on human development and its relationship to play, recreation, or leisure, it is abundantly clear that the kind of play a child experiences has enormous developmental consequences. Vander Zanden argues that in broad and general terms leisure activity and play make at least five major contributions to the development process. These are summarized as follows:

1. Through play, children make motor and sensory discoveries; they learn about the properties of things.

2. Play prepares children for life, but on their own terms. Children at play can experience themselves as active agents in their environment, not merely as resting ones.

3. Play provides opportunities for rehearsing adult roles, a process called **anticipatory socialization.**

4. Play helps children build their own individual sense of identity. It allows them to get outside themselves and view themselves from other perspectives.

5. Play allows for both reality and fantasy. It is a pliable medium that enables children to come to terms with their fears—of villains, witches, ghosts, lions, dogs, etc. Through imaginary episodes, children can harmlessly confront these creatures and perhaps even triumph over them.[11]

Not included in the Zanden list is the relationship of play to physical growth and development. It is now to this topic we turn.

Leisure Activity and Physical Development

When parents talk about newborn infants, the discussion often flows around physical attributes such as height, weight, and mobility. A frequent statement made by new parents goes something like this, "I can't believe how fast she is growing!" This reflects the fact that rapid growth is one of the most notable features of the first few years. Physical development occurs more rapidly during the first three years than at any other time in a person's life. By the first year, a person's brain will reach two-thirds of its adult size. Infants generally learn to sit alone around six months. It is around this same time that they master rolling from stomach to back. Most babies are able to crawl by nine to ten months. Babies can usually stand unsupported by 13–14 months; walking comes about a month later. By age two, most toddlers are able to run, climb, and manipulate objects rather well. The combination of these three physical skills coupled with what parents see as unbounded energy produces a developmental phase both dreaded and enjoyed by most parents. The phrase, "The Terrible Two's," suggests the essence of this delightful but challenging period. During this period of rapid development, play is the principal means by which new skills are learned and practiced, and through which coordination and muscle strength is promoted. As someone once keenly observed, "Play is the work of the child."

Before adolescence, boys are slightly stronger than girls, but the differences are only slight. After the adolescent growth spurt (usually in girls around age 10 and in boys around 12–14), the male's larger muscles, larger heart and lungs, and greater capacity for carrying oxygen in the blood provide the male with the strength and endurance for highly competitive and physical activities. This does not mean, however, that women are necessarily inferior to men in strength and endurance. A cursory look in any gymnasium will reveal some very powerful women.

That physique influences one's leisure is not a particularly new notion. The idea that an individual's inherited physique helps determine an individual's character has its roots in folklore and mythology. Some of these early myths suggest that the depth, color or shape of a person's eyes can reveal personality traits. Strength and beauty have long been associated with valor and virtue. People with slight builds have often been judged as artistic or effeminate. In the 1800s the idea that physical features were related to behavior became formalized by Franz Joseph Gall in his theory of "*phrenology*." This theory, which assumed a relationship between the shape of the skull and behavior, was later refuted by anthropologists and psychologists.

Of more recent origin is William H. Sheldon's theory that one's inherited physique predisposes one to certain emotional, cognitive, and behavioral traits.[12] Initially, Sheldon set out to classify human body types. After an intensive study of photographs, Sheldon and his colleagues concluded that all body types fall within three classifications: *endomorphic* (fat), *mesomorphic* (muscular), and *ectomorphic* (frail). These three classifications are not to be taken as mutually exclusive, but rather as often being present in varying degrees in the same person. For example, a person may be ectomorphic above the waist, mesomorphic through the legs and endomorphic in the middle—an all too common complaint.

Sheldon proposes that each component is associated with different temperaments, and as such, by knowing an individual's *somatotype,* an individual's temperament can be predicted. He proposes three universal dimensions: *viscerotonia* (a love of food and comfort), *somatonia* (a craving for physical action), and *cerebrotonia* (an inclination for restraint, inhibition and apprehensiveness). According to Sheldon, body type is a stimulus for certain responses from one's social environment, which then shapes an individual's temperament according to cultural expectations. Hence, in a society where leisure activities include football, basketball, and baseball, forces are put into action early in one's life that direct the mesomorphic toward such activities, and those of less athletic somatotypes into less athletic endeavors. The extent to which Sheldon's theory adequately explains the relationship between physical characteristics and leisure remains to be seen; nevertheless, it does provide a theoretical basis for arguing that leisure behavior may be influenced by anatomical and physiological factors.

Activity Deprivation and Development

The relationship of leisure to development can be viewed from a perspective contrary to that provided in Sheldon's formulation. Here, we are interested in the influence leisure activities have on physical development. There is good evidence that physical development is strongly influenced by the play patterns of early childhood. In a now famous study involving Iranian orphanages during the 1960s, it was demonstrated that when children are deprived of physical play, their physical development is adversely affected. In this study, children in two orphanages were studied. Due to understaffing, overworked attendants seldom handled the children. The children had no toys and were never put in a sitting position or placed on their stomachs. Once a child was able to sit on the floor, there were no toys, no play furniture, and no play apparatus. *The net result of this type of child rearing was severe motor retardation.* The results clearly demonstrated the developmental role of physical play in child development. As a control, a third orphanage was studied which employed acceptable child rearing practices. In this orphanage, the children were frequently handled, were placed in playpens at four months, had many toys, and were given considerably more play opportunities than their less fortunate counterparts. The children in this orphanage showed normal motor development.[13]

In a study of 288 infants from Yucatan, Mexico, it was found that in the first three months Yucatan children developed manipulative skills faster than a sample of U.S. children. However, by 11 months they were far behind the American sample on all motor skills. The explanation of this turnabout can be in part attributed to the differences in play behavior between the two groups. American children were encouraged to play in a much more unrestricted manner than Yucatan children, given more objects and afforded greater freedom of movement. Papalia and Olds summarize the restrictive child rearing pattern of the Yucatan parents thusly:

> the more advanced manipulative abilities of Yucatan babies may arise from their not having toys to play with. As a result, they discovered play with their fingers at earlier ages. Their delayed skills in moving about are probably related to several conditions in their lives: as infants, they are swaddled, which restricts their freedom of movement, as older children, they continue to be restrained by being held more in the arms or on the hips of their parents and older brothers and sisters, by sleeping in hammocks (which become net cages compared to the open space of a firm-mattressed crib), and by not being put on the ground to play.[14]

That there are certain windows for physical development is most dramatically demonstrated by the fact that if a child is born with cataracts, unless the cataracts are promptly removed, the child will lose his/her ability to see, even if the cataracts are removed at some later time. This is a classic example of how the brain requires stimulation to become structured for normal functioning. Light hitting the retina is required to stimulate the development of the visual centers of the brain. Without this stimulation, the ability to see is lost and the developmental window of opportunity closed forever.

Gender Differences

There is a plethora of studies which demonstrate a difference in the play behavior of boys and girls (Lehman and Witty, 1927; Britt and Janus, 1941; Smity and Conolly, 1972; Rubin, 1977; Barnett and Chick, 1986). Fundamentally, these and similar studies suggest that certain aspects of play behavior may be predicted solely on the basis of gender. The following list nicely summarizes the differences generally observed in the play of young boys and girls:

1. Boys tend to be more boisterous and aggressive.

2. Boys' play involves struggles for dominance.

3. Boys tend to be more competitive than girls.

4. Girls tend to avoid conflict by establishing rules, etc.

5. Girls tend to be more empathetic in their play.

6. Girls are less likely to avoid "tomboyish behavior" than boys are to avoid "sissy behavior."

There is evidence to support the notion that some of the differences in play behavior between the sexes is the result of the basic biological differences between boys and girls. At about the sixth week of gestation, embryos destined to become males are exposed to relatively large quantities of androgens (substances producing or stimulating the development of male characteristics). These hormones stimulate the formation of the male body structures, destining the developing male to greater physical strength and greater tendency toward aggressive and physical play behavior.

Testosterone has been shown to be related to aggressive behavior in neophylic animals, including humans. Prolactin (a hormone secreted by the pituitary gland, which, in association with estrogen stimulates breast development and formation of milk during pregnancy) has been demonstrated to produce motherly behavior in virgin male animals (Papalia and Olds, 213). Papalia and Olds cite a study by Crowley (1962) which showed the relationship between *idiopathic hypogonatropic hypogonadism* (a disorder resulting in abnormally low amounts of male hormone being produced at puberty) and spatial skills. When the subjects suffering from this disorder were compared to a sample of normal males on their ability to identify certain geometric designs camouflaged by distracting lines, the normal group did far better than those with low hormone levels.[15]

Further evidence showing the relationship of gender related constitutional predispositions is cited in Glietman (516).[16] In a longitudinal study, 70 men and women were first observed as infants and then again as adults. A strong correlation was observed between aggressive behavior as infants and aggressive behavior as adults among the men in the subject pool. No such correlation was found among females. The researchers argue that this difference resulted not from a biological predisposition, but rather from socialization practices which legitimize aggressive behavior in males and limits aggressive behavior among females. The greater predisposition for aggression among males may interact with socialization practices which sanction aggression among males and prohibit it among females. This bias in socialization practices is illustrated clearly by a cursory analysis of gender specific games and recreation activities, as well as a review of the content of much of our television and movie productions.

It is suggested by Iso-Ahola that under situations of extreme stimulus deprivation, anatomical and biochemical changes can occur which can have far reaching effects. He points out that rearing animals in conditions of complete stimulus deprivation affects the production of ribonucleic acid. A decrease in this acid minimizes the body's ability to synthesize protein, which, of course, is essential for physical growth and repair. On the other hand, he presents evidence to suggest that opportunities for optimal stimulation contributes to the development of the cerebral cortex.[17]

The Importance of Healthy Gestation

Development, in general terms, begins at the moment a spermatozoa penetrates an oocyte. At the moment of this union a series of events are initiated that cascade forward in an increasing dance between DNA and cellular metabolism. The cellular structures at first are fragile and simple. But within just hours, cellular differentiation begins to occur setting the stages for organ and anatomical development. For the first eight weeks this developing structure is known as an embryo. By the ninth week all of the organ systems are in place, and the embryo takes on the recognizable form of a human being. From the ninth week to roughly the ninth month it will be called a fetus. During that period it will grow to be on average 22 inches long and weigh about 6–7 pounds. Fragile and rapidly changing, the fetus is totally dependent upon the mother to survive. And, although the mother's body provides the ideal environment for gestation, there are always risks that a developing fetus will face. Once outside of the mother's womb, new risks await the newborn infant.

There has been a great deal of research examining the relationship of certain prenatal and postnatal factors on healthy growth and development. In reviewing these studies two facts seem to stand out: (1) the developing fetus, and later the infant, is particularly susceptible to harm from certain chemicals, and (2) stress during gestation and during infancy can have extremely deleterious effects on the developing child. These effects are not limited to morphological development, but are manifest across the board in physical, cognitive, psychological, and social development.

For example, thalidomide was approved in 1950 as a drug for morning sickness in pregnancy and also as a sedative. What in reality was touted as a very safe drug turned out to have horrible side effects. Nearly 15,000 children were born with disturbing physical abnormalities, principally missing limbs. In addition, it was later discovered that thalidomide also produced mental retardation and autism. The thalidomide disaster turned our attention to the role that seemingly harmless chemicals might have on the developing fetus or the very young child. As a result, numerous chemicals have been identified that are associated with anatomical deformities and neurological problems. Some of these chemicals have been also associated with dysfunctional behaviors in later life.

There are roughly 80,000 chemicals registered with the Environmental Protection Agency. Some of these have been identified as posing risk to the very young, and in some cases the developing fetus. For example, lead has been shown to adversely affect intelligence and contribute to adverse social behavior. Polychlorinated biphenyls (PCBs) are known have the capacity to cross the placenta to cause damage to the developing brain *in utero*. It is well established that mercury compounds are potent neurotoxins, and certain pesticides have been linked to both brain and anatomical disorders.[18] In addition to the risk that environmental chemicals pose to the developing fetus and infant child, are the so-called recreational drugs. Science has known for quite sometime now that such aberrations as dyslexia, attention deficit disorder, intellectual retardation, and autism can be caused by *in utero* exposure to alcohol, cocaine, heroin, and probably nicotine.

Stress also has a deleterious impact on prenatal and postnatal development. Again, the problem is associated with chemicals that have a negative influence on the developing brain. Here, however, the chemicals are produced by the body itself. Cortisol, often called the "stress hormone" seems to be the main culprit. There are indications that when infants (and presumably later-term fetuses) are exposed to stress, the increased amount of cortisol in the body may affect the development of the hippocampus.[19] In addition, there is conclusive evidence that abuse in early life affects the development of the corpus collosum, the neural bridge between the right and left hemispheres of the brain.

Dr. Martin H. Teicher's research[20] has demonstrated that childhood abuse can produce the following four specific changes in both brain structure and function:

1. Stress resulting from child abuse may lead to structural changes in the limbic system predisposing a child to epileptic seizures as well as inappropriate emotional responses.

2. Children exposed to high levels of stress are more likely to experience unusually high levels of electrical activity in the brain. These readings are often associated with self-destructive or aggressive/violent behavior.

3. Stress in the very young or developing fetus can result in a deformed corpus collosum which prevents children from effectively integrating the functions of the two hemispheres.

4. Children exposed to high levels of stress tend to show deficient development of the left hemisphere of the brain. This in turn may be associated with depression as well as hindering the child's ability to process and understand certain types of information.

What should be clear from the foregoing is that the developing fetus must be protected from both stress and dangerous chemicals. Similarly, the developing infant is also at risk of adverse developmental consequences if exposed to abuse, stress, or environmental toxins.

PLAY AND COGNITIVE DEVELOPMENT

Cognitive development refers to the growth of human properties essential to the process of acquiring knowledge. As Zanden states, "It encompasses such phenomena as sensation, perception, imagery, retention, recall, problem solving and thinking."[21] This process is dependent upon a complex array of biochemical and neurophysiological events. Contrary to early thinking, a child is not born as a blank slate awaiting information, nor is a child a preprogrammed automaton. The debate between "nurture versus nature" is coming to an end. A careful look at the developing brain makes it clear that nature and nurturing work hand in hand to achieve important developmental goals.

At birth, a baby's brain has already developed to an amazingly sophisticated level: the child can hear, see, smell and demonstrate some degree of muscle control. The brain stem is completely functional and thus heart rate and breathing are automatic, the digestive system is wired and functional, and the endocrine system is in place; however, the wiring process is just beginning in the cognitive parts of the brain. It is during the first few months of life that the brain demonstrates more activity than at any other time, and much of this activity involves the creation of neural pathways that set the stage for all subsequent cognitive growth. In fact, it is estimated that by age two, a child's "brain contains twice as many synapses and consumes twice as much energy as the brain of a normal adult."[22]

At birth a child will have as many as 100 billion separate brain cells. Many of these cells are connected through a complex system of long nerve fibers known as axons and short bushy fibers knowns as dendrites. It is the axon that sends a message and the dendrite that receives. When axons are produced they can travel a considerable distance to connect with the appropriate dendrites. Dendrites and axons don't actually touch, they come very close to on another, but maintain a very small gap called a synapse. Messages are passed over the dendrite by electrically charged chemicals known as neurotransmitters. What determines the nature of the patterns that are produced is the nature of the child's experience. Every time a child experiences some kind of sensory stimulation, there is a tiny corresponding burst of electrical energy that leads to the production of a neural connection. The neural pathways that ensue become largely permanent, even though later on connections not utilized may be destroyed.

The important lesson to be learned here is that the first few years of life are critical to every subsequent life experience to follow. There is no time in an individual's life where the capacity to learn and the capacity to develop platforms for subsequent cognitive development is as great. Thus, it is absolutely essential that parents come to recognize that not only is it important to enjoy time with their child, but it is essential that time be characterized by play activity that produces neural patterns that will be most beneficial to the child.

Over the years, there have been several studies that demonstrate the importance of early play experiences in the developing child. According to Zelazo and Kearley, at some point early in infancy, children begin to generate ideas. They refer to this stage as *cognitive metamorphosis*. This is believed to usually occur between nine and 16 months. It is not clear as to the extent that cognitive metamorphosis can be encouraged through play, but this study does demonstrate that there is a high correlation between play complexity and age. So certain of this relationship are Zelazo and Kearley that they concluded that play can be used as an indicator of the cognitive level of babies.[23]

Not only can play be used as an indicator of intellectual ability, but some studies indicate that it makes a major contribution to its development. As a child explores and manipulates his/her environment, a sense of competence occurs. This provides the basis for subsequent exploration. New situations are arousing and challenge the developing cognitive and motor skills of the developing child. Redundant situations lose their arousal potential and the child is motivated to seek out new and stimulating activities. Conversely, situations that tend to be too arousing compel the child to withdraw and look for other less arousing opportunities. By providing a child with play items appropriate to his arousal needs, a parent supports the natural learning process found in play and recreation. When a child is prevented from experiencing optimal arousal, or when a child is subjected to too much arousal, the net result is a reduction in learning.

Adaptation and Organization

Piaget postulates that children's play is dependent upon cognitive structures that are presumed to be inherent to the process of maturation and development. These structures are referred to as *schemas* and are the *basic cognitive units*. Cognitive schemas are primarily the function of the child's interaction with the environment. As time passes, the child accumulates knowledge, which gives rise to new schemas. Two general principles govern this process: (1) adaptation and (2) organization. Adaptation is the process children use to produce new cognitive structures. Organization involves the integration of all schemas into one overall system. *Adaptation* is dependent upon *assimilation* and *accommodation*. Assimilation involves incorporating new information derived from experience into a child's existing cognitive structures; accommodation is the process by which children change their cognitive structures to better fit their perceptions of their environment. These two processes operate together to produce changes in the child's conceptualization of the world and appropriate reactions to it.

As pointed out earlier, Piaget identified four major phases in the development of the child: sensorimotor (birth to two years), pre-operational (two to seven years), concrete operations (seven to eleven years), and finally, a stage of formal operations. Each of these stages is characterized by specific cognitive capabilities. During the first stage, the child is limited to thinking about sensory input and the manipulation of objects. Thinking during this phase does not involve symbols. The use of symbolic thinking follows, where a child is able to think about objects without the object being present. The use of mental representation of things and events allows them to become proficient at classifying, dealing with numbers, and understanding the principles of conservation. Eventually, the child learns how to think in abstract, as opposed to concrete terms.

The form that children's play takes can be viewed as a function of the stage of development in which the child is currently operating. Sensorimotor play tends to involve the exploration of the environment through motor activity and the senses. During the preoperational phase, children are able to imitate actions or objects and can play games where one object stands for another (symbolic play). During the concrete operational phase, children are able to use representational symbols in logical patterns permitting word plays and jokes that depend upon reversal and transformations. In the formal reasoning stage, play reflects the ability of the individual to go beyond a concrete situation and think in abstract terms and hypothetical situations.

Play is not only a function of development, but also a factor contributing to it. It is chiefly through play that children learn about and understand their relationship to their environment. Starting with the most fundamental concepts, a child begins to acquire information which enables him to think in an increasingly sophisticated fashion. Simple explorations, through play, often provide children with essential insights and understanding. Piaget was a champion of this view even to the point of advocating the use of play in the otherwise formal environment of the modern school:

> Children should be allowed to do their own experimenting and their own research. Teachers, of course, can guide them by providing appropriate materials, but the essential thing is that in order for a child to understand something, he must construct it himself; he must re-invent it. Every time we teach a child something, we keep him from inventing it himself. On the other hand, that which we allow him to discover himself will remain with him visibly . . . for all the rest of his life.[24]

The balance between accommodation and assimilation is seen as the basis for intelligence. The counter balance between these two cognitive functions is referred to by Piaget as *equilibrium*. As new responses are added to cognitive structures, the perceived constraints of the environment are carefully evaluated against previous experience. This produces a dynamic which permits increasingly complex thinking. This becomes the basis for new accommodations. As Ellis states:

> Change in assimilatory processes produce new accommodations and the accommodatory changes alter the cognitive schemata and the assimilatory constraints placed on immediate experience. The individual's complexity spirals upward over time as assimilation and accommodation interact.[25]

As the child learns about his/her environment, he/she tests these learnings by manipulating objects in the environment to determine if they respond in ways predicted by recently assimilated information. When results are as predicted, the child develops a sense of competence which serves to validate both assimilated information and the child's perception of self. This process of *affectance-competence* plays an important role in helping an individual learn about the environment and her/his relationship to it.

Central to stage theories, such as Piaget's, is the notion that people are somehow inherently motivated to pursue activities that contribute to the developmental tasks of each of the phases. There is little doubt that the play of children and young adults contributes to the tasks of each of these phases, but just what motivates people to engage in play behavior in the first place? Particularly useful to this discussion is the work of anthropologist Desmond Morris, who argues that all mammals are fundamentally stimulus or novelty liking. This observation suggests that the more intelligent an animal, the greater its probability of participating in "non-utilitarianism" or playful behavior.[26] This observation gives rise to the idea that neophylic (stimulus seeking) animals possess some kind of stimulus seeking drive.

Ellis explored this area in 1973.[27] His work led to a book entitled *Why People Play*. In his formulation, he argues that sensation seeking behavior is rooted in the reticular arousal system, a structure in the brain which modulates incoming sensory data allowing only stimulation to the cerebral cortex which has a high probability of producing a level of arousal optimal for the context in which the stimuli is perceived.

In this theory, it is argued that in order for a stimulus to be viewed as possessing arousal potential, it must be viewed as novel, complex, or possess significant uncertainty. When a stimulus possesses too much arousal potential, the individual receives too much stimulation and will engage in behaviors designed to reduce the stimulation. The state of too much arousal is referred to as *supraoptimal arousal*.

The inverse situation is where too little arousal is present. This state is referred to as *suboptimal arousal,* and usually triggers strategies to increase the level of stimulation reaching the cerebral cortex. Suboptimal arousal (frequently referred to as boredom) comes as the result of the absence of new information to assimilate or new situations requiring the accommodation of old information. In a situation such as this, there is high congruity between existing information and context. Situations of this sort lack the novelty, complexity, or uncertainty required to produce elevated levels of arousal, and thus, leads to arousal seeking behavior. It is through this type of exploratory or sensation seeking behavior that many play behaviors are invented. Through searching for novelty, complexity or uncertainty, the developing individual acquires new information which provides the basis for subsequent learning.

Unfortunately, not all attempts to minimize suboptimal arousal leads to productive behavior. Too frequently, arousal seeking leads to watching television, which may result in exposure to incorrect ideas about society and even physical reality. Stimulus seeking must not be confused with what may be called *epistemic behavior* or knowledge seeking behavior. Knowledge seeking has the same characteristics as stimulus seeking, but it involves more formal operations and abstract thinking. Not normally classified as play, these explorations may take the form of reading, studying, philosophizing, etc. That this type of arousal seeking is not as frequent an occurrence as stimulation seeking is manifest in a study by Kohlberg and Gilligan[28] in which they reported that almost half of American adults never reach the formal operations stage. In their study, a sample of adults was asked to perform certain tasks requiring cognitive development typical of the formal operations stage. The percentages of those passing the task by age group are presented below:

- ages 10–15: 45%
- ages 16–20: 53%
- ages 21–30: 65%
- ages 45–50: 57%

These relatively discouraging statistics might be due in part to the tendency of people in this society to engage in leisure activities which are principally stimulating to the limbic system, but don't tax the cerebral cortex. In many respects, we are a society of spectators, far less a society of critical and creative thinkers. It is doubtful that contemporary American culture encourages play that contributes to high levels of cognitive development. As Papalia and Olds point out:

> Even if young people have the necessary neurological development to reach the stage of formal reasoning, if they have not been encouraged in this direction culturally and educationally, they may never attain this highest level and final qualitative leap of cognitive development.[29]

Creativity and Leisure Behavior

One of the most important cognitive skills is the ability to think in creative terms. Essentially, creativity is the ability to see things from an unusual perspective, to solve problems in a unique and novel fashion. That creative thinking is related to leisure is relatively easy to see. Creative thinking occurs when an individual is free to examine alternative solutions to some problem. The extent to which this occurs is in part dependent upon the individual's ability to function without constraint from external forces. That is to say, a creative person must possess what psychologists refer to as *internal locus of control*. Internal locus of control is related to the two principal components of the leisure state of being—perceived freedom and intrinsic motivation. Consequently, creativity and leisure are closely related.

That leisure and creativity are closely linked can be illustrated by a review of studies showing the relationship of play to creativity. (It can be presumed that play is representative of leisure activity in that it is characterized by perceived freedom, intrinsic motivation, and optimal arousal.) Of the many studies dealing with this problem (Leiberman, 1965; Simonton, 1975; Feitelson and Ross, 1973; and Hirshfeld and Hirshfeld, 1977) a study done by Bruner and reported in Iso-Ahola[30] is most revealing. In this study, Bruner tested the assumption that learning through play produces optimal arousal, which leads to creative problem solving. To test this notion, he divided his subject pool into four groups of children. The first group was shown how to do part of the assigned task. The second group was shown how to do the entire task. The third group played with the tools used in the solution but was given no further information. The fourth group received no input at all. The results were as predicted: The children who received no training but played with the tools solved the task as well as the students who had seen the entire solution. Iso-Ahola concludes his discussion of this study by stating, "It is clear that an appropriately stimulating play environment enhances problem solving ability in children."[31]

Papalia and Olds (1984) summarized 61 studies dealing with creativity. Following is a review of their findings:

1. Social class is positively related to creativity.

2. Family size appears unrelated to creativity.

3. Highly creative children often have a younger sibling close in age.

4. Girls are more likely to be verbally gifted, boys tend to show creativity in figural tasks.

5. Creative children usually have parents who are secure, uninhibited, and unconventional.

6. Creative children usually have parents who are enthusiastic about their personal leisure pursuits.

7. Creative children are granted both freedom and responsibility.

8. Creative children often come from homes possessing little cohesion.

9. Creative children usually have parents who are not rejecting, hostile, or detached.

10. Perceived freedom is essential to creative growth. As Papalia and Olds state, "The most consistent and best supported finding to emerge from this review—is that parental vigilance, authoritarianism, dominance and restrictiveness inhibit the development of creativity."[32]

The evidence seems clear. Play and leisure are closely related to creativity. What applies to children may, to a lesser extent, apply to creativity in adults. People need a sense of freedom and intrinsic motivation in order to be creative. People who are constantly directed and molded are not likely to possess the confidence and spontaneity essential for the creative process.

That play is a contributing factor in cognitive development seems relatively well established. To apply this knowledge in a way that will give a youngster an opportunity to achieve his cognitive potential is a serious challenge to parents and schools alike. By recognizing the powerful influence of play in cognitive development, parents and educators can tailor their respective responsibilities in a way that will provide youngsters with a rich opportunity for intellectual and creative growth.

Personality Development and Leisure

As pointed out earlier, one of the major problems associated with a discussion on personality as it relates to leisure is the difficulty we have in finding a universally accepted definition of the word "personality." From one perspective, personality attempts to deal with the whole person. In its literal sense, the word "personality" means the state or quality of being a person. In a sense then, personality theories encompass the other three divisions of human development presented in this chapter. It can be argued that if otherwise disparate theories of personality have something in common, it is the tendency to integrate a great many aspects of human behavior into a single theoretical framework. To attempt to integrate the sum total of human attributes into a section within a chapter of a handbook on leisure is beyond the scope of human capability. Consequently, in addressing the question of personality and leisure, personality will be defined in accordance to *Webster's Dictionary*, ". . . an individual's emotional and behavioral tendencies." Inasmuch as one's perception of the conscious and unconscious self is at the heart of emotional and behavioral tendencies, this discussion will focus on the relationship of leisure to such variables as *self-esteem, self-image,* and *psychological adjustment.*

In explaining emotional and behavioral tendencies, social scientists have devised a number of theories. Freud makes four basic assumptions about personality: (1) the unconscious portion of the mind has a great deal to do with behavior; (2) sexual and destructive instincts comprise a large portion of the unconscious mind; (3) these impulses are protected from the scrutiny of society by the conscious mind; and (4) in disguised form, subconscious motivations break through the conscious barrier to influence behavior.[33] As pointed out earlier, Freud identified five separate stages of development. These stages each had a specific role to play in the development of an individual's personality. If something went wrong during these stages, he theorized that the effect would continue into adult life by way of a behavioral characteristic. To Freud, pleasure gratification was viewed as a strong motivator, and the pivot point upon which the direction of personality development was determined. For example, during the oral stage, a child takes pleasure in eating, nursing, and exploring objects orally. For the most part, this form of pleasure is dependent upon other people. If a child is deprived of oral pleasure or is over-indulged, a dependent and passive personality may emerge in adulthood. Similarly, Freud argues that during the anal stage severe or over gratification during toilet training can produce a person who is either disorderly, destructive, and messy, or one who is orderly, stingy, and obstinate. During the next phase, children resolve issues surrounding their sexual identity and how they relate to members of the same and opposite sex. Again, unresolved issues are believed to carry on into adulthood. Freud feels that all of this usually occurs before a child's sixth birthday.

In considering psychoanalytic theory as an explanation of personality development, one must remember that Freud's psychoanalytic theorizing was based on his work with neurotic patients. Consequently, reflected in this formulation is the skewed experiences and viewpoints of the mentally and emotionally disturbed. Had Freud based his theory on a random sample of a normal population, his theorizing may have taken a different turn. As it stands, however, it is reminiscent of the old saying, "As the twig is bent, so grows the tree." As such, it leaves little room for self-determination, free will, or rational thought as causal factors in personality development.

Raymond B. Cattell proposes that human behavior is a function of structural units which make up the personality. These structural units are the relatively stable traits which allow us to describe and predict an individual's nature. To Cattell, the source from which traits spring is less important than that they exist. Like many psychologists, Cattell believes that most traits are acquired through early socialization, but he does view some as being of physiological in origin. Like Freud, he believes that traits are established early in life and that once traits are established, social forces have little effect on them. Cattell is the author of a widely used personality test, which is frequently used to create personality profiles. If traits are relatively stable, as theorized by Cattell, and if they provide the structural units of personality, it is logical to assume that research could show a relationship between Cattell's personality traits and leisure behavior.

Unfortunately, at this point there is little evidence to support this assumption.[34]

Unlike trait psychologists, those who accept social learning as the basis for personality development view traits as less than stable. They view behavior as a function of situation interacting with previous experience. They disagree with trait theorists regarding the power of socialization in adolescent and adult life. Albert Bandura and Richard Walters are the foremost proponents of this approach.[35] According to their formulation, human beings, as a result of their superior cognitive abilities, have the ability to think with insight and foresight, and consequently, consciously influence their behavior. Following this notion, this theory emphasizes: (1) learning from models as opposed to learning through personal and direct experience; (2) the symbolic and cognitive aspects of learning as opposed to stimulus followed by response; and (3) self-regulation modulated by external behavior reinforcement. Like many theories, the results are not yet in. For example, the role of modeling in personality development is not clear; similarly, the extent to which personality formation is influenced by rewards remains a question yet to be fully examined.

The Myers-Briggs Type Indicator

Within recent years, it has become popular, particularly in educational settings, to measure personality types through the use of the Myers-Briggs Type Indicator (MBTI). This instrument was developed by psychologist Isabel Briggs Myers. She based her instrument on the theoretical work of her mother Katherine C. Briggs, who in turn was an adherent to Carl Jung's theory of personality. Essentially she theorized that the human personality could be measured along four bipolar dimensions. These are:

1. extroversion—introversion

2. sensing—intuition

3. thinking—feeling

4. judging—perceptive

You have heard people talk about being an ESFP or an INTJ etc. These letters represent the initial letter of the bipolar dimensions on which they scored the highest. To break the Myers-Briggs code you need to know the abbreviations for each of the traits. Here they are (after Drummond[36]):

E=**Extrovert:** one who relates more easily to other people.

I=**Introvert:** one who relates more easily to ideas.

S=**Sensing:** one who prefers to work with concrete, known facts.

N=**Intuition:** one who prefers to look for intuitive, conceptual relationships.

T=**Thinking:** one who bases judgments on objective analysis and logic.

F=**Feeling:** one who bases judgment on more personal, subjective values.

J=**Judging:** one who prefers a planned, organized way of life.

P=**Perceptive:** one who prefers a flexible, spontaneous way of life.

There are essentially 16 different personality types according to this instrument.

David Keirsey published *Please Understand Me,* a book for the popular press in which can be found a version of the Meyer-Briggs.[37] This instrument is called the "Kiersey Temperament Sorter"[38] (KTS), and is often used in classes and is readily available on the internet. One difference between the MBTI and the KTS is that the KTS assumes that the 16 types can be lumped together into four temperaments. The KTS and the MBTI are similar but not the same.[39]

The MBTI and KTS are frequently used in personal counseling, career guidance, increasing the effectiveness of educational programs, team building in human resource management, and self-enrichment. The MBTI is viewed by many as well researched and of significant practical value.[40]

If you haven't taken either the KTS or MBTI, you can get an estimate your personality type by estimating where you would fall on the following continuum. (Modeled after Porthouse)[41]

WHICH SIDE OF THE CONTINUUM DO YOU MOST IDENTIFY WITH?

Extrovert ⟷	**Introvert**
Typically: social, external, gregarious, talkative, intensive, energetic, interactive, broad in scope, outgoing	Typically: territorial, internal, reflective, few relationships, low energy, narrow
Sensor ⟷	**Intuitive**
Typically: sequential, present, realistic, down to earth, factual, inspired, practical, specific, convergent, general	Typically: random, conceptual, head in the clouds, theoretical
Thinkers ⟷	**Feelers**
Typically: objective, firm-minded, legal minded, just, personal, impersonal, analytical, logical, detached	Typically: subjective, fair-minded, humane, involved
Judgers ⟷	**Perceivers**
Typically: decided, fixed, in control, closed, structured, definite, scheduled, organized, closed-ended	Typically: flexible, tentative, adaptable, open, spontaneous, unplanned, unstructured

To take the KTS as well as receive a personal analysis of your scores, I suggest you visit the internet. There are a number of sites that will be of interest to you, but the one I recommend is: **http:// sunsite. unc.edu/personality/keirsey/html** or your could access **http://sunsite.unc.edu** and find personality tests through the SunSITE Directory. In addition to the test, there is a wealth of information on personality theory with special reference to the Myers-Briggs.[42]

What value might come from taking the KST? Assuming that the KST, or any other personality inventory, models the human personality with some degree of accuracy, I can see two values coming from taking such a test: (1) it provides the individual with a better sense of self, and thus may contribute to increased self-awareness and perhaps self-esteem; (2) it might help an individual understand how he or she relates to others, and thus contribute to better interpersonal relationships.

It is important to recognize that these instruments are not perfect, nor are they measures of mental health. They simply give an indication as to the extent to which a person's approach to life can be related to selected variables. In the KST and MBTI, it is assumed that most people will fall into one of 16 different combinations of four sets of opposing variables. It is important to recognize that no attempt is made to value one personality type over another. All have equal validity, all are equally good. In each personality type you will find examples of people who are famous, successful, and who have made outstanding contributions to society. For an extensive list of famous (including fictional) people by personality type I suggest, once again, that you visit SunSITE at **http://sunsite.unc. edu/pub/academic/psychology. personality/type. info/famous.types.**

Leisure and Personality Research

To date, there appears to be little research where the above and other personality theories have been related to questions of leisure. This is not surprising when one considers the complexity of this type of research undertaking. In spite of the claims of leisure practitioners regarding the relationship of leisure to personality variables, few credible studies have been produced. Turning to Iso-Ahola, we read:

> But what is known about the effects of leisure experiences on personality? The answer is very simple: very little is known because systematic research is conspicuously lacking. Merely to correlate participation in various recreation activities with selected personality traits does not reveal when, why, and how leisure creates the effects it does in various persons.[43]

Studies dealing with the relationship of personality to leisure are faced with a variety of problems. Initially, one must determine a theoretical basis for his or her research. A responsible researcher will do this for two reasons: (1) social science can only progress if research projects are designed to test the validity of theories; and (2) a theory is essential for it provides the logical framework from which a hypothesis can be drawn. In respect to personality studies, attention has to be paid to the dynamic nature of the human condition; and as they relate to leisure, attention must be paid to the variety of interpretations explaining and identifying the leisure condition. To deal with these concerns, Iso-Ahola provides the following guidelines:

> the following four parameters have to be considered as part of a continuous process of change: (1) dimensions of personality, (2) situational social influences, (3) type and degree of leisure involvement, and (4) an individual's developmental stage. The effects in turn may be one of three: (1) they may improve, (2) they may deteriorate, or (3) a person may maintain his present level at a given personality dimension. The resultant change in personality may be measured in absolute or relative terms; the former refers to change within a person, and the latter to a person's change in relation to other individuals on a particular personality dimension . . . it is important to realize that leisure involvement itself does not lead to any changes in personality. Rather, what an individual is able to derive psychologically from leisure participation is critical.[44]

Self-Esteem and Leisure

In a study done in 1971 by Koocher, boys ages 15–17 who were participants in a YMCA program were divided into three groups.[45] One group consisted of boys who knew how to swim and who had passed the swimming test at the beginning of camp. The second group consisted of boys who refused to take the swimming test or failed, and the third group consisted of boys who learned to swim during the 12 day camping period. All participants were given a self-concept test at the beginning of the program and at the end. The results showed the learners improved in self-concept, whereas the other two groups showed no change. This type of study is typical of studies done in recreation and leisure and exemplifies studies showing relative change on a personality dimension. This type of study is important because it does lend credibility to the claims made by recreation practitioners that leisure has a positive effect on self-image. More specifically, this study illustrates the role that learning new recreation activities has on how one views himself. If in fact learning new leisure skills brings about a desirable change in personality, then it makes sense that individuals whose background includes a history of successful leisure skill acquisition will have a stronger self-concept than those who don't.

Psychological Adjustment and Leisure

Another area related to personality and leisure is that of psychological adjustment. Studies dealing with this area suggest that a rich variety in recreational experiences is inversely correlated with neurotic tendencies (Cavanaugh, 1942; Hendry and Douglass, 1975). That early leisure socialization may have a relationship to adult psychological adjustment was demonstrated by Brooks and Elliott (1971). In their study it was shown that children who experienced leisure satisfaction were better adjusted 20 years later than children who were not as fortunate.

It is important to recognize that active leisure involvement doesn't always correlate with psychological adjustment. Under some circumstances, passive recreation seems to show a higher correlation with adjustment than active leisure. For people whose work may be highly active or physically tiring, leisure patterns may take the form of relaxation and stimulus avoidance behavior. In situations where a passive pattern is an appropriate response to leisure, physical activity may be correlated with poor psychological adjustment (Bishop, 1973).

Leisure and Social Development

When we speak of social development, we are basically referring to the acquisition of skills and knowledge associated with successful interpersonal involvement. It is assumed that as one matures, he or she interacts with others in such a manner as to reinforce earlier interaction, and sets the stage for future social patterns. The extent to which these interactions involve leisure activity is the extent to which one's development is influenced by leisure, and conversely, leisure involvement is a function of one's past experience. Again, we see human development and leisure as a two way street—each influencing the other. The process wherein social factors influence development is referred to as "socialization." The process whereby social factors affect leisure involvement is referred to as "leisure socialization."

In more specific terms, socialization can be thought of as the process whereby an individual acquires self-concept, an understanding of who he/she is in relationship to his/her society. Modern social psychologists attempt to explain this process through *social learning theory*. In this theory, the effect of modeling is emphasized. It is argued that the acquisition of new responses is dependent upon exposure to a model for the new response. This notion may have important implications for parents who are concerned about the effect of television on the behavior of their children; for that matter, it has important implications for all of us regarding the possible socializing influence of television and theater.

In a now classic study testing the social learning theory, children were shown a film in which a large plastic "bobo doll" was treated in an abusive manner by an adult. The adult walked over to the doll and ordered it out of the way. Obviously, the doll could not comply, so the adult punched it out of the way. This was followed by kicking, additional punching, and even hitting it with a mallet. In addition to striking the doll, the adult also abused the doll verbally by repeating phrases such as, "Sockeroo, stay down," or "Right on the nose, boom, boom." One experimental group saw the film up to this point, while another group saw a final segment wherein the malicious adult was disciplined. After the film viewing, all of the children were placed in a room containing toys including the Bobo doll. The children who did not see the concluding segment of the film imitated the behavior of the adult model. The children who were witness to the entire film were less inclined to aggressive behavior.[46]

Television

Research on the effects of TV have been accumulating since the 1950s.[47] With few exceptions, the results of these studies have produced results similar to the Bobo doll studies—watching violence on TV tends children to aggressive behavior. A report issued by the National Institute of Mental Health concludes that television encourages aggressive behavior in at least two ways: (1) children (and possibly adults) come to view aggression as acceptable behavior and (2) children (and possibly adults) imitate what they see on television. Next time you go to a movie, pay attention to the behavior of the patrons as they leave. You should not be surprised to see imitative behavior even on the part of adults.

That viewing television violence has a serious impact on the viewer is clearly illustrated by Eron's study of the viewing habits of 427 young adults. This longitudinal study (a longitudinal study is one that is done over a long period of time) revealed that the best single predictor of a young man's aggressiveness at age 19 was the programs he liked to watch at age 8. In a follow-up study, it was found that the parents of aggressive children were less inclined to monitor the shows watched by their children.[48]

Russell points out that viewers of television violence are more likely than nonviewers to display aggresive and violent behavior. In addition, she points out that some individuals develop a "victim" mentality from watching television violence. These people tend to exhibit paranoid behavior; they tend to carry guns, be distrustful of others, and demonstrate self-protective behavior. She also talks about the "bystander effect." This refers to the notion that television violence can desensitize an individual to violence and its effects. These individuals are more likely than others to be callous toward victims, and apathetic toward people who carry out violent acts.[49]

Watching television may have other developmental consequences. Russell asks, "When too much time is spent watching television, is the development of social interaction and communications skills impeded? Is growth, experimentation, creativity, and the development of physical and mental skills stifled?" Kelly points out another problem with television, and that is it portrays an unrealistic image of life. It presents a caricature, a distorted view of how things really are, thus giving viewers an unrealistic benchmark against which they can measure their lives and define and evaluate their behaviors.[50]

Children absorb a tremendous amount of information from an afternoon of watching television. And given the fact that if the set has cable or satellite capabilities, the child will have his/her selection from as many as 100 channels. The larger the number of channels the more difficult it will be for the child to seek other recreation. There will always be something to catch the viewer's interest. And, of course, this is not just a problem for children. Adults have been known to be captivated by television. But, the developmental implications make television particularly detrimental to children. Nancy Paulu[51] summarizes the concerns of many educators, counselors, and psychologists regarding the harm that too much television can do to children:

1. It can expose children to too much sex and violence.

2. Children can be unduly influenced by the junk food and toys advertised in commercials.

3. It can give children a poor model for good behavior before they have developed a clear idea of what is right and wrong.

4. Young children do not have the experience and wisdom to understand complicated plots or scary scenes.

5. Sitting passively in front of the set for extended periods of time can slow young children's social and intellectual development.

Television isn't in and of itself evil. There are some wonderfully uplifting and educational programs. However, the unfortunate truth is that most of the programming possesses little positive developmental value. Kaufman citing a UCLA study points out the following:

1. In television, perpetrators of violent acts go unpunished 73% of the time.

2. About 25% of violent acts involve handguns.

3. About 47% of violent situations present no harm to the victims and 58% depict no pain.

4. Only 4% of violent programs show nonviolent alternatives.

5. About 85% of programming on premium movie channels is violent compared to 44% on the broadcast networks.[52]

The government has been slow to take action, even though it has been recognized for a long time that television is not a benign form of recreation. It was in 1990 that Congress passed the Children's

Television Act which required the FCC, when reviewing TV broadcast license renewals, to consider the extent to which television programs meet children's educational needs. In July, 1996, the White House, the four major networks, and the National Association of Broadcasters agreed to broadcast at least three hours of educational programming per day. The Telecommunications Act of 1996 now requires the manufacturers of television sets to install the new "V-chip" into all new sets. This chip will allow parents to block out programs they don't want their children to see. These actions taken by the government are important, but the ultimate solution to the problem of children and television rests with the parents.

What can parents do? Obviously one solution is to turn off the set. A more realistic approach would be for parents to help children develop good television viewing habits. Nancy Paula makes the following suggestions for bringing this about:

1. Limit televiewing to two hours a day. Keep a diary of what children watch.

2. Learn about current TV programs and videos; select good ones.

3. Plan with your children what they will watch and schedule these programs. Turn the set off when programs end.

4. Watch television with your children, interact with them regarding what they watch.

5. Follow-up TV with activities or games. There may be benefit in selecting games that relate to the content of the program.

6. Make certain that TV isn't used as a baby-sitter.

Parenting Practices

It has often been theorized that parental behavior provides a model for the developing child. Lynn Barrett and Garry E. Chick of the Leisure Behavior Research Laboratory at the University of Illinois recently examined this notion. They hypothesized that a parent's leisure attitudes, participation in leisure activities, and their personal leisure satisfaction would be indicative of the role structure of the parents and be reflected in their children's orientation toward play. In this study, 97 preschool children enrolled in several local day-care centers were rated by their teachers on five playfulness factors: physical spontaneity, social spontaneity, cognitive spontaneity, manifest joy, and sense of humor. Both parents were then asked to respond to the Leisure Satisfaction Scale, the Leisure Attitude Scale, and identify their participation in leisure activities.[53]

The results of this study indicate that playfulness in children is only moderately related to the leisure of their parents. The strongest relationships were cross-sex typed, i.e., the leisure behavior of mothers tended to correlate more closely with their sons than daughters, while fathers showed a stronger correlation with daughters than sons. The most playful boys tended to have mothers who were "very satisfied" with their leisure. These mothers reported that their leisure provided them with social, aesthetic, educational, and physical benefits. Boys were more influenced by their mother's activity preferences than by their father's choices.

This study is illustrative of the kinds of problems one has in examining a hypothesized relationship which is part of an incredibly complex dynamic. The apparent ambiguity in the findings of this study are consistent with the complex nature of human development. One problem Barnett and Chick were faced with, which is typical of any study of this type, was the fact that socialization is not the only factor influencing personality development. Recent studies on infant temperament make it very clear that heredity plays a role in shaping personality. One infant may be passive and relatively happy, whereas another may be aggressive, despondent, or assertive. Thomas, Chess, and Burch have shown conclusively that such traits persist for at least two years and much beyond.[54] This poses a significant problem for the researcher because it may well be that the child's temperament determines to some extent the manner in which he or she is treated by the parent. In a sense, the infant's temperament serves as a socializing influence on the parent, just the reverse of what social learning theory predicts.

An additional problem with the Barnett and Chick study is its failure to recognize that the developmental stages of development between parent and child mark a rather astronomical gap. The leisure behaviors appropriate for pre-schoolers are significantly different from the behavior appropriate for young and middle-aged adults. Preschool children (two-five years) are characterized by physical activity. Just having emerged from the sensorimotor stage, they demonstrate significant progress in coordination and muscular development. The net result is that children during this period focus on activities involving both fine motor skills and gross motor activity. In addition, the child is just learning to use symbols in the thinking process, which permits the child to incorporate language and perceptual images into their play. Parents, particularly fathers, are less likely to exhibit active recreation in the presence of children. Parents tend to engage in more passive recreation at home, and participate in active recreation away from home (at health clubs, jogging, playing tennis, etc.). Consequently, the leisure behavior of the parent may be inconsistent with the developmental needs of the child, and give the appearance that no leisure modeling is occurring or that the child's behavior is more consistent with the behavior of the parent of the opposite sex.

The notion that leisure satisfaction among mothers appears to be the most significant predictor of playfulness in boys, but not girls, may find explanation in the fact that girls are socialized to behave in a "ladylike" manner. Boys are socialized to more aggressive and seemingly more playlike behavior. What may be at work here is more the influence of perceived freedom in the home than any specific modeling.

The fact that playfulness in the home environment is in part a function of a parent's cognitive style has been demonstrated. By correlating creativity scores in children with measures of cognitive style in parents, it was shown that "children's creativity improves as the playfulness of the home environment is increased."[55]

In a home where a mother expresses a high degree of satisfaction with her leisure, it would not be surprising to find an atmosphere characterized by high degrees of perceived freedom and intrinsic motivation. Such a home naturally would provide a rich environment for a child to develop a strong play orientation. In homes where the mother is the dominant socialization force, it is consistent with social learning theory to show a correlation between a mother's leisure satisfaction and a son's playfulness. Similarly, it is not inconsistent to show a relationship between a father and daughter on this measure. Young fathers may be less satisfied with their leisure simply because of their dedication to their careers. A preoccupation with work is not uncommon for young fathers. A young mother, who has chosen to spend her days with her children may find great satisfaction from her interaction with her children, thus reinforcing her perception of her leisure satisfaction and her capacity to socialize leisure and quite likely gender specific behavior.

One further limitation in this study is found in the difficulty associated with controlling for other socialization factors. As already illustrated, it appears that television has a profound effect on children. Certainly in some families, the principal modeling influence is television, while in other families, television plays a minor role. And to what extent did teacher, peers, siblings and others play in determining the playfulness of the children in the study? Another question that needs to be answered relates to the amount of time parents spent with their children.

In this review of the Barnett and Chick study, it must be pointed out that the intent is not to be critical of two well respected researchers, but rather to illustrate the difficulty inherent in trying to validate the various theories advanced to explain the ways in which people acquire leisure behaviors. As pointed out earlier, the socialization process overlaps the other areas of human development and consists of a wide array of interlocking factors, including physical characteristics, temperament traits, and social factors such as economic forces, sociocultural values, and patterns of childrearing.

In order for a study to provide conclusive answers to leisure socialization questions, it must account for the interplay between these and other pertinent variables. Hopefully, this review of the Barnett and Chick study has served to illustrate the complexity and difficulty inherent in this type of undertaking.

What is certain is that effective parenting is absolutely essential to effective growth and development in children.

Competition vs. Cooperation

In a capitalistic society, the value of competition largely goes without question. Basically, in this society, there seems to be an implicit faith in the value of competitive behavior. So it is not surprising to learn that American children are more competitive than children from other countries. Similarly, children from parents of high socioeconomic status are more effective competitors than children from lower socioeconomic strata. Prior to age two there appears little urge on the part of children to compete; however, once in the preoperational stage, children begin to recognize the nature of competitive behavior.

This corresponds with the child's increasing ability to recognize concepts such as value and possession. Once a child has begun to exhibit competitive behavior it tends to increase until about age eleven.[56] Following an extensive review of studies dealing with competitive play behavior (particularly Little League baseball), Iso-Ahola summarized his findings:

1. Competitive tasks lower the quality of interpersonal relationships, whereas cooperative tasks tend to enhance social relationships.

2. In competitive rather than cooperative situations, children tend to be more anxious, tense and less secure.

3. Cooperative tasks enhance social perspectives, which in turn is related to social adjustment, effectiveness of communication, personal identity and self-awareness, moral judgment, open-mindedness and acceptance of individual differences.[57]

In reference to Little League Baseball he draws the following conclusions:

1. Other things being equal, cooperation is superior to competition because of the positive effects of the former on interpersonal and intrapersonal behavior. . . . With major emphasis on ingroup cooperation and minor emphasis on intergroup competition, Little League is psychologically healthy, assuming that competition between teams does not become too serious.

2. Self-serving causal attributes for team outcomes suggest that players are capable of coping with winning and losing. However, there are reasons to believe that repeated and uncontrollable failures give rise to feelings and inferences of helplessness.

3. Intensive involvement by coaches and parents in Little League has turned children's recreation into work. The use of external rewards and sanctions has reached a point where players have to infer extrinsic reasons for their participation. This clearly reduces the player's intrinsic interest in Little League Baseball and makes it seem more like work. . . .

4. Before and after the baseball season, players rate higher than nonplayers on self-concept and certain socially desirable characteristics (e.g., leadership and emotional adjustment).

5. . . . due to its highly structured nature, Little League does not provide players with skills and characteristics (e.g., creativity, innovation) needed for change and improving the prevalent society; if anything, it will only reinforce those traits that tend to maintain the status quo.[58]

From this point of view, Little League programs are contributing very little to child development. It is not that youth sports don't contribute to a person's development, it is rather that the elements of the youth sport's experience may have contradictory effects. In addition, because of the progressive exclusion that occurs in youth sports, there is a possibility that as youngsters are eliminated from the more prestigious sports groups, deleterious effects on both the favored and the unfavored may occur. Speaking to this point, John Kelly has this to say:

> More than those who lose a particular contest, there are those who lose out in the progressive exclusion model of school sport. As more and more are left out of participation and asked to take secondary supporting roles for the few who still play, most young men and women become losers. They are left and judged unqualified to compete. The consequences of this filtering that begins in elementary school and sport programs for the very young have yet to be measured.[59]

It is interesting to note that children are less likely to emphasize winning in youth sports than parents and coaches. Clark states that there is a significant difference on the emphasis adults and children place on winning. Clark cites a national survey of young people between ages 10–18 who were asked to rate the importance of winning in relationship to why they chose to participate in youth sports; winning was not even in the top ten reasons for girls, and only number seven for boys. When asked what they would change about sports, both genders indicated they would prefer less emphasis on winning. Clark also points out that attitudes change with age. The older the child, the more emphasis he or she places on winning.[60]

Many, if not most, people have a belief that youth sports are good, that they build character and promote fitness. Those claims may have some validity, but on the other hand, the indications are that too much emphasis on winning may have negative consequences. Too much emphasis on winning makes sports an extrinsically motivated experience, and where this occurs the joy inherent in activity may be supplanted by anxiety. Where winning is emphasized, the relative distance between victory and defeat is exaggerated, and victory may be viewed as success and defeat as failure. Parents and coaches can do a great deal to assure that children benefit from sports. By emphasizing the value of participation and activity and diminishing the importance of winning, by focusing on the individual growth and development of each player, and recognizing the validity of fun in youth sports, coaches and parents can help youth sports help youth achieve their physical, social, and emotional potential.

In our discussion of leisure socialization, we have only scratched the surface. So broad is this topic that it could easily fill an entire textbook. The purpose of this discussion has not been to conduct an extensive review of related literature and studies, but rather to point out some of the salient issues surrounding the process whereby one gains basic knowledge about leisure, develops attitudes and values associated with play, and learns various leisure skills.

As presented earlier, much of this learning occurs in childhood (about 50% of one's adult activities can be traced to childhood) and is the result of modeling, imitation, and identification with behavior of significant others.

In this cursory look at social development and leisure, several important interesting areas have been neglected. This is due to the limiting effect of time and space, not the result of a lack of interest in the topic or lack of attention to detail. Although the limiting influence of time and space can justify omitting certain related areas, it would be remiss to ignore one final concept. It is important that the student of leisure recognize that leisure socialization does not end with childhood. It is an ongoing process that causes us to continually grow and develop. This process can be facilitated by seeking leisure activities that promote feelings of self-confidence, by engaging in activities that are intrinsically rewarding, that contribute to feelings of perceived freedom, and activities that are optimally stimulating.

Just as social development goes well beyond childhood and continues to influence behavior and emotions throughout life, so do all other aspects of human development. In the next chapter, we will look at human development as it relates to leisure throughout the rest of the life cycle.

NOTES

1. Statt, D. *Dictionary of Psychology.* (New York: Barnes and Noble Books, 1981): 94.

2. Freud, S. *A General Introduction to Psychology.* (Garden City, New York: Doubleday, 1943).

3. Gleitman, H. *Psychology.* (New York: W.W. Norton and Company, 1986).

4. Erikson, E. H. *Childhood and Society.* (New York: Norton, 1963).

5. Piaget, J. *Play, Dreams, and Imitation in Childhood.* (NY: Norton, 1962).

6. "Talking, Singing to Baby Is Vital to Brain Development." *Star Tribune.* Friday, April 19, 1997 (http://www. hbci.com).

7. Parten, M. W. "Social Play Among Preschool Children." *Journal of Abnormal Psychology and Social Psychology.* (1932): 243–269.

8. Smilansky, S. "The Effects of Sociodramatic Play on Disadvantaged Preschool Children." (NY: John Wiley and Sons, 1968).

9. Gunn, S. L., and C. Peterson. *Therapeutic Recreation Program Design: Principles and Procedures.* (Englewood Cliffs, NJ: Prentice-Hall, 1978).

10. Gunn and Peterson, 157–172.

11. Zanden, V. *Human Development.* (NY: Alfred Knopf, 1978): 363–364.

12. Sheldon, W. *The Varieties of Temperament: A Psychology of Constitutional Differences.* (NY: Harper, 1942).

13. Papalia, D. R., and S. W. Olds. *Human Development.* (NY: McGraw-Hill, 1986): 100.

14. Papalia and Olds, 101.

15. Papalia and Olds, 213.

16. Glietman, H. *Psychology.* (NY: W.W. Norton Co., 1986): 516.

17. Iso-Ahola, S. E. *The Social Psychology of Leisure.* (Dubuque, Iowa: Wm. C. Brown, 1980): 83.

18. Weis, Bernard, and Philip J. Landrigan. *The Developing Brain and the Environment: An Introduction.* (http://ehpnet1.niehs.hih.gov/docs/2000/supl-3/intro.html)

19. The hippocampus is associated with the capacity to remember as well as the sense of smell.

20. Teicher, Martin. "Child Abuse and the Developing Brain." *Cerebrum* (2000): 50–67.

21. Zanden 247.

22. Nash, Madeline. "Fertile Minds: From Birth a Baby's Brain Cells Proliferate Wildly, Making Connections that May Shape a Lifetime of Experience; The First Three Years Are Critical." *Time*. February 3, 197, Vol. 149. 05 (http://www.time.com/time/magazine/1997/dom/97023/ cover0/ html).

23. Zelaso, P. R., R. B. Kearsley, and J. Ungerer. *Learning to Speak: A Manual for Parents* (Hillsdale, NJ: l. Erlbaum Associates, 1984): 85–117.

24. Piaget, 27.

25. Piaget, 66.

26. Morris, D. *The Human Zoo*. (NY: Dell Publishing, 1974): 23.

27. Ellis, M. J. *Why People Play*. (Englewood Cliffs, NJ: Prentice-Hall, 1973).

28. Kohlberg and Gilligan (1971).

29. Papalia and Olds, 325.

30. Iso-Ahola, 97.

31. Iso-Ahola, 96.

32. Papalia and Olds, 263.

33. Freud, 143.

34. Iso-Ahola 108–109.

35. Bandura, A., and R. H. Walters. *Social Learning and Personality Development*. (NY: Rinehart and Winston, 1963).

36. Drummond, R. J. *Appraisal Procedures for Counselors and Helping Professionals*. (Englewood Cliffs, NJ: Prentice-Hall, 1996): 259.

37. Keirsey D. *Please Understand Me*. (Del Mar, CA: Prometheus Nemesis, 1998).

38. Keirsey D., and M. Bates. *Please Understand Me: Character and Temperament Types*. (Del Mar, CA: Prometheus Nemesis Book Co. 1984).

39. Layne, V. "Myers-Briggs Psychology: A Brief Primer." (http://www.web.mit.edu/) (June 1, 2001).

40. See: Psychiatry on Line (http://www.gold.net/ users. html) (April 21, 2001).

41. Porthouse, W. Summary of the Myers-Briggs Type Indicator MBTI (http://longwood.cs.ucf.edu/porthous/ mbscores.html) February 16, 1998.

42. SunSITE is one of the best sites on the internet. It is operated by the University of North Carolina, Chapel Hill, in cooperation with Sun Microsystems. It is an eclectic collection of art, educational, political, and recreation information. It is worth visit, if for no other reason than the potential it holds for discovery. Be prepared to spend some time if you pay it a visit, it is full of interesting things to do, to see, and to learn from.

43. Iso-Ahola, 210.

44. Iso-Ahola, 210–211.

45. Iso-Ahola, 211–212.

46. Glietman, 500.

47. Zanden, 86–90.

48. Papalia and Olds, 224.

49. Russell, 181.

50. Kelly, J. *Leisure*. (Boston: Allyn and Bacon, 1996): 261.

51. Paulu, N. *Parents' Resource Almanac*. (http://www.family.storeware.com/) (May 10, 2001).

52. Kaufman, R. *Kill Your Television: Children and TV*. http://www.netreach.net/people/kaufman/children.html. (Jan. 2, 1997).

53. Barnett, L., and G. Chick. "Chips off the Old Block: Parents' Leisure and Their Children's Play." *Journal of Leisure Research* 18.l4 (1968): 266–283.

54. Glietman, 506.

55. Iso-Ahola, 100.

56. Iso-Ahola, 115.

57. Iso-Ahola, 116.

58. Iso-Ahola, 126–127.

59. Kelly, 205.

60. Clark, M. A. "Winning, How Important Is It In Youth Sports?" http://www.educ.mus.edu/units/Dept/PEES/ysi/ spotlightf94/winning.html (Jan. 3, l997).

REFERENCES

Bach, R. *Jonathan Livingston Seagull*. New York: Avon Books, 1970.

Bandura, A., and R. H. Walters. *Social Learning and Personality Development*. New York: Holt, Rinehart and Winston, 1963.

Barnett, L., and G. Chick. "Chips off the Ol' Blocks: Parents' Leisure and Their Children's Play." *Journal of Leisure Research*. 1968, 18, No. 4, 266–283.

Bishop, D. W. "Psychological Adjustment and Leisure-Time Activities." Final Report for Grant MH 17913, Department of Recreation and Park Administration, University of Illinois, Urbana-Champaign, 1973.

Britt, S. H., and S. Q. Janus. "Toward a Social Psychology of Human Play." *The Journal of Social Psychology*. 1941, 13, 351–384.

Brooks, J. B., and D. Elliott. "Prediction of Psychological Adjustment at Thirty from Leisure Time Activities and Satisfactions in Childhood." *Human Development*. 14.1 (1971): 51–61.

Callois, R. *Man, Play and Games*. New York: Free Press, 1961.

Carlson, Neil R. *Psychology*. New York: Allen Bacon, Inc., 1987.

Cattell, R. B. *Personality and Motivation*. New York: World Book Co., 1957.

Cavanaugh, J. O. "The Relation of Recreation to Personality Adjustment." *Journal of Social Psychology*. 1942, 15, 63–74.

Clark, M. A. "Winning, How Important Is It In Youth Sports?" http://www.educ.mus.edu/units/Dept/ PEES/ ysi/spotlightf94/winning.html (Jan. 3, l997).

Csikszentmihalyi, M. *Beyond Boredom and Anxiety*. San Francisco: Jossey-Bass, 1975.

Drummond, R. J. *Appraisal Procedures for Counselors and Helping Professionals*. Englewood Cliffs, New Jersey: Prentice-Hall, 1996.

Dyer, W. *The Sky Is the Limit*. New York: Avon, 1978.

Ellis, M. J. *Why People Play*. Englewood Cliffs, New Jersey: Prentice-Hall, 1973.

Erikson, E. H. *Childhood and Society*. (Second Edition). New York: Norton, 1963.

Feitelson, D., and G. S. Ross. "The Neglected Factor." *Play and Human Development*. 1973, 16, 202–223.

Freud, S. *A General Introduction to Psychology*. Garden City, New York: Doubleday, 1943.

Gleitman, H. *Psychology*. New York: W.W. Norton and Company, 1986.

Gunn, S. L., and C. Peterson. *Therapeutic Recreation Program Design: Principles and Procedures*. Englewood Cliffs, New Jersey: Prentice-Hall, 1978.

Hendry, L. G., and Douglass, L. "University Students: Attainment and Sport." *British Journal of Educational Psychology*. 1975, 45, 549–560.

Hirshfield, S. F., and S. L. Hirshfield. "The Use of Games in Developing Analytical and Combinatorial Reasoning." *Journal of Creative Behavior*. 1977, 11, 101, 104.

Iso-Ahola, S. E. *The Social Psychology of Leisure and Recreation*. Dubuque, Iowa: Wm. C. Brown Company Publishers, 1980.

Kaufman, R. *Kill Your Television: Children and TV*. http://www.netreach.net/people/kaufman/children.html. (Jan. 2, l997).

Keirsey, D. *Please Understand Me*. Del Mar, CA: Prometheus Nemesis, 1998.

Keirsey, D., and M. Bates. *Please Understand Me: Character and Temperament Types*. Del Mar, CA: Prometheus Nemesis Book Co. 1984.

Kelly, J. *Leisure*. Boston: Allyn and Bacon, 1996.

Layne, V. "Myers-Briggs Psychotypology: A Brief Primer." http://web.mit.edu/dagoura/www/Working-Drafts/ psychotypology.html.

Lieberman, J. N. "Playfulness: An Attempt to Conceptualize the Quality of Play and of the Player." *Psychological Reports*. 19, 1278.

Morris, D. *The Human Zoo*. New York: Dell Publishing, 1974.

Paula, N. *The Parents' Resource Almanac*. http:// family. starwave.com/resource/pra/BONUS82.html (Jan. 3, 1997).

Papalia, D. R., and S. W. Olds. *Human Development*. New York: McGraw-Hill, 1986.

Parten, M. "Social Play Among Preschool Children." *Journal of Abnormal and Social Psychology*. 1932, 243–269.

Piaget, J. *Play, Dreams and Imitation in Childhood*. (Trans. G. Gattegno and F. M. Hodgson). New York: Norton, 1962.

Porthouse, W. *Summary of the Myers-Briggs Type Indicator MBTI*. http://longwood.cs.ucf.edu/porthous/mb-score. shtml.

Psychiatry On-Line. "Using Myers-Briggs in the Workplace—an extract." http://www.gold.net/users/ ad88/mbwp.html.

Russell, R. *Pastimes: The Context of Contemporary Leisure*. Chicago: Brown and Benchmark, 1996.

Rubin, K. H. J. "Play Behaviors of Young Children." *Young Children*. 1977, 32, 16–24.

Sheldon, W. (with S. S. Stevens). *The Varieties of Temperament: A Psychology of Constitutional Differences*. New York: Harper, 1942.

Simonton, D. K., "Sociocultural Context of Individual Creativity: A Trans-historical Time-Series Analysis." *Journal of Personality and Social Psychology*. 1975, 32, 1119–1123.

Smilansky, S. *The Effects of Sociodramatic Play on Disadvantaged Preschool Children*. New York: Harper John Wiley and Sons, 1968.

Smith, P. K. and K. Connolly. "Patterns of Play and Social Interaction in Preschool Children." *Ethological Studies of Child Behavior*. Cambridge: The Cambridge University Press, 1972, 62–65.

Statt, D. *Dictionary of Psychology*. New York: Barnes and Noble Books, 1981.

Zanden, J. W. V. *Human Development*. New York: Alfred Knopf, 1978.

Zelaso, P. R., R. B. Kearsley, and J. Ungerer. *Learning to Speak: A Manual for Parents*. Hillsdale, NJ: L. Erlbaum Associates, 1984.

CHAPTER 6

PERSPECTIVES ON WORK: LEISURE OR DRUDGERY

Ernest G. Olson with Katherine Martinez

We went to become, not to acquire.

—ELBERT HUBBARD

A few years ago, while sunning on a beach, a young professor met a woman whom he inadvertently offended. As strangers often do, she asked, as a matter of introductory conversation, "What do you do for work?" He quickly responded; he didn't even have to think about his answer, "I don't work, and you?" She went on to tell him that she was a teacher, and then conjectured as to the source of his "wealth."

"Actually, I'm a teacher, too," he said.

"What! I thought you said you didn't work! Teaching is an enormous responsibility, very difficult, very challenging. How could you possibly say that teaching isn't work?"

He went on to explain that he loved his "work," and to him it was so enjoyable that he couldn't think of doing any other kind of job. He explained how it provided him with perceived and perceptual freedom and intrinsic satisfaction. The extrinsic satisfaction was important too, but there were countless ways to make money. What was important to him was the intrinsic benefits that he received as a teacher. No, to him teaching didn't seem like work. She calmed down immediately and said she understood, but he sensed a bit of envy.

The ideal, of course, is to discover early the type of career that you enjoy most, and not quite so ideal, but very important, is learning how to discover leisure in those jobs that aren't quite so satisfying.

The Meaning of Work

In primitive times, people had to be self-sufficient. Survival depended upon their ability to protect, feed, clothe, and shelter. The work of primitive people *was not rewarded by financial gain,* but rather by survival. Civilization altered this model. Organized communities produced specialization and soon ecomonic systems were devised. One's specialization allowed one to generate income which provided the means to procure the products or services of other specialists. Thus, work became associated with income, but the net result was, as it had been in earlier times, the acquisition of food, clothing, and shelter.

From an economist's point of view, work is usually an activity for which there is remuneration. This point of view is of practical value to a social scientist because money provides an efficient way to measure value in society. Unfortunately, it fails to account for work done for which there is no direct payment. Examples of this are the homemaker who works daily in the house, or the unemployed individual who exerts energy in seeking a job or the self-sufficient individual who directs his/her energies to producing food, clothing, and shelter.

In physics and mechanics, work refers to the energy of a force acting against some resistance, resulting in the displacement of the source of the resistance. Work is equal to the product of the force and the distance of the movement. Unlike social definitions, the time factor doesn't enter into the physical science of work. The ability to work for any period of time is associated with the concept of power. *To the physical scientist, work is energy to create movement.*

Borrowing from physical science, one can argue that work is any activity in which one uses energy to bring about a change in something. From this standpoint, work is associated with any human activity that is directed toward any goal or objective. Work can range from mowing a lawn to playing a vigorous game. From this viewpoint, work is nothing more than the application of force or energy.

Ann Harriman, following her study of work patterns among managers and professionals, concluded that work is the *set of meaningful activities by which an individual defines himself or herself.* Work provides intrinsic rewards; it may or may not be undertaken for its own sake and not because it is prescribed by one's role as job holder or by any other social or family role. It is akin to the notion of a "calling or vocation."[1]

To Harriman, a job is how one *earns a livelihood;* work is something else. This is a logical perspective, and one that corresponds to Neulinger's Model. It is important to note that in common parlance, work and job often are used synonymously. This is manifest in how people use the word "work" in their daily conversations. When one is at his place of employment, one is at work. Or, when one is going to one's job, one is going to work. As summer approaches, students are heard to say, "What will you do for work?" When a person receives employment, one has found work. When one loses a job, one is out of work.

I Owe, I Owe, It's off to Work I Go.

—Linda Lucky

The Purposes and Importance of Work

Clearly, one's job is important from the standpoint of financial reasons. Few of us are born with discretionary wealth, most of us have to "work" in order to survive. But in addition to the monetary value of work, there are other important outcomes.

Extrinsic Rewards Other Than Money

Normally, when one thinks of extrinsic rewards, money is the first thing to come to mind. But for many people, one's employment may provide them with a number of non-monetary, yet extrinsic, values. *Status* is an important reward for work. *Recreational-opportunity* afforded under the heading, "employment recreation," may be thought of as an extrinsic reward. *Schedule-flexibility* is an extrinsic value that attracts many people to jobs such as teaching. In fact, for many people, time is viewed as being as important as money. In one survey workers, when offered the choice between more time off or money, opted for the time off (Harriman 8). These are but a few of the non-monetary extrinsic rewards offered by one's employment.

Work provides people a social group with whom to associate and identify. Such a group is important for at least two reasons: (1) it provides a group against which one can mirror one's social, emotional, and economic characteristics and (2) it provides a community within which one may socialize, contribute, and seek support.

Intrinsic Rewards

Although extrinsic rewards such as salary, benefits, favorable scheduling, career advancement, etc., are important, intrinsic rewards are equally significant factors to consider in choosing the ideal career. Intrinsic rewards are derived directly from the work experience itself. Consider your current job (or if you are not employed, think about your academic studies). What do you like about your job or field of study? Chances are you will be considering intrinsic factors such as socializing with colleagues, helping others, making a difference, critical thinking, enjoyment of the task itself, a feeling of accomplishment, etc.

Assets v. Liabilities

In choosing the ideal career for you, it is important to consider both the assets (the extrinsic and intrinsic rewards) as well as the liabilities. Liabilities are the negative factors of a job such as physical danger, long work hours, stress, travel, etc. Regardless of how satisfying a career may be, liabilities will still exist. Understanding what your career liabilities are will be a starting point to determining a course of action to combat them. For example, in the law enforcement field, the potential for physical harm is extremely high. Some solutions would be to maintain peak physical conditioning, participate in routine law enforcement training, and to follow health and safety policies.

Importance to Society

A society unwilling to work is ultimately doomed. The progress of any culture is, certainly in part, related to the productivity of its members. It would also appear that freedom is an essential component to successful economies, suggesting that successful work in contemporary society may be more similar to current thinking about leisure than early thinking about work.

The Importance of Work in Your Life

Those of us who study leisure have often suggested that work-time will eventually give way to leisure-time, that people will be required to work less, and hence, will be given the opportunity to enjoy more free-time. In fact, it wasn't more than a decade or two ago that we were very much concerned about what people were going to do when faced with the unprecedented leisure the near future guaranteed. We were afraid that unprecedented leisure would pose more problems than benefits, largely because people were so accustomed to being externally directed. The big fear was that the majority of people would not know how to use leisure to their advantage. At present, the indicators are that as a society, we are spending more hours at work than we did at the end of World War II. We have not become a society of leisure. The 1991 Harris Poll revealed that the average American worker "works about forty-seven hours per week spent at and getting to one's job . . . this is up from 40 hours per week in 1973. Our worries about unprecedented leisure seem to have been unfounded, at least for present and the near future.

Why? Paul Wallich tells that we have developed a "workaholic economy." He states,

> *Provisional and managerial employees supply the most obvious lesson . . . once people are on salary, their cost to the firm is the same whether they spend 35 hours a week in the office or 70. (1) This is apparent even in such diverse fields as medicine and education. To encourage extra production, more universities are offering performance pay, while in HMO's the physician who keeps costs down and sees the most patients can receive a handsome bonus. In regard to factory workers, it is more profitable to ask 40 employees to labor an extra hour each than to hire one more worker to do the same 40-hour job. Given the expense of benefit packages, it is often more profitable for a company to pay overtime, than to hire new employees. The net result is that employees, regardless of their job, are working more hours.*[2]

This development, coupled with the consumer-based economy, results in the situation getting more hectic! Even two-career households don't generally generate enough money for a family to acquire all of the "things" that "money can buy." There are always new things to buy, and things we must have. Our high technology society makes products almost obsolete at the time of the creation. The cost of education is constantly increasing, medical costs are increasing, and the cost of living always seems a step ahead of most Americans. For people living on a minimum wage "it now takes between sixty and eighty hours of work per week to feed a family."[3] As a consequence, in many households both spouses work, many teens are forced to work, and many individuals have more than one job. The great irony is that many of the things we buy are for leisure purposes, but unfortunately, many of us simply don't have time to enjoy them. So much for the leisure society.

Forty-years ago people worked 12 hours a day, and it was called economic slavery. Now they work 14 hours a day, and it's called moonlighting.

—Robert Orben

Faced with what appears to be a decline of leisure time, it becomes increasingly important that people find employment that offers them more than just a salary. Unfortunately, many people find dissatisfaction with their jobs. Hughes cites a study that shows that even though highly career oriented, only one in four workers between ages 18–50 are satisfied with their jobs. Some simple mathematics make it clear how damaging an unsatisfying career can be to one's lifestyle. Even if an individual only works eight hours a day, this amounts to 1/3 of their available time. Add to that eight hours travel time, and incidental but related activities, and it is not unreasonable to argue that one's work accounts for as much as 10 hours per day. Factor in six to eight hours for sleep, and you have six to eight hours remaining in which to attend all other activities: take the kids to school, bathe and groom, eat, do domestic chores, shop, household maintenance, yard work, television, family activity, paying bills, and the list goes on. For many people time for discretionary activities is generally nonexistent.

Consequently, it becomes extremely important that one select a job that offers some of the opportunities and benefits associated with leisure. In seeking a career one should be mindful of the extent to which the job offers the principal elements of leisure: (1) perceived and perceptual freedom, and (2) intrinsic satisfaction. When a job is rich in intrinsic satisfaction, when people feel that they have a significant say as to how they are going to complete their tasks, when there is a genuine sense of pleasure associated with their work, and when pleasant interactions are associated with the workplace, it can be said that one's work offers some of the benefits of leisure.

The old adage goes, "If your work makes you sick, you should call in well." It has been clearly established that jobs that are primarily extrinsically motivated, that offer little intrinsic satisfaction or that are essentially devoid of perceived or perceptual freedom, "erode self-identify, stifle initiative, and impair mental health, leading to injuries, absenteeism and unwanted staff turnover."[4] The article goes on to say ". . . stress-related disorders can arise from monotonous tasks, authoritarian supervision, time pressure, tight schedules, lack of stimulation, coercion, harassment and poor employee to employee interaction."

Behold the little turtle. He only makes progress when he sticks his neck out.

—James Bryant Conant

Calling in well is often an act of courage. Many of us remain in unsatisfying situations because we are afraid of an uncertain future. Many people stay in bad marriages for the same reason. William Shakespeare said, "Doubt is the thief that makes us fear to tread where we might have won." Many of us dream of a different life, a better career, but day in and day out continue to plug along, inwardly knowing that we will never make a change. It is just too frightening. However, there are those who take the chance.

Stephan Duncan called in well. He was studying accounting, his future was defined for him. He was going to be an accountant. After hearing a lecture on "calling in well," he approached his instructor and asked what he thought about calling in well if your major was making you ill. In the course of their discussion it became clear that Stephan's greatest desire was to fly high performance jet aircraft. Although competent in accounting, he felt he was best qualified to fly jets. It was the thing he wanted most to do. His instructor suggested two alternatives (1) become a very successful accountant and buy his own jet, or (2) since at that time there was a need for air force pilots, enlist in the air force. Two weeks later Stephan enlisted in the air force. A year passed and the instructor received a note in his mail box saying that Lt. "Been Through the Sound Barrier" Duncan had called. Stephan was on a training mission and was just checking in. Later they had lunch, and Stephan regaled his instructor with stories about flying a jet fighter. Stephan took charge of his future by calling in well and working for a future that he could enjoy.

Happiness is essentially a state of going some where, wholeheartedly, one-directionally, without regret or reservation.

—William Sheldon

Choosing the Right Job

The Bureau of Labor Statistics provides us with projections regarding career opportunities in the future. A quick look at the best paying and fastest growing occupations for the next 10 years are essentially those that require the most education and training. Occupations which require a bachelor's degree or above will average 23 percent growth, almost double the 12 percent growth projected for occupations that require less education. The most jobs for those with a college degree will be for teachers, who are projected to account for about 20 percent of all jobs available for college graduates. Eight of the 146 occupations surveyed will account for about 50% of new jobs: registered nurses, systems analysts, blue-collar worker supervisors, general managers, top executives, and four teaching occupations—elementary school teacher, secondary school teachers, college faculty, and special education teachers. The fastest growing occupations in general include: personal and home care aides, home health aides, systems analysts, computer engineers, software specialists, physical therapy assistants, electronic pagination systems workers, occupational therapists, physical therapists, residential counselors, and human services workers.[5]

In considering a career or a career change it is a good idea to look at such projections. Making a reasonable career choice, in part, will rest on the projected opportunities available to you. A good resource for you, and this is available at almost any library, is the *Bureau of Labor Statistics Monthly Labor Review*. Another source is the *Occupational Outlook Quarterly*, or the *Occupational Projections and Training Data*. Both are produced by the Bureau of Labor Statistics. Much of this information is available on the Internet at:

http://stats.bls.gov/oco/coc/2003.htm or http://stats.bls.gov/news.release/eco.toc.htm.

Faith Popcorn (yes, that is her pen name) is the head of an organization that does market projections for business. In her book, *The Popcorn Report* she identifies 10 trends that her organization believes will have an impact on business in the United States up to the year 2010. Her analysis goes beyond that of the Bureau of Labor Statistics and considers the social and psychological factors at play as well as the implications of such factors. It might be particularly helpful for those of you who have an entrepreneuring spirit.

The haves and the have-nots can often be traced back to the dids and the did-nots.

—D. O. Flynn

One of the obstacles to a career of your choice is failure to prepare properly. Everyone would like a well-paying, satisfying career. But when faced with the preparation required for such jobs, many people feel they just don't have the time. Students often say that they feel life is passing them by, that they need to get out and start making a living. Consequently, many students decide not to go on to graduate school, or not to take a major that might require an extra year or two. In effect, it is a career that passes them by, not life.

PERSONAL NOTE: I once talked to a working mother who said she wanted to be a teacher, but going to school part-time would take her almost eight years to get her credential. I pointed out to her that those eight years would pass regardless of whether or not she went to school, and wouldn't it be better to have her teaching credential at the end of that time? A friend of mine said he really wished he had studied law. "What's stopping you?" I asked. He said that it was his age . . . he'd almost be sixty when he graduated. My response was, "Well, wouldn't it be better to be sixty and a lawyer, than be sixty and still wishing you had gone to law school?" As some anonymous writer once said, "The saddest words of tongue or pen are just four words—it might have been."

The point is obvious. To become what one desires requires preparation and perseverance. As Henry Ford said, "Getting ready is the secret to success."

Some Practical Tips

1. **To paraphrase Shakespeare, "To your own self be true."** So many people choose careers for the wrong reasons. They are told by their parents what to study, or because they believe that to be successful they must be either an accountant, doctor, engineer, or lawyer. Some select a career strictly for the money it offers. Regardless of your motivation, once you start a career path it is difficult to leave it. Consequently, it is important that you find a career track that you will enjoy. One way to enhance the possibility of a "successful" career is to choose a career for which you are well suited. People who are spatially gifted and highly creative will probably be very unhappy in careers that deny them the opportunity to exercise their unique talents. If you are a right hemisphered person, look for a career in advertising, art, music, creative writing, or graphic art. If you are left hemisphered, then choose accounting, engineering, or research. The frustration that comes from not finding your niche may make it difficult for you to enjoy your work, and for that matter achieve your career goals. You simply cannot have a leisure lifestyle if you are unhappy in your work.

2. **Decide what is more important to you.** The geographical area in which you live and work, the industry in which you work, or the discipline itself. If you like living in a rural setting, and this is the most important factor for you in choosing a career, then you will have to be very flexible. I know of one young man who was so committed to living in a rural setting that he accepted work as a correctional officer at a remote prison rather than work in an urban setting as a business manager. The greatest employment opportunities are found in urban areas, so you will have to decide what is most important—where you live or what you do. Chances are you will have to compromise. As for the industry you work in, some industries are growing and expanding and employment opportunities are good for qualified individuals. Other industries are cutting back and dwindling.

In making a career choice, you need to evaluate the extent to which you value the industry, and the extent to which opportunities exist in that industry. Some people really don't care about the industry, they just want to work in their discipline—be chemists, work in public relations, do social work, etc. Where they work and with whom is secondary. Generally speaking, all of these factors will have to be taken into consideration. For example, some people may find a conflict between the job and where it is located, or find employment out of their discipline. You see, finding a job is more than just finding a job.

3. **Don't overlook the possibility of finding employment in related disciplines.** You may find that you really don't want to work as an accountant, but what other careers are available? Well, for an accountant, law enforcement might be an attractive alternative. One discipline the FBI recruits from is accountancy. You studied psychology, but you really don't want to be a psychologist or counselor. If you possess people skills, and are suitably creative, you might find a career in public relations or advertising interesting. Don't lock yourself in a box. You are more than your degree, and if your personality and talents compel you in a direction different from your discipline, look for those fields which can accommodate both your training and talent. My tax preparer is such a person; although trained in the academic side of physical education, her propensity toward quantitative analysis coupled with her entrepreneurial interests which led her into the field of tax preparation. Today she has her own tax service and does very well.

4. **If you have a good idea, are creative, and independent—you just might want to try your hand at being your own boss.** One of my students, when I taught at San Diego State University, was such a person. Although she graduated in recreation and leisure studies, she had talents and skills that tended her toward public relations. In fact, during her short tenure in the recreation field, much of her work was of a public relations nature. Eventually, she set out on her own and established herself in the field of public relations. Today she holds the controlling interest in one of the most prestigious public relations firms in Northern California.

5. **Do your research.** Good decisions cannot be made without good information. Today there is no reason for not having good information about the geographical areas in which you might reside, the industries in which you might work, or the opportunities different disciplines afford. The Internet is filled with information, as is your library (*Ward's Business Director, Moody's Industrial Manual, Standard and Poors Register of Corporations* to name but three library resources). A quick call to a prospective employer will often produce an annual report. Before taking a job make certain you do your homework. For example, find out if a company is privately owned or public. A publicly owned company is controlled by a board of directors responsible to shareholders, important jobs in such a company are more objectively awarded than in "family businesses." Find out exactly what you would be doing on the job—if you wouldn't like the routine, you probably wouldn't like the job. Find out about the opportunities the job offers. Of course, eventually you will get down to pay and benefits. Benefits can add a lot to your base pay, and investment programs can be quite beneficial in the long run. But remember, don't put all your eggs in the salary basket, no amount of financial success will compensate if your job makes you sick, disrupts your life, or prevents you from enjoying a leisure lifestyle.

6. **Learn from the "Peter Principle."** *The Peter Principle* was first introduced in a book of the same title by J. Laurence Peter, educator, philosopher, and humorist. Dr. Peter's book describes the pitfalls of bureaucratic organizations. He argues that in a hierarchically structured organization, people tend to rise up through the administrative ranks to a "level of incompetence." In other words, people continue to get promoted as long as they are demonstrating competence. Once they reach their level of incompetence, they cease to function effectively, become unhappy, and tend to compromise the efficiency and effectiveness of the organization. According to Dr. Peter, when managers stop getting promoted, it is because they have exceeded their potential. No wonder so many organizations are in trouble! Shortly following the publication of *The Peter Principle,* Dr. Peter published *The Peter Prescription.* In this book he suggests a solution to the Peter Principle—don't allow yourself to be promoted to a position for which you aren't qualified or prepared. In other words, stay at your level of competence.

GIVE THIS A TRY

Are You a Workaholic?

1. Do you work more than 45 hours per week?
2. Do you think about your job while you are doing other nonwork activities?
3. Do you feel anxious when you are not at work or are being productive?
4. Do you tend to feel guilty when not at work?
5. Do you talk more about your work than other aspects of your life?
6. Do you get irritated when someone tells you to stop working so hard?
7. Do you constantly worry about having enough money?
8. Do you find that your work has interfered with your personal or family life?
9. Do you find yourself being critical of others who don't share your passion for work?
10. Do you find it difficult to engage in recreation and leisure?

If you answered yes to any of these questions, you may want to take a few minutes and examine the degree to which your life is dominated by work. If you answered yes to all of these questions, you may need to seek professional assistance. One good source is found at http://www.workaholic-ananymous.org/.

A Few Words about Workaholism

In analyzing the meaning of the word work earlier in this chapter, Ann Harriman provided a definition that related work to being a means by which we define ourselves, akin to the notion of a calling or vocation. In many cases this statement is true, since the ideal career mirrors our personal skills and interests. However, there is a fine line between passion for your work and workaholism; a compulsion to work incessantly, devoting more time and energy than necessary. An example is found in a man who retired from the military after more than 20 years of service, worked another 20+ years for local law enforcement, and after less than a month after his retirement party, he returned to his job as a volunteer. When asked why he came back to work, he stated that he was bored and he would work until the day he died. His identity was completely tied into his career, and he felt that if he wasn't working, he wasn't living. In this case, his life was so tied into his career that he hadn't developed a leisure lifestyle to replace his work lifestyle. One key to a fulfilling life is to maintain balance between work and leisure.

Work is more than a foil against which one measures the value of leisure. It provides us with financial resources and rewards. It contributes directly to leisure by providing us with the means to recreate, and under some management schemes, it becomes a source of pleasure and personal satisfaction. You spend a lot of your life in the workplace and at work. It is important that you consider carefully what it is that you want to do for a job. Look at financial reward, intrinsic reward, locale, advancement opportunities, company philosophy, and how career will mesh with your interests, attitudes, and values. It is a good idea to look at trends as well. Technology and culture often combine to eliminate certain jobs that just a few years ago were popular and viable.

If your work makes you uptight it will have an adverse affect on your health and happiness. On the other hand, a job that you enjoy will make an important contribution to the quality of your life. If you've found the ideal job—great! If you haven't, don't waste another second, start formulating a plan to get the job you want in the area where you want to live.

NOTES

1. Harriman, A. *The Work/Leisure Trade Off*. (New York: Praeger Scientific, 1982): 12.

2. Wallich P. "A Workaholic Economy." The Analytical/Economist." www.uakron.edu/eduecone/201/hw/wallich. html (October 17, 1996).

3. Hughes, J. ed. *Eco-Socialist Review*. 5.2 (1991): 3.

4. For the entire article see "A Workaholic Economy," by Paul Wallich at www.uakron.edu/eduecon/e201/hw/wallich.html.

5. http://stats.bls.gov/oco/coc/2003.htm (June 1999).

REFERENCES

Bammel, G., and L. L. Burrus-Bammel. *Leisure and Human Behavior*. Dubuque, Iowa: Wm. C. Brown, 1986.

Harriman, A. *The Work/Leisure Trade Off*. New York: Praeger Scientific, 1982.

Hughes, J. (ed). *EcoSocialist Review*. 5(2) Summer, 1991 http://www.dsausa.org/ESR/Work.html.

Wallich P. "A Workaholic Economy." *The Analytical/Economist*. www.uakron.edu/eduecone/201/hw/wallich.html (October 17, l996).

Peter, J. L. *The Peter Prescription*. New York: William Morrow and Company, 1972.

Peter, J. L., and Raymond Hull. *The Peter Principle*. New York: William Morrow and Company, 1970.

Popcorn, F. *The Popcorn Report*. New York: Double Day, 1996.

CHAPTER 7

PERSPECTIVES ON LEISURE VALUES AND ATTITUDES— WHAT ARE YOURS?

Jennifer Piatt

"Decisions put us in charge of our lives. We find out who we really are every time we make a real decision because we make use of our own priorities and values."

—THEODORE I. RUBIN

What exactly are values? What do they mean to you? Do you have the same values I do? Do your personal values reflect your culture and family? Or, have you re-evaluated life's priorities and have a value system independent from the values you were raised with?

Each one of us has different **core values** that have been instilled in us by influential individuals throughout our lives, as well as life experiences. The people who help shape our values might be our parents, grandparents, teachers, mentors, friends, co-workers, or others who have had a strong impact on life choices. These are the incredible people who come into our lives and become influential in the important life choices we make—from what career to pursue, how to handle finances, and how we want to raise our family. What we do with our lives and the values we hold play an important role in the outcome of our lives, as well as how others perceive us. Values affect our belief system, attitudes, ethics, and the choices we make daily. Deciding who to include in our lives, what career choices to make, and how to live our life come from values. Our values reflect to others, "This is who I am and this is how I have chosen to live my life."

Questions you may ask yourself as you read this chapter and evaluate what values are important in your life include:

- What do I look for in coworkers, friends, or business partners?
- When I complete a project at work, how do I want others to view my work?
- What type of experiences do I want to have in my life?
- In what direction do I see my life going?

After reading this chapter, you will be able to:

- Define the term "leisure values" and explain how these influence behavior.

- Illustrate the difference between instrumental values and terminal values.

- Explain the importance of attitudes toward leisure values.

- Describe the correlation of leisure attitudes and the impact they have on your life.

- Understand what role belief systems play in defining values.

- Articulate how values influence ethics.

- Outline how your personal values affect your leisure beliefs and attitudes.

ATTITUDES

Attitudes, important to the values clarification process, are different than beliefs and values. Attitudes play a significant role in the development of determining our leisure values and are basically one's like or dislike of a specific situation, person, or object (Wikipedia, 2007). Negative, positive, or neutral, attitudes are a driving force behind behavioral change and directing one's life course. It is through your attitude that you decide what the positives and negative attributes of your life are.

Theories of attitudes stem back to learning theories and conditional responses to both negative and positive feedback we receive throughout our lives (Fishbein & Azjen, 1975). Doob (1947) explains attitudes as learned, implicit, and anticipatory response to a specific situation, or object. Yet, many theorists have taken the definition a step further, explaining it as the evaluation process of the meaning of the response to the situation or object being confronted (Fishbein & Azjen, 1975; Osgood, Suci, & Tennebaum, 1957). Fishbein & Azjen (1975) indicate most attitude theories agree with their definition of attitudes "as a person's location on a bipolar evaluative or affective dimension with respect to some object" (p. 9). Ultimately, you don't have an attitude about something, until you evaluate the object, person, or issue and have an emotional response to it (Nelson & Quick, 2006).

The ABC (affect, behavioral change, and cognition) model of attitudes further explains the complexity of defining attitudes (Rosenberg & Holland, 1960). Affective refers to the psychological response of the object being evaluated. This is when you are indicating whether you like the object, or dislike it. Behavioral change looks at what is the behavioral intention or response the individual is planning. You may choose to be supportive, hostile, angry, jealous, or neutral toward the object (Nelson & Quick, 2006). And, finally, the cognition component of the model is the mental evaluation of the object to form the attitude. This reflects the individual's perception and/or belief about the object (Nelson & Quick, 2006).

Attitudes are developed on different levels from individual, cultural, and societal influences. Social influences on all three of these levels can influence an attitudinal change within ourselves, thus either leading or misleading us to our values. For example, think about the ever-too-popular slogan "keeping up with the Joneses." As individuals, most of us want to be financially stable and want to be perceived by others as "successful." Unfortunately, the American culture's attitude of "success" is in terms of material possessions and what we own (i.e., large homes, expensive cars, name brand clothes, etc.). Society as a whole influences our attitudes towards what "success" looks like by buying into the notion that wealth means success. Personally, some of the most unhappy, negative people I have met have loads of money and lots of possessions associated to their name. What is your attitude toward materialism in the United States? And, how do you define "success"? What attitude, biases, judgments, and beliefs do you associate with the word "success"?

BELIEFS

Beliefs are developed out of the attitudes we hold toward different aspects of our environment. Fishbein & Azjen (1975) state "We defined beliefs in the term of the probability that a given object is related to some attribute, i.e., to some other object, concept, or goal" (p. 9). Beliefs play the role in what we determine as truth—that to be real and true. Researchers in the social sciences, including the study of leisure, have developed numerous theories that contradict one another trying to prove what they "believe" to be true. The more we know about something, the stronger our beliefs become. If we know little to nothing about something, it is difficult to believe it to be true.

This goes with our beliefs about what a leisure lifestyle entails, and what the "ultimate" life looks like to us. It is important to be aware of how your attitudes influence beliefs you have about different aspects of your life. This includes what you believe to be your dream job, ideal mate, and what is important to you in your life. When you form a belief about a specific area of your life, there is a relationship to the evaluation (attitude) that took place about the object (Fishbein & Azjen, 1975). Ultimately, your attitude about anything in your life is a direction reflection of your belief system. Each one of these plays a significant role in how you determine what your values are.

Understanding Our Values

"When something is important to us, when it is viewed as worthwhile, desirable, or consequential, such thing is said to have *value*. Values permeate society and influence all aspects of social life. They can be viewed from a *societal, group or individual perspective*. Values have a profound influence on what we view as leisure, and the types of leisure activities in which we choose to participate" (Olson, 2001). Personal values, leisure values, and cultural values combined make up who we are. They help us in making the choices we do and deciding how we want to live our life.

Each decision you make, regardless of what it is demonstrates what your true values are that you practice in your everyday life. "Because everything we do reflects our values, every decision is a choice between competing values" (Passe, 1999, pp. 124–125). Think about it. Have you ever been in a situation where you have had to make a difficult choice between being honest and possibly hurting someone's feelings, or "avoid" the truth and save hurting the person's feelings? Take for example your roommate has a new significant other whom you cannot stand. They ask you what you think of them. Are you honest with them and tell them that you dislike the person? Do you choose politeness and tell them that the person seems to be wonderful? Or, do you avoid confrontation and walk around the subject asking a question about the significant other such as "So where did you guys meet?" It is very possible that you will not want to hinder your friendship with your roommate and will be dishonest with them to their face about your true feelings of their significant

other. Therefore, you compromise honesty to prevent your roommate's feelings from getting hurt.

This situation illustrates what is called a *value conflict*. It occurs when we have to make a choice between two values that we strongly believe in. A value conflict you are very likely to experience as you graduate from college is the balance between work and personal life. There will be some tough decisions to make between loyalty to family versus loyalty to work, or quality of live versus making lots of money. As stated by Passe ". . . choosing between conflicting values is not always so simple, and that the choice needs to be discussed so that each individual can make his or her own decision" (p. 125). This is why it is important to understand the relative strength of your values.

Cultural Values

Cultural background plays an extremely important part in your values. "It is easy to see how one's culture influences leisure choices. Since we make our leisure choices within a social context, the dominant values of the society will determine to a large extent what activity choices are available" (Olson, p. 70). Your cultural background influences everything from foods you choose to eat, work habits, areas of the world you decide to live, to your family value structure. Culture plays an important role in society, and how we engage in the social context. The society we live in encourages us to demonstrate certain values and beliefs.

Olson explains the importance that cultural background plays in clarifying what our values are:

"Social values evolve and in the process new values emerge. What was viewed important to society a few years ago may now seem outdated and possessing little value. This is clearly demonstrated in our leisure choices. At one time, Sundays were reserved for religion not recreation, sex reserved for the bedroom not the television screen, and leisure was viewed merely as a reward for work. Obviously, these values have changed, and just as they have changed so will our contemporary values. For example, Kelly (1992) suggests that in the next few decades cultural values will change to influence American leisure in the following ways:

1. The value of religion in the United States is diminishing. Consequently, religious values such as sacrifice, worship, and adherence to the

Puritan Work Ethic, are also lessening. There are those who are concerned that decline of religion will mark a decline in moral values, and that society will engage in leisure that will be characterized by excess and degradation. Kelly doesn't see it this way. Rather he views a decline in religious values as having important implications for leisure. A reduction in the importance of religion may lead to an increase in the value of the leisure ethic. The value of intrinsic motivation (satisfaction), freedom, and personal expression in leisure may increase.

2. Decisions regarding the environment may be influenced by an increasing appreciation for the role that leisure has in enhancing the quality of life. Today such decisions are based on economics. In the near future, Kelly believes that decision regarding outdoor recourses will be based more and more on their leisure value.

3. Kelly believes that in the future, there will be a general value shift from extrinsic motivations to the intrinsic. In today's value orientation, we often have to legitimize our leisure behavior in terms of social benefits, economic gain, or personal development. Kelly believes that our value-orientation is moving toward greater emphasis on intrinsic values. He believes that we will come to a time when a leisure activity "... need not be good for the community, family, employment status, or social prestige if it yields a full measure of personal satisfaction (p. 179).[1]

The society in which we live influences the kinds of leisure activities we value. Cultural values create common threads among a society, and although they evolve and change, they persist as a powerful force in determining the kinds of recreation and leisure people choose. But, among the members of any society there will be variation in leisure choices. That difference is reflective of the variation one finds in personal values." (Olson, pp. 70–71)

Although we take it for granted, our cultural background, whether it be one culture or a mixture of several cultures in our family, plays an important part in making us who we are, and what we believe in. This includes the most obvious family traditions of how each of us spends the holidays, to looking at ourselves more in depth. It is important to look at what role we play in our own lives, as well as society as a whole and the impact our cultural background

plays in the process of clarifying what our values are, as well as what our belief systems is made up of and what our attitude of leisure is.

Personal Values

There are different factors that influence our personal values. First, the experiences we have had in life, including negative and positive, influence why some values are more important to us than others. Think of a time when a friend or significant other lied to you about something, or hid something from you. Possibly, this has encouraged you to become a more honest and trustworthy person because you do not want to do this to someone else. Did your parents encourage you to further your education even though you had to work through several obstacles to obtain your college education? If so, you will probably state that education is something you strongly value. Family upbringing plays an important part in deciding the values in your life. Those values your parents strongly believed in were no doubt exercised in your home and encouraged to live by this set value.

There are two different types of values: instrumental and terminal values. Olson (2001) states, "Terminal values are those that reflect a person's belief about ends to be achieved, and instrumental values reflect beliefs about how one might achieve desired ends. In other words, instrumental values are the means to achieving terminal values" (Olson, p. 71). Instrumental values assist in describing how you want to be perceived by others. They also include how you perceive yourself and what you stand for through your belief system. They describe our human character. These values include, but are not limited to: self-worth, spiritual belief, and sense of accomplishment, freedom and service to others. On the other hand, terminal values are described through life's activities and experiences. They reflect why we live and what we live for. A good question to ask yourself regarding terminal values is, "Do you practice what you preach?" Terminal values include, but are not limited to: knowledge, good health, wealth, independence, and leadership.

As stated earlier, what we believe relates directly to those personal values that we feel are the most important in our lives. Olson puts it this way:

"Beliefs are related to values in that beliefs refer to what we know about the world, and values relate

more to what we find desirable in the world. Beliefs play an important role in determining leisure choices. We only select activities that we will produce positive outcomes. What is considered a positive outcome is determined by our values. If there is a low congruence between what one believes about a recreational activity and what one values, the probability is low that such an activity will be included in one's recreation. Conversely, where there is high congruence between values and the degree which we believe an activity produces valued outcomes, the probability of participation is increased." (p. 72)

Leisure Values and Needs

The leisure choices you make and how you choose to spend your leisure time, whether it is at work, or time away from your career, reflect what you value and what is most important in your life. For instance, let's say your family is something you strongly value. When people ask you if your family is important to you, your immediate answer is, absolutely! Several of your recreational activities and leisure habits probably stem from your family, and how you were raised. If you include family in your leisure activities, this is probably something that is very important to you and you make a point to include this in your life. The big question most people have to ask themselves is: Do my leisure values and attitude about leisure reflect what is important to me, and reflect how important leisure is in my life? Do you practice what is important to you in your leisure life? If your family is important to you, do you make time to engage in recreational activities with your family on an ongoing basis weekly?

Your leisure values motivate you to do the things that you do in your free time. Some people value thrill seeking activities in leisure, where others want serenity and peace in the outdoors. Some people value time spent with friends and family, where others enjoy being by themselves in their free time. Beard and Ragheb (1980) discuss six categories of leisure motivation. These categories are as follows:

1. Psychological: sense of freedom, enjoyment, intellectual challenge

2. Educational: intellectual stimulation

3. Social: rewarding relationships with other people

4. Relaxation: relief from stress

5. Physiological: staying fit, healthy, weight-control

6. Aesthetic: appreciation of beauty

These six categories were reduced to the following:

1. Intellectual: expand interests, satisfy curiosity, and expand knowledge

2. Social: be with others, interact with others, belonging

3. Competence Mastery: challenge, achievement, competition

4. Stimulus Avoidance: relax physically, relax mentally, relieve stress, escape (pp. 20–33).

Leisure values relate directly to your **leisure beliefs,** and especially to your **attitude about leisure.** This in turn **motivates** you to make the leisure choices that you do. How you demonstrate your values in your daily life illustrates to the people around you what you believe to be true. These are the standards you live by. Your beliefs, attitudes, and values work together to compose a portrait of yourself. Think about your leisure values. What are they? Now, think about your beliefs of leisure, and lastly what is your attitude about leisure? Do they complement each other?

Values Clarification

Values Clarification is simply that—clarifying those values that are the most important to you. It is the process of looking at yourself, how you view yourself, how you feel others view you, and how you are going to practice your values through your daily actions. Kinnier states "Values Clarification is both a theory and an intervention. The theory was inspired by humanistic writers such as Maslow (1959) and Rogers (1961), who believed that individuals are responsible for discovering their own values through the process of honest self-examination and open-minded search for truths about life" (Beard and Ragheb, p. 72). Individuals who are responsible, honest, and have integrity act on those values they believe in, and not the values of others. "Value Clarification is the process of deciding and clearly stating what you believe. It fosters self-confidence and places you in control of your life. Value Clarification is the reviewing and assessing of your values periodically. It is necessary in order to maintain a clear understanding of who you are, what you want, and where you are going in life" (Finch, 2000).

Look back at the previous discussion of cultural, personal, and leisure values. How will your values in each of these areas balance each other? Something to think about is what compromises you will have to make in your life to demonstrate those values that are important to you. If time spent with your family is important, what compromises with your future career will you have to make? If your company transfers you far away from your family, will you change careers so that you can be by your family, or is your profession important to you so that you will sacrifice only seeing your family a few times a year? Values Clarification helps you in outlining what are your most important values and assist you in values conflict resolution.

If we do not take the time in our lives to look at our values and evaluate those values that are important, our life has no direction, unclear goals, and we tend to just let life pass us by. We do not use our time, energy, or personal resources to the best of their ability. We may even forget what we stand for and start to compromise those values that are important to us. Values Clarification helps us clarify the direction we want our lives to go. It gives us a sense of purpose and a positive direction to take our life in. "According to Values Clarification theory, an individual who is confused or unclear about his or her values will tend to behave in immature, over conforming, or over dissenting ways. In contrast, the *clarified person* is likely to exhibit many of the characteristics of Maslow's self-actualized person, such as behaving in a calmly confident and purposive way" (Kinnier, 1995, p. 18). How wonderful! Clarify your values, stand up for what you believe in, and you become a confident, independent, and positive person because you are doing what you believe to be right.

Values Clarification is an ongoing process that continues throughout out our lives. Think back to what your values were in high school. Friends and social recognition may have been high on your ranking order of importance of values in your life. Now, think about certain life situations you have gone through. You may have compromised, or even changed, your view of values after experiencing a life-changing experience. A good example is losing a parent. Before this, you may have always thought

family was important, but never really took the time to include family in a large part of your daily life. This may change after losing a family member and realizing that you need to make time for more family involvement in your life. While you are in college, membership to a fraternity, or sorority may be very important to you, or you may detest membership to an organization. Then, you get married and have children, and you once again need to re-clarify what values you are willing to live for, and make compromises in your life to uphold those values.

"As an intervention, values clarification consists of thought-provoking exercises and hypothetical choice situations designed to encourage participants to think about (or discover) their own values" (Kinnier, p. 19). Kinnier goes on to draw from Raths, Harmin, and Simon who stated:

> *All strategies do two things. First, they focus our attention on life. They bring to mind our attitudes, feelings, activities, goals, aspirations, interests, beliefs, and worries. Or they raise some of the confusing issues of life including relationships, hope, power, generosity, justice, and the rest. Second, they help us deal with life more skillfully and more comprehensively. They give us practice in choosing freely, seeking alternatives, anticipating consequences, recognizing what we prize and cherish, standing up and affirming what we care about, acting on our choices and prizing, and doing so with some consistency. (Kinnier, p. 150)*

I have found that students have a difficult time with the values clarification exercise, and I hear over and over again that every value listed on exercise 2 is important to them. How do you choose honesty over integrity? This reconfirms why values clarification is so important. Remember back to the discussion of values conflict? This is a good time to ask yourself, for what value am I willing to make sacrifices? Students have also commented that they were surprised with the results of the values clarification exercise. They frequently point out that the exercise helps them better understand why they value certain friends, have preferences in recreation, and are interested in career of choice. Other students have re-evaluated their life-paths, and made changes in their priorities and behaviors.

Questions to ask yourself when starting the values clarification process: What am I committed to? What would I be willing to die for? What am I willing to live joyously or enthusiastically for? What is freedom? What is peace of mind? What is security?

What is power and authority? What comprises happiness in me? What is love? What kinds of beauty do I need in my life? How do I think goodness is rewarded? How would I like people to think of me? Do I need ethical standards and integrity in my life? What do other people mean to me? What do I want my legacy to be?

Values may be discussed in terms of how they relate to our life's goals, objectives, and direction in life. Values are a source of meaning and satisfaction in life. "Every person has their personal **objectives** based on their **values, needs, desires** expressed by their **ideas, opinions** and conditioned by their **biases, attitudes, interests,** which determines their **decision making** or **leisure behavior**" (Finch, 2000).

Finch goes on to define the following terms:

Objective:	Short range, measurable, statements that relate to our goals. They are meaningful to use and are attainable.
Values:	Sources of meaning and bring satisfaction to our lives. It is why we live.
Needs:	They motivate our actions. They are things that are strongly desired.
Desires:	Also motivations to action. This represents only what is desired, not what is needed.
Ideas:	Conceptions of reality that are vague and hazy because of the lack of complete and factual information.
Opinions:	Evaluations based on what you know, consider probable or estimate. They are beliefs not based on facts.
Biases:	Conceptions based on misinformation.
Attitudes:	This is affected by all the concepts defined. It is how you feel or think about something and produces a behavior.
Interests:	Motivates action. It is when you are concerned our curious about something.
Perceptions:	What we perceive based on acquired knowledge as well as our experiences in life (Finch, 2000).[2]

Something to Value

Values determine to large measure one's life-path. They stem from various aspects of our lives, and in turn, affect all aspects of life. We have values that are important to us that relate to our culture and social context, as well as those that are instilled in us from the time that we were young children. Values become important to us through the process of formal learning, as well as through the socialization power of life experiences, both positive and negative. Values clarification helps us define what our most important values are and give us the opportunity to take an in-depth look at how we want to live our lives on a daily basis, as well as put us in control of what direction we want our life to go. Values need to be reviewed at various times through out our lives, and constantly evaluated for their self-actualization potential. Without knowing what our values are and what we stand for, our lives have no direction and no sense of purpose. A person with strong values that she or he is aware of and demonstrates through thoughts, opinions, and actions is an independent, self-confident, and quite likely a successful individual—a person capable of living and enjoying leisure to the fullest.

NOTES

1. For more from Kelly, interested readers are directed to his book *Leisure,* published by Prentice Hall (1992).

2. The material from Finch comes from a course packet entitled "RLS 122: Perspectives on Leisure Course Packet." This material was used in an upper-division intensive writing course on leisure in 2000.

REFERENCES

Beard, J. G., and Ragheb, M. (1980). Measuring leisure satisfaction." *Journal of Leisure Research,* 12, 20–33.

Doob, L. W. (1947). The behavior of attitudes. *Psychological Review* 54, 135–156.

Finch, William J. *Recreation and leisure studies 122: Perspectives on leisure, course packet* California: Hornet Bookstore, 2000.

Fishbein, M., & Ajzen, I. (1975). *Belief, attitude, intention, and behavior: An introduction to theory and research.* Reading, MA: Addison-Wesley.

Kelly, John R. (1990). *Leisure.* Englewood Cliffs: Prentice Hall, 1990.

Kinnier, R. T. (1995). A reconceptualization of values clarification: Values conflict resolution. *Journal of Counseling & Development, 74,* 18–24.

Nelson, D. L., & Quick, J. C. (2006). *Organizational behavior: Foundations, realities, & challenges (5th ed.).* Macon, OH: Thompson Learning.

Olson, E. (2001). *Personal development and discovery through leisure* (2nd ed.). Dubuque, Iowa: Kendall/Hunt Publishing, 2001.

Osgood, C. E., Suci, G. J., & Tannenbaum, P. H. (1957). *The measurement of meaning.* Urbana: University of Illinois Press.

Passe, J. (1999). The value of teaching values. *Social Education.* 63:2, 124–125.

Rath, L., Harmin, M., & Simon, S. (1978). *Values and teaching: Working with values in the classroom,* (2nd Edition). Ohio: Charles E. Merrill.

Rosenberg, M. J., & Hovland, C. I. (1960). Cognitive, affective, and behavioral components of attitude in Hovland, C. I., and M. J. Rosenberg. Attitude organization and change (pp. 1–14), New Haven, CT: Yale University Press, in Pratkanis, A. R., Breckler, S. J., and Greenwald, A. G. (Eds.), *Attitude structure and function,* Hillsdale, New Jersey, Lawrence Erlbaum Associates Publishers.

Wikipedia. (2007). Attitudes defined. Retrieved on July 31, 2007 from http://en.wikipedia.org/wiki/Attitude_%28psychology%29.

CHAPTER 8

PERSPECTIVES ON CREATIVITY: A KEY TO LIFE BALANCE

Dr. Carol Stensrud[1]

"Creativeness often consists of merely turning up what is already there. Did you know that right and left shoes were thought up only a little more than a century ago?

—BERNICE FITZ-GIBBON

INTRODUCTION TO THE CREATIVE PROCESS

INTRODUCTION TO CREATIVITY

Creativity is a topic vital to a person's well-being, life balance and quality leisure lifestyle. It is a topic not unlike leisure, a bit hard to put your finger on, but recognizable when you see it. In many respects, creativity holds the key to the unfolding of one's personality. Creativity allows you to meet your unconscious need to express your individuality, to test your limits, and add definition to your existence. J. B. Nash describes creativity as one of the loftiest pursuits in which you can become involved. He argues that it is only through the application of creativity that one can truly acquire and understand leisure. To Nash creativity is not limited to play or leisure, but can have applications in all aspects of one's life. We use creativity not only to express ourselves through dance, art, poetry, theatre, painting, ceramics, woodworking, food making, party making, love making, etc., but to solve our daily challenges. The questions of how to pay the bills, start a new career, raise a family, maintain one's sanity during crises, spark a romance, or have a fabulous life are all answered through personal creativity. In a very real sense creativity is critical to our very survival. It is creativity that allows us to meet life's problems head on, knowing that we possess the ability to solve any challenge that life throws our way!

CREATIVITY—THE PROCESS

Creativity can be thought of as being similar to, and in some circumstances, a form of play. To begin the creative process, we often begin by playing with ideas, notes, shapes or forms, and/or words. By playing with various ways to solve a problem, the creative mind begins to explore alternative solutions. An artist like Matisse would develop his paintings by playing with various combinations of colors in the background. One of his paintings depicted a woman on the couch. He experimented with various backgrounds: one blue, another red, and so on. His playing with changing colors and proportions would continue until he felt he had found the most aesthetic combination. Once the combination had been found, it was then a matter of producing the final project. At this point, much of the fun of experimentation ended and gave way to the technical process of painting. Play had evolved into work. The creative process begins by playing with ideas, exploring and experimenting with them, and slowly shifts to the procedures necessary to bring the creative product to fruition. In between playing and working often comes a time of rest, re-visiting ideas, and incubation.

Creativity is a blend of play, rest, incubation, and work. Creativity is a function of both the right and left hemispheres of the brain. Creative people listen to the right hemisphere more often than less creative people. Creative people often employ left brain distracters in order to free the right brain to speak more clearly to them. One example of this is the "drawing with your non-dominant hand" exercise, which automatically relinquishes your preconceived ideas about how something is supposed to appear. The effectiveness of this strategy is the result of the left hemisphere's capacity to store preconceived solutions to old problems. When a new problem is presented the brain attempts to adapt an old solution to the new problem. When faced with a distraction, such as drawing with the non-dominant hand or drawing the picture upside-down, the left brain gives up and allows the spatial capabilities of the right hemisphere to take over.

EXERCISE IN A BOX

Take out a pencil and paper. Using your non-dominant hand, draw a picture of YOURSELF on a horse. How did it feel doing this? Try doing this again with your dominant hand. Compare. Which drawing would you say was more free? More creative?

Creativity involves serendipity, intuition, surprise, "turning left," and making mistakes! The creative process often is described as having a life of it's own at a certain stage. The writer, computer program, inventor, artist, etc., will often describe the creative process as starting off as free-willed by the inventor. Then, after a period of immersion into the process, the process itself begins to take over. The unconscious begins to play into the process. Gut feelings, serendipity, and intuition fuel the creative process at this stage. This is when the process feels as if it has a life of it's own.

Surprise is a significant element in the creative process. Go into a ceramics lab when a pottery firing is about to take place. You will see the delight and disappointment of the surprise element. Glazes, clay, and heat are all put together with some notion of the outcome; however, nature makes it impossible to predict exactly what will occur. This is true of all experimentation in life. Creativity embraces surprise and a "let's see what happens" attitude.

"Turning left" is a concept that indicates one is going against the grain or doing things in a different way. What would happen if we did things backwards? What if we ate desert, wrote the ending, signed the painting, or put our shoes on . . . first? This kind of out of the box thinking is one of the processes used in creativity.

Mistakes are also a key to creativity. Yes, before the final prize painting is painted, there are many that are duds. In photography, for every picture that is a "take" there are 35 shots on the editing floor. For every minute of utilized television, there is close to an hour of video shot.

Mistakes, making them, understanding them, analyzing them, sifting through them, and even trying to make them are part of the creative process. Creative people often come to a phase of not liking what they are making. The painting you cannot stand at one point will most likely be one of the better paintings, as it unfolds and creative discontent moves it further along towards completion. Sometimes when a painting is working too well, is too settled, or too understandable, I will intentionally make a mistake. I might use a non-corresponding color; or put an x where there should be an o. Concomitantly, if the painting is truly a mistake, after some time of working to solve the unanswered question, I will tear it up and those pieces of a painting will be wondrously reincorporated into a new painting. Mistakes are to be celebrated in the creative process. Without them, there would be no creativity.

Can Creativity Be Learned?

Once upon a time, perhaps when you were in kindergarten, you made a snowman during arts and crafts time. Your teacher made rather rude comments about how you did not follow the lines or graded you harshly on your project. This adult voice . . . "YOU ARE NOT CREATIVE" came down from the heavens and from then on . . . you knew you were not creative. Other people were, you just were not in line when creativity was handed out.

Creative people ignore most criticism. In fact, they might relish the idea of not having their process be appreciated by the majority. That perhaps is what they are striving for, something new, different, and most likely foreign, confusing and even repulsive. Wow! What a life goal!

Creativity can be fostered. It is not handed down one day to some but not to others. We all have creative abilities. . . . We just need to foster them. Yes, some will take it further than others will, but we are ALL creative.

Environment, culture, and family play significant roles in creative potential. Parents who emphasize being right and staying inside the box will tend to produce children who are less creative than more liberal parents. Cultures that give children precious toys to only look at in glass boxes will foster less creative children than cultures that emphasize creative play experiences, such as puppetry or drama. If you are intent on giving a child a gift from the toy store, you might be well advised to buy whatever you desire, then throw the toy away and give the child the box! To the developing creative mind, the box can be anything, the toy is always limited by the minds of the adult creators.

I was lucky! My mother loved to play. She also worked very hard as a nurse and raised two twin children as the primary breadwinner. One of my early play toys was a child size chalkboard set up near the kitchen. I can remember hours of joyous messing around on the chalkboard. Mom sewed a little, enough to make costumes for Halloween and various silly plays, including "The Nutcracker," that my twin brother and I produced in the basement after seeing it live at the holidays . . . this was all in preschool.

One early school experience in kindergarten was that of being taken to the principal for getting into a fight. I am not an aggressive person; however, this girl had TAKEN MY PAINTING EASEL! Of course, it was not mine, nor had she taken it. I had already developed the passion for color and art that remains with me today. My creativity was fostered as a child, both at home and in school.

Adults can foster their own creativity, or take it out of the closet and dust it off.

How Do We Foster Creativity?

My simple life recipe for any lifestyle change is:

Want it

Find it

Get it

Keep it

Hold on to it for YOUR LIFE!

The first step is *wanting it.* By developing an understanding of what creativity can do for us and how it can contribute to our quality of life, we can begin to appreciate and truly want to experience more creativity.

Why want it? Let's brainstorm. Do you know the rules of brainstorming? (Peek ahead in this chapter if you don't.) This is one of the key processes to being creative in home, work, or personal life. Brainstorming is one of the ways to generate the ideas with which to play, needed in the beginning of the creative process.

EXERCISE IN A BOX

Brainstorm 10 reasons why YOU should bother with fostering your creativity (see p. 97).

Why Bother with Fostering Creativity?

Compare your list to mine:

1. It's fun! (*see kids in the bathtub with colored bubbles and soap*).

2. Lets off steam (*see poet pouring heart out*).

3. Helps us solve life's problems through unique ways (*see a collage made up of old love letters*).

4. Offers us windows to our souls (*see a dancer choreographing her autobiography through dance*).

5. Opens us up to our subconscious (*see painter finishing a painting of the universe*).

6. Provides opportunity for lifelong challenges (*see computer programmer inventing new product*).

7. Assists us in our work (*see boss encouraging five creative approaches to be developed to solve one company problem*).

8. Assists us in our family life (*see parents inventing an "our family only" ritual on Thursday nights*).

9. Assists us in our everyday life (*see yourself making dinner out of a "nothing makes sense" list of on hand ingredients*).

10. *Assists us in our love life* (see yourself creating a unique surprise for your honeybunch based on five of his/her favorite things).

11. Assists us in reaching our goals (*see yourself brainstorming on how many different ways you could approach finding a more fulfilling job*).

12. Fulfills us! (*see a child beam as he/she finishes a real snow man outside*).

13. Provides us memories! (*see the framed collage of mementos you collected while on a travel adventure*).

14. Offers opportunities for self expression (*see the hair raising performance of a women's Chicano theater troupe performing radical poetry combating stereotypes*).

15. Offers opportunity for building community (*see the knitters club, puzzle making club, woodworkers club, gardening club, community art fair, cooperatively run gallery, community mural, intergenerational theater troupe, WEB gallery of art by individuals who are autistic, artists in residency in schools, prisons, and hospitals, etc.*).

Now Are You a Believer?

What Makes a Person Creative?

The next step in being creative (after knowing what benefits it holds) is believing in your own abilities to be creative. People have a notion that creativity is inherited. I am firm believer that if people give creativity a chance and really research the right voice for creativity, they will find themselves being creative. My brain is not very creative when it comes to technology or machines. I will look at a gadget and have no process by which to decipher how to turn it on, put it together or fix it. I have technodyslexia. Another person may look at the same gadget and without any experience with it, creatively turn and manipulate things in a discovery mode, in order to figure it out, and of course do so. One of the keys to confidence in being creative is believing in the unknown, participating and going forth. One block to creativity is searching for the right answer. A more go-with-the-flow approach is needed in order to be creative.

EXERCISE IN A BOX

Draw a person who is creative. What do they look like? Do you fit the picture? Do you have some preconceived idea about what a creative person looks like?

One of the *labels* that artists and other *out-of-the box* types of individuals endure is that we are all crazy, alone, alcoholics, and a bit scary. This is simply not true.

Creative people are of all types, shapes, and styles. I can remember once when a tour bus came to a coastal California city full of women from Japan. They were all dressed like tourists with little white sun visors, modest sweat suits, etc. They jumped out of this bus, and literally took over this beach area and made a GIANT installation artwork from materials found on the beach. One artist literally made a field of ribbons running from various natural points, rocks, bushes, etc., over the cliff side edge into the ocean. Installation art is a bit hard to describe, as it is temporary and usually life size or larger than life. The point being, one might have thought by seeing this bus that it was a commercial tour bus full of middle aged tourists. No way! These were prominent bonsai artists in Japan that had come here to the U.S. to do installation art that reflected nature and ecological issues.

EXERCISE IN A BOX

Draw yourself as a creative person. What is new, if anything?

ATTITUDE IS EVERYTHING

Being creative is more of an attitude than a function or activity. This attitude includes several factors defined by Roger Van Oech (1998),[2] one of the first persons to offer creativity training in the Twentieth Century. These factors are:

1. Belief in one's own creativity . . . nurturing and fostering your own creative spirit.

2. Freedom from habit . . . knowing that the old way may not work.

3. Creative discontent . . . asking how can I make this better?

4. Not afraid of failure . . . investing in the process rather than the outcome.

5. Not afraid of others' perceptions . . . knowing that others may not view being outside of the norm as safe or good.

Can you imagine the crazy looks that some of our earliest computer inventors received when they began to describe their dreams of the World Wide Web? How many mistakes or changes occurred in the process of developing this technological wonder? Did this stop the progress or help it? The creative process involves a spirit and attitude of belief in one's self, doing things differently, ignoring the opposition, being ever curious as to how to make things better and lastly. . . .

NO FEAR.

STRATEGIES TO ENHANCE CREATIVITY

CREATING FROM WEALTH

Creating from wealth is another strategy suggested by Van Oech. This process suggests that creativity will be spurred by surrounding yourself with a wealth of stimuli . . . whatever you are creating will dictate this. An example would be the arts and crafts project of making a collage. If you surrounded yourself with many resources such as magazines, old calendars, paper mementos, greeting cards collected over time, a few postal stamps, stickers, rubber stamps, and . . .

feathers, twine, sequins, leaves, cat hair, and glue, you would come up with something totally different than if you were to use only one magazine. The combining of elements often develops creativity. The more elements surrounding you in this creative process, the more possible combinations and permutations on the theme are possible.

So, if you are planning a creative meal, get the cookbooks out! Writing a poem, get the poetry books out, the thesaurus, inspirational items such as photos, etc. Planning a big research project? Go swim in the library for twenty relevant sources. Indulge! Over do! This is one of the ways to foster creativity. Creating from wealth serves to start the idea pumps running.

CREATING FROM POVERTY

This creative technique, the opposite of creating from wealth, is also developed by Van Oech (1998). The old adage, "poverty is the mother of invention" may have something to do with this creativity enhancing technique. This process suggests that your creativity is cheered on by the need to *make do,* or make something from nothing, fill in, or make it happen with what is available. An example of this type of process would be the amateur chef, who finds that there are no noodles left for his famous dish just before the guests are coming. He substitutes rice and the dinner dish becomes a fabulous success. Another example of this process would be to give a group of artists newspaper (that is all) for their art materials. The challenge would be for them to make a piece of art. The results could be wonderful, diverse, and inspiring. Creating from poverty is also enhanced by taking something away. This subtractive process often inspires a new view, approach, or thought process in the person's creative endeavors.

As an artist, I had what is called a breakthrough when I was infected by Lyme disease and my hands became arthritic. This experience made me unable to hold a painting brush therefore I began to use sponges or the flat of my hand. Now, much of my art is done without brushes and it has a freer and *outside-the-box* feel to it than if I was painting with a brush in the traditional way. We, the authors of this text, do not recommend the creating from poverty strategy for approaching academic research or report writing. Using the right tool in the right place is part of the creative process.

Brainstorming

Brainstorming is a process also suggested by Van Oech (1998) as a means of enhancing creativity. You may be familiar with this process. It is basically a process by which a topic, question, or idea is presented to a small group or individual. Brainstorming can be used to develop a new home, find a new job, decorate a child's room, make a sculpture, write a research paper, plan a meal, or solve a problem. It is a very useful creative tool.

How do you brainstorm? With the foundation being the topic presented, brainstorming means generating as many ideas as possible related to the topic. Let's view a brainstorming process related to planning a graduation party for family and friends. The topic is *graduation party . . .* now let's brainstorm ideas.

- Outdoors
- Barbecue
- Catered
- On a boat
- At a funpark
- At the beach
- At the house
- Potluck
- Entertainers
- Music
- Games
- Prizes
- Gifts

Each person or persons generate as many ideas as possible regarding the topic in order to bring to light the various options that might be possible.

Brainstorming Has Rules. These Rules Include:

1. **Quantity is important.** Generate lots of ideas without comment or criticism. The quality or validity of presented ideas will be decided later in a sifting through process to decide what is the best route to take.

2. **All ideas are honored.** In a brainstorm process, you and the members are not to be condemning each other's ideas, i.e., "Oh, that is real bright!" Even if you complete the brainstorm by yourself, please try not to limit your thinking with negative thoughts. Often unreasonable or far-fetched ideas spur alternatives that are reasonable and usable with some adaptations.

3. **Stick to the big picture rather than the details.** It is easy to get derailed in an initial brainstorming process by analyzing the details, i.e., what to cook at the barbeque, how to get people to the beach for the party. Just go with the idea generation process first, without thinking through all the details, which would bog down the process.

4. **Brainstorming can have themes or "overlays" in order to direct the thought.** For instance, if you were using the topic of planning a graduation party as the main idea, an overlay could be *low cost*. This would point your ideas in a direction much different than if the topic overlay was *high cost* or *sporty* or *cultural* or *formal* or *casual*.

5. **Note taking helps with the brainstorming process.** Record all your ideas on paper. This can be done creatively also by using nontraditional methods, such as writing on a brown paper sack!

6. **Use markers.** Markers, a cardboard box, or making a wall mural of ideas noted (this is done in business and organizational worlds) work really well. Creativity seems to be cultivated if people are provided creative means. Try a little color, larger paper, and a more *let loose* style of recording ideas. Go outside, and sure enough you will have better results.

7. **Time crunch helps with creativity.** Give yourself a little pressure in the brainstorming process. The party planning process could work like this: Get your recording materials together, present the challenge of planning the party to your three friends, and limit yourself to 10 minutes for the initial brainstorming process. This works better than stretching it out for a weekend.

8. **Sift the best ideas out from the batch of options. You can then begin to plan the details of actualizing the idea into reality.** The party may end up being at a beach with wonderful low cost fish and chips provided for all. Games will be organized for the kids and a silly awards ceremony made up by the graduating senior as

a way of thanking his/her family and friends for the support provided during the college years. This is only one version of the numerous options that could be developed based on brainstorming the party planning process.

More Suggestions

Piggybacking is another concept explored by Van Oech. It is the process by which one notion, idea, or thought is combined or added on to another notion to produce a new and creative end result. The concept's name comes from the children's physical game, where one child rides on another's back—the "piggyback ride." An example of piggybacking in the art world would be the artist who works on paper going to view a sculpture show. On returning to the studio, inspired by the sculptures, the artist might begin to explore how paper could be made three-dimensional into a sculpture. Many painters add dimensions to their painting surfaces, some subtly through collage, others more boldly through the insertion of the real world object.

An example is Jim Dine's famous heart painting (6 feet square) of bright painted colors, with a blue builders metal clamp sticking out of it. He may have piggybacked an object in his immediate surroundings into his painting. Why? Because adding the clamp makes the painting work and gives it a subversive psychological implication that is fun and different. Piggybacking could also be used in baking. Take making bread for instance. You decide to make rolls from a mix and get creative and add them to the top of you casserole . . . you are piggybacking. Combine a favorite poem into your research paper and you are piggybacking. One of the most famous examples of piggybacking is the roller blade, invented by outdoor metric speed skaters in the 70s in order to be able to train in non-ice weather. Yes, the combination of an inline ice-skate shoe and the roller skate (which used to be a quadrant of wheels) has become a phenomenal hit in the world of sports equipment. The roller blade is a great example of piggybacking.

Renaming is the last of the suggestions for creativity enhancing techniques, once again, coined by Van Oech (1998). Renaming is a process by which you develop a list of adjectives: formal, wild, outdoors, indoors, small, fast, fun, serious, and then apply these adjectives to the theme, topic, or idea you are working on.

Just for Fun!

Make a list of adjectives as suggested above. Use at least ten in your list, please. Now, pick a topic you would like to get creative about. For example, plans for this weekend's leisure activities. Now go down the adjective list and figure out the outcome of a weekend's leisure if you apply the word *outdoors* to it, or *fast*, or *serious* etc. You can see how this process injects new ideas into your thought process and enhances creativity.

Your Topic? _____

Adjectives List:

1.

2.

3.

4.

5.

6.

7.

8.

9.

10.

Now rename your topic by adding the adjective to it. *Dinner* becomes a *picnic* when added to the adjective *outdoors*.

Creativity Contributes to Life Balance

Creativity is an important element in the recipe of life balance. Being creative helps us forget the worries of the day. Creativity helps us move into the right brain functions, which are usually shut out during most of our straight ahead, straight-line processes required at work. Creativity helps us get in touch with the soul, spirit, and inner voices of wisdom. This in turn assists us tremendously with our preventative and ongoing physical and mental well-being activities. We believe that creativity is a key to being fully human, with creative endeavors being viewed by Nash as paramount in human activities.[3]

Life can be whatever you want it to be. Much of our lives we are anesthetized by the television and media into a state of stupor, in which creative thinking is discouraged. We believe that creativity assists you with the go-for-it attitude. You only live once, as far as we know, and to live without creative input into your life is to live a life that is not truly yours. The famous *autotelic*[4] personality is one that follows his or her own drum beat. Experience shows that the *autotelic* personality tends to be happier and more fulfilled than the externally directed individual.

Creativity Is for Everyone

People of all ages and abilities are creative. Visit the Website of the National Arts and Disabled Center on Arts for the Disabled, NADC, at *http://nadc.ucla. edu* for a view of the extensive programs worldwide that promote inclusion in and access to creative endeavors for people with disabilities.

VSA, Very Special Arts, is a national organization promoting artistic involvement for persons with disabilities. VSA has recently founded a program called Start with the Arts which trains school teachers, parents and parks and recreation professionals how to include children with disabilities in everyday creative activities thus promoting equal access to creativity by all. You can check out the various programs of VSA on the web at *www.vsarts.org*.

Creativity Resources for You!

You May Want Some Further Guidance in Creativity

There are many resources that will prove helpful. Books on the creative process can be found in many local bookstores. They may be in the self-help, motivational or psychology section, or in the art section. Some of my favorites are those that call on you to doodle or do something along with the book's content. Books about any subject can also assist you in the *gathering of ideas* stage of creativity. Visiting a Perspectives on Creativity: A Key to Life Balance 161 library or good bookstore is a highly recommended regular exercise for the creative person.

Classes May Be Helpful

You can take classes to enhance creativity at a university, community college, or through an adult education organization. You may want to explore creativity via artistic means. If you do, your horizons are wide open for classes. Visit a local art center, gallery, and studio for information. Art store bulletin boards are also usually helpful for finding classes and even private tutors in art. Your local parks and recreation agencies may offer dance, art, poetry, pottery, sewing, singing, or cooking for a reasonable fee. There are also many private schools at which to train in the creative arts. Surf the web and your local phone book and you will find many opportunities to enhance your creativity.

Take a look at some resources:

- Parks and recreation classes
- Adult Education opportunities
- Continuing Education through colleges
- Art centers and art retreats
- Community organizations such as YMCA or Women's Workshop
- Art galleries/studios and workshops
- Bookstores
- Local art commissions
- Cultural groups, such as a local Latino Club sponsoring salsa lessons
- Talk with people who are creative and ask what they are doing

Now Go Create Something!

When you feel uncertain about your ability to be creative, you are moving away from becoming a more creative person. Don't doubt your ability. Don't question your potential for creativity. Give yourself permission to explore your creative potential. Recognize your creative potential. Move toward it. Embrace it. Create something.

NOTES

1. A personal note from Dr. Carol Stensrud, CTRS, RTC—I am honored to write this chapter on creativity. Being creative has been a wondrous source of life's adrenaline for me. You may know me as a professor, *leisurologist,* and recreation therapy consultant (all of which I consider creative professions). In my private life I am proud to be a working artist who also teaches workshops on creativity. I choose many of my analogies in this chapter from the world of art and more specifically painting. However, I want to convey that creativity is not about making art; it is about life. Each suggestion related to how to become more creative (often presented through artistic terms) is about living life fully, robustly and with heart and soul. Art is not a choice. It is air.

2. Van Oech, Roger. *A Whack on the Side of the Head: How You Can be More Creative.* (Warner Books, Revised Edition, 1998).

3. Nash, J. B. *Philosophy of Recreation and Leisure.* (Dubuque, IA: Wm. C. Brown, 1960).

4. *Autotelic* refers to someone who is self-directed.

REFERENCES

Olson, Ernest G. *Personal Growth and Development through Leisure.* (Dubuque, IA: Kendall/Hunt, 2000).

Nash, J. B. *Philosophy of Recreation and Leisure.* (Dubuque, IA: Wm. C. Brown, 1960).

Van Oech, Roger. (1998). *A Whack on the Side of the Head: How You Can be More Creative.* (Warner Books, Revised Edition, 1998).

CHAPTER 9

PERSPECTIVES ON LEISURE WITHIN HEALTH PROMOTION

This textbook focuses on leisure: what it is and how professionals can promote and foster leisure opportunities. The perspectives on leisure presented include addressing concepts such as values, attitudes, and balance as well as the role of the professional to promote and advocate for leisure opportunities. This chapter focuses on perspectives on leisure from a health promotion perspective. When reviewing the information presented, it is important to keep the focus and context on the overall goal of health promotion which is to help people improve their quality of life. Leisure fits right in given that leisure encompasses many facets of health and focuses on three recurring themes of freedom to choose, intrinsic motivation (things to feel good and that are in line with our attitudes and beliefs), and pleasure or things that make us feel good. When we have the freedom to choose activities that are based on intrinsic motivation and that make us feel good, we seek opportunities that are in line with quality of life indicators. This chapter further explains health promotion and the role of recreation, sport, and park administration professionals to promote health and a quality of life.

What Is Health?

Let's begin by defining and explaining health. Health is "a state of complete physical, social and mental well-being, and not merely the absence of disease or infirmity" (World Health Organization). Health is a dynamic state or condition that is multidimensional, a resource for living, and results from a person's interactions with and adaptation to the environment and therefore exists in varying degrees unique to the individual." Health is no longer discussed in a binary perspective (sick or not sick). It is not only influenced by many things but also influences many things like health status, health outcomes, as well as quality of life (Report of the 2011 Joint Committee). Health is multidisciplinary, so let's explore those dimensions of health.

Dimensions of Health

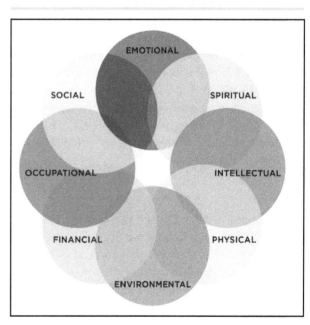

**Eight Dimensions of Wellness.
SAMHSA: Substance Abuse and Mental Health Services Administration**

Available at https://www.samhsa.gov/wellness-initiative/eight-dimensions-wellness.
Source: Substance Abuse and Mental Health Services Administration

---

Contributed by Melinda Novik. © Kendall Hunt Publishing Company.

Physical Health

This dimension focuses on the bio-physiological functioning of the body as well as the health behaviors in which individuals engage (both healthy and unhealthy). These include behaviors such as diet, physical activity, sleep, sexual activity, alcohol, tobacco and other drug use as well as how we drive our cars. Physical health also includes how our bodies respond to internal and external stimuli and the relationship that we have with medical care. Finally, physical health requires an understanding of the many determinants of health outcomes so that we can help others to delay the onset of negative physical conditions like injuries, illness, and diseases.

Social Health

This dimension focuses on those relationships we have with other people and the reciprocal influence that a person has on those people and vice versa. This dimension focuses more on the quality of our interpersonal relationships rather than the quantity of these relationships. An aspect of social health is the support that we receive from our family, peers, and co-workers. Social health as a dimension is changing due to the prevalence of social media and networking sites. While many people have hundreds or thousands of Facebook friends or Twitter or Instagram followers, our connections with people may diminish and be inversely connected with the time we spend on the sites. Developing and maintaining meaningful, reliable, and trusting connections and relationships is indicative of positive health outcomes.

Intellectual Health

This dimension includes our personal capacity for information as well as how we access, understand, and apply that health information in our behaviors. Intellectual health also encompasses a need to be stimulated and challenged mentally on a regular basis and being involved in stimulating relationships and environments. Intellectual stimulation can delay the onset of neurological diseases like dementia and Alzheimer's disease. A recreational example of stimulating our intellectual health would be rock climbing in which climbers are having to be critical thinkers and problem solvers on the fly, all while being challenged physically.

Spiritual Health

This dimension focuses on the morals, values, beliefs, and attitudes one possesses related to overall health and health behaviors and how those aspects influence health decisions. Spiritual health can also be related to Maslow's Hierarchy of Needs and the desire for self-fulfillment and self-actualization and finding peace, meaning, and purpose for our own lives. While many people find meaning and direction from formal religions, spiritual health is not relegated merely to religion. People find meaning and value in their lives and develop beliefs and attitudes about health from a variety of factors including their families, peers, and culture as well as their own personal experiences.

Emotional Health

This dimension focuses on the accurate identification of feelings and the manner in which people cope with those feelings. I liken emotional health to the use of emojis. Emojis are used to express one's feelings. When using emojis, it is important to first identify what we are feeling. We wouldn't use a crying, sad-faced emoji to articulate our feelings of joy. Emotional health is similar in that we must first identify the appropriate feeling then choose the healthiest manner/behavior in which to express that feeling. Our emotional health affects our physical health, our stress levels, our sleep patterns and many other aspects of health that can lead to negative health outcomes. Finally, emotional health relates to social health and the importance of having healthy, satisfying interpersonal relationships.

Financial Health

Simply put, this dimension relates to a person's financial situation. However, a person's financial situation can be very subjective and can depend on a person's values, beliefs, and priorities. There is research indicating that a financial threshold exists and that more money (past a point) does not equate to more happiness (Jebb, Tay, Diener, & Oishi, 2018). However, money is necessary when it comes to those services and opportunities that may not be affordable, like health care. The good news is that parks, leisure, and recreation activities can often be maximized with little to no money.

Environmental Health

This dimension focuses on the physical surroundings as well as the accessibility, availability, and affordability of health care and other health services as well as health-promoting opportunities. This dimension of health incorporates aspects related to how we are influenced by our physical surroundings but also the influence we have on our physical surroundings. This could include taking care of our environment, monitoring our ecological footprint, recycling and reusing, as well as choosing active transportation options. Our campus has two different colored sidewalks, the typical gray concrete and a maroon hue. The maroon sidewalk also has a bike stamped into it every few feet to designate it as a biking section. This allows for those who walk in-between classes to stay on the natural colored sidewalk and those who ride their bikes to have a safe, non-congested area in which to travel.

Occupational Health

As a dimension of health, this refers to one's satisfaction, happiness, and sense of fulfillment from their place of employment. There are many things that influence one's satisfaction, happiness, and sense of fulfillment, and those many things are the other dimensions of health such as the interpersonal/social relationships we have with our co-workers. Our sense of fulfillment relates to our spiritual health and can be referred to with occupational health given the context of career fulfillment. Financial health and the idea that we are paid equitably relates to our satisfaction with our current state. When a person is not satisfied and fulfilled at work, they tend to miss more work or are not productive at work, have lower morale, and are more likely to quit. These issues can also carry over to their home and family lives. Most worksite health programs exist to address many of these occupational health issues (in addition to saving money on insurance costs).

Mental health is not a specific dimension of health, rather it is a summed aspect of health. Mental health has constantly been given more attention in our culture and is often considered as a component of health along with physical and environmental health. Mental health (and the related disorders and diseases) can be seen as a combination of emotional, spiritual, intellectual, and social dimensions of health as well as the way in which our brain responds and functions in a bio-physiological manner.

THINK ABOUT IT . . .

How are these dimensions of health related to leisure and recreation?

If you remember in Chapter 1, leisure was described as "a time to 're-create' oneself, mentally, physically, emotionally, and spiritually. It is a time to grow personally and socially." The benefits of leisure included an opportunity "to re-create oneself mentally, physically, emotionally, and spiritually."

Therefore, it is impossible to discuss leisure without an understanding of health and the many dimensions. It is also important to realize that leisure (and health) goes beyond the reaches of physical health. In this time when mental health has been receiving more and more attention and more acceptable to discuss, leisure has a very important role in helping people improve their mental health.

All of these dimensions of health influence each other. A person's physical health (behaviors) can be a result of their interpersonal and social relationships and what behaviors other people (family, peers) promote. I often ask my undergraduate students if they would bring in donuts to class for breakfast. The majority say no because it is a health class and donuts are not healthy. However, they admit to eating donuts every once in awhile. Their reasoning for not bringing in donuts for breakfast is not based on their own attitudes but rather the social acceptability of eating donuts in a health course and how interpersonal relationships do influence our personal health decisions. Related to spiritual health, a person may place their health as a top priority in their life (values, attitudes) and would not compromise their exercise time for any other reason. Related to emotional health, many people use health behaviors (healthy and unhealthy) as a means to cope or deal with their feelings. There is a reason emotional eating is called emotional eating. People can turn to food to celebrate a happy occasion or to make them feel better when they are feeling sad or lonely.

However, physical health influences our other dimensions of health. Being active can help improve our mood (emotional health), allow us to spend time with friends (social health), challenge our minds (intellectual health), improve our attitude about physical activity (spiritual health), and help us stay in tune with our physical surroundings (environmental health). It is hard to talk about one dimension of health without considering its relationship with the other dimensions of health which is why wellness is defined as "an approach to health that focuses on balancing the many aspects, or dimensions, of a person's life through increasing the adoption of health enhancing conditions and behaviors rather than attempting to minimize conditions of illness" (Report of the 2011 Joint Committee) and is often illustrated in a wheel or circle as shown below. Wellness is an important concept because it goes beyond the physical dimension of health and highlights the importance of all of the other dimensions of health in creating whole or holistic individuals who can strive for the highest quality

of life rather than focus on merely preventing or delaying the onset of (physical or mental) disease.

What Is Health Promotion?

Health promotion is "any planned combination of educational, political, environmental, regulatory, or organizational mechanisms that support actions and conditions of living conducive to the health of individuals, groups and communities" (Report of the 2011 Joint Committee). Health promotion can be seen as a multilevel approach to influencing health behaviors. A part of health promotion is health education which can be described as "any combination of planned learning experiences using evidence-based practices and/or sound theories that provide the opportunity to acquire knowledge, attitudes, and skills needed to adopt and maintain healthy behaviors" (Report of the 2011 Joint Committee).

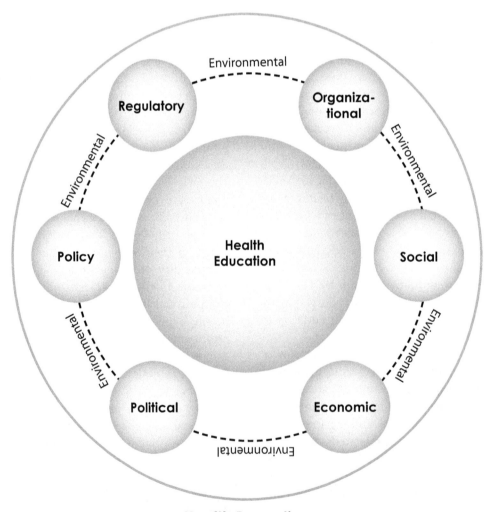

Health Promotion
Source: McKenzie, Neiger, Thackeray, 2017

How can we use the ecological perspective to understand recreation, sport, and park administration's influence on health and quality of life?

RSPA professionals may not focus primarily on individual health behaviors like fitness and exercise. Rather, RSPA may focus on a connection with the environment, to other people, to a more spiritual and connected state of being. These foci include the individual factors (spirituality) but also the interpersonal (social relationships), institutional, community, and policy factors. RSPA professionals require knowledge of social, cultural, and environmental issues which ties in with health and health promotion. RSPA professionals may be tasked with implementing opportunities for recreation and leisure within institutions or organizations, within neighborhoods, communities, and cities. They may even be asked to write, advocate for, or implement policies related to health and wellness that make recreation and leisure more accessible, available, and affordable for individuals and groups of people.

An ecological perspective helps us to understand how we relate to others and our physical surroundings. Using an ecological perspective to understand health and the various levels of influence on a person or group of people, we examine the individual, interpersonal, institutional or organizational, community and public policy factors (Rimer, Glanz, & National Cancer Institute, 2005) that create conditions conducive to the health of individuals. We understand that health and health behaviors do not exist in a vacuum in the sense that we are constantly interacting with others and our environment and that those interactions affect how we think about health and ultimately act.

Health education focuses on a person's (or group of people's) capacity for health related to their ability to understand and apply information and translate that information into behaviors (intellectual health). Health education also assumes that people must have positive attitudes (spiritual health) related to health and healthy behaviors in order to then act in a healthy manner. Finally, one must possess the appropriate skills (and confidence in their skills) to then perform the healthy behaviors. While the concept of health education is great; it primarily focuses on individual levels of influence and does not consider the many other levels of influence on a person's health, health status, and health promoting behaviors.

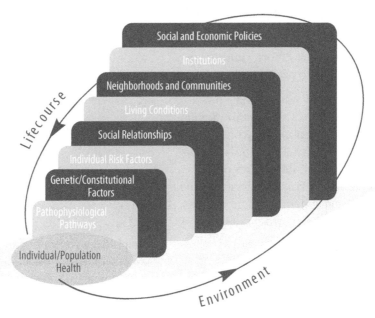

A Multilevel Approach to Epidemiology

Source: Smedley BD, Syme SL (eds.), *Institute of Medicine. Promoting Health: Strategies from Social and Behavioral Research.* Washington, D.C.:, National Academies Press, 2000.

This is where health promotion fills the gaps. We know that if people are left to their own devices (knowledge, attitudes, skills), they do not always act in the most healthy of ways. Therefore, we must also consider the external factors (social, environmental, political, regulatory, and organizational mechanisms) that influence our health decisions. Health promotion seeks to create "conditions of living conducive to health," which in essence is to make the healthy choice the easy choice and, vice versa, the unhealthy choice the hard choice. Health promotion seeks to equalize the negative personal and individual influences so that people are surrounded by health and healthy options. By improving the physical environment like installing bike racks or lockers and even charging for parking spaces, walking may be an easier option than driving. By adopting policies that support active transportation, employees are encouraged to bike or walk to work. Another example would be an organization that offers locker rooms so that those who bike or walk to work have a place to get ready for work. Combining health promotion efforts like these examples along with health education (informing people of the benefits of walking or biking as well as encouraging these options to influence positive attitudes about active transportation) would make active transportation more likely.

THINK ABOUT IT...

What role does recreation, sport, and park administration have in health promotion?

Health promotion includes educational, political, environmental, regulatory, or organizational mechanisms that support actions and conditions of living conducive to the health of individuals, groups, and communities. RSPA focuses on providing organized leisure activities, understanding the impact of leisure on individuals and societies, and a knowledge of social and natural environments (all in an effort to create conditions conducive to healthy living) (MSU Department of Kinesiology). In essence, the goal is the same: to promote quality of life. RSPA can be seen as a component of heath promotion; the difference is merely in the daily focus of activities.

Health education is a component of health promotion. However, health promotion encompasses so many other levels of influence on a person's health status and health behaviors. The ecological perspective looks to understand the internal and external influences on a person's health and includes the intrapersonal (individual), interpersonal (social), organization, community, and public levels of influence. This perspective ties in very well with the definitions and health education and promotion and further exemplifies that health is not contained within an individual. Further, efforts to improve individual health, health behaviors, and health status need to include these multidimensional and multifaceted aspects.

Health Outcomes and Determinants

While an understanding of health promotion is important, it is not complete. It is also important to understand the leading causes of death and how we can look at these outcomes from a leisure perspective.

1. Heart diseases
2. Cancers
3. Chronic obstructive pulmonary diseases
4. Unintentional injuries
5. Stroke
6. Alzheimer's disease
7. Diabetes
8. Pneumonia and influenza
9. Nephrotic syndrome
10. Suicide

While it is interesting to gain perspective about the leading causes of death, what is possibly more insightful is to understand which factor led to those causes of death. The determinants of health are considered the "personal, social, economic, and environmental factors that influence health status" (Report on the 2011 Joint Committee). In addition to considering these as determinants of health, the specific behavioral risk factors are also often referred

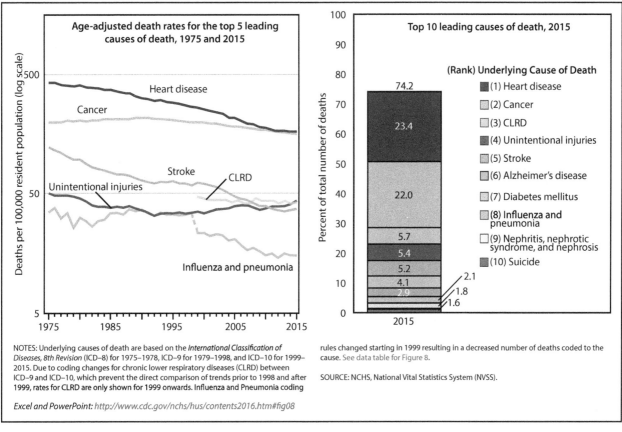

Leading Causes of Death in 1975 and 2015: United States, 1975–2015

to as "*actual*" causes of death because these are the behavioral reasons that many develop those health outcomes highlighted in the above table.

1.   Poor diet and physical inactivity

2.   Tobacco

3.   Alcohol

4.   Medical errors

5.   Toxic agents

6.   Microbial agents

7.   Firearms

8.   Motor vehicle

9.   Sexual behavior

10. Illicit drug use

What cannot be ignored when understanding these behavioral determinants of health or actual causes of death is the role of the social, economic, and environmental factors that influence these

behaviors. This is why in this chapter we also discuss the various dimensions of health and look at health within an ecological perspective. This is also why it is so important to understand the combination of different mechanisms as is stated in the definition of health promotion.

In order to put health (outcomes and determinants) into a recreation, sport, and parks perspective, we can look toward the Healthy People 2020 Objectives (Healthy People 2020). Within the physical activity topic area, there are two specific objectives that focus on increasing leisure time.

PA-1—Reduce the proportion of adults who engage in no leisure-time physical activity. The target for 2020 is 32.6% of adults aged 18 or older that engage in no leisure-time physical activity (LTPA). Between 1997 and 2015, the rates of no engagement in LTPA steadily declined, going from 39.8% in 1997 to 30.0% in 2015. RSPA professionals have a big role to play in continuing this downward trend by not only providing opportunities for LTPA but also to advocate policies and environmental mechanisms that support LTPA. Further, by decreasing the

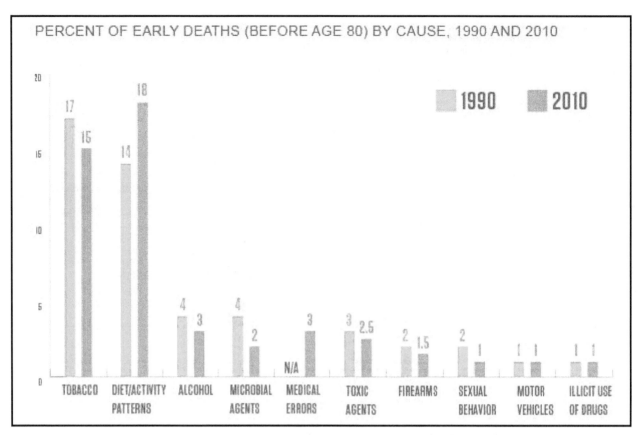

Poor Diet, Lack of Exercise Impede Progress on Reducing Early Deaths

Note: Deaths due to medical errors not calculated in 1990.
Source: J. Michael McGinnis, "Actual Causes of Death, 1990–2010," Workshop on Determinants of Premature Mortality, Sept. 18, 2013, National Research Council, Washington, D.C.

proportion of adults that do not engage in LTPA means that adults are more physically active which addresses the overall goal of getting adults (and families and children) more active.

THINK ABOUT IT . . .

How do the two Healthy People 2020 leisure objectives relate to the concept of health promotion?

Remember that health promotion includes educational, political, environmental, regulatory, or organizational mechanisms that support actions and conditions of living conducive to the health of individuals, groups, and communities. In order to improve leisure-time physical activity, people need knowledge, positive attitudes, and skills to be active. Moreover, people need cultures,

communities, environments, and policies that support leisure-time physical activity. RSPA professionals will be called upon to advocate for a change in culture, environment, and policies to facilitate conditions that support leisure activities throughout the lifespan.

PA-15—Increase legislative policies for the built environment that enhance access to and availability of physical activity opportunities. This objective focuses community-scale policies, street-scale policies, and transportation and travel policies for the built environment. By providing more community and city level opportunities and incorporating the built environment via political forces, leisure and physical activity opportunities may become more of the norm and foster cultures of change in which recreation is at the forefront.

Levels of Prevention

While considering the perspective of wellness and that approach to balancing all of the dimensions of health while also seeking to adopt health promoting behaviors, it is important to consider the roles that health and wellness play in prevention. Prevention can be defined as behaviors, situations, or conditions that delay the onset of a negative health outcome. There are three levels of prevention: primary, secondary, and tertiary. When considering the levels of prevention, it is important to consider the context in which we think about negative health outcomes. Primary prevention is focused on delaying the onset of a physical or mental disease, illness or injury, or those behaviors in which we engage in to keep us "healthy." Secondary prevention is focused on early detection and those resources we utilize to identify and diagnose the presence of a disease, illness, or injury. Tertiary prevention is focused on treating or managing a diagnosed disease, illness, or injury. Health behaviors can and are used at each level of prevention; the focus is on the context of the prevention and whether we are engaging in specific behaviors to stay healthy or to identify or treat a negative health outcome. Exercise and physical activity is a behavior that can be considered at each level of prevention. When we are disease-free, we are active to remain in a state of disease-free. Exercise can also identify the presence of a disease, injury, or illness in the context of a graded exercise clinical test or when we are engaging in other activities and notice a pain in our body that prompts us to get checked out by a medical professional. Finally, exercise can be considered treatment for someone who has been diagnosed with a physical or mental disease as a mode to either get them back to a state of health or slow down the decline of their physical or mental functioning and delaying the onset of premature death due to the disease.

In addition to the general causes of death and actual causes of death, there are also specific risks associated with participating in leisure activities. Those include an increased risk of skin cancer due to participation in outdoor activities, accidents, and injuries (Healthy People 2020). As RSPA professionals, it will be critical that you include educational messages about these risks and foster cultures, environments, and policies that include prevention as normal and expected behaviors and even required for participation.

Think About It . . .

What role does recreation, sport, and park administration have in the prevention of disease, illness, and injuries?

There have been and are many safety requirements related to leisure activities. Orientations, waivers, equipment requirements, and trained staff are great examples of risk reduction. RSPA professionals continue to promote safety and risk reduction through educational, environmental, and policy strategies. I recently brought my children to a rock climbing gym. What do you think happened from the time we walked in the door to when they started climbing? We had to sign waivers. We were oriented to the equipment. My children were provided appropriate equipment (shoes and harnesses). We were told the rules of the facility, and one rule was not to wear the rock climbing shoes into the bathrooms. Why? Because shoes carry a lot of bacteria and that bacteria can be transferred to the holds which then get onto people's hands. And we know that hands touch eyes, noses, mouths, and so many other surfaces. So this simple policy of not wearing the rock climbing shoes into the bathroom is a great way to prevent the spread of disease.

Final Thoughts

So what does all of this health education and health promotion discussion have to do with recreation, sport, and parks administration? Great question! The National Recreation and Park Association (NRPA) highlights the importance of parks and recreation professionals in the overall health of our nation. The stance that the NRPA acknowledges and the role that parks and recreation opportunities have addresses health issues such as obesity and chronic disease that are often a result of a sedentary lifestyle, providing meal opportunities to address hunger as well as providing opportunities for social interactions and mechanisms in which people can feel more self-fulfilled. Furthermore, the NRPA has many supporting points that include components of environmental health and accessibility and availability of physical activity opportunities and activities as well as the presence and location of facilities like parks, gardens, and community centers. Finally, the NRPA includes health and wellness as one of the three pillars for parks and recreation professionals. Therefore, an understanding of health and wellness is vital in future professionals' abilities to do their job well and to understand how to fit into the grander approach of health promotion and to be able to co-exist with other health education and health promotion professionals.

One example of the coordination of parks and recreation professionals collaborating to improve the health of a community is through shared or joint use agreements in which city park officials partner with public schools to allow for school playgrounds to be utilized by the communities after school hours. These are facilities that typically are not in use after school hours but readily accessible by many urban neighborhoods. There are many local and state policies that address this issue and the benefit of this type of partnership in promoting overall health (Shared Use of School and Community Facilities). This is a great example of health promotion and incorporates the environmental, political, and organizational mechanisms that allow for physical activity to be more attainable.

THINK ABOUT IT . . .

How can you support the field of health education and promotion?

While you may not call yourself a health education/promotion specialist, what you do is within the realm of health education and health promotion. By understanding the role that you have in promoting health and quality of life, we can all work together to make our neighborhoods, schools, cities, states, and nation environments that are conducive to healthy living. Improving quality of life among individuals and communities requires a multilevel, collaborative effort. So let's join forces to work together!

REFERENCES

Eight Dimensions of Wellness. SAMHSA: Substance Abuse and Mental Health Services Administration. Retrieved from https://www.samhsa.gov/wellness-initiative/eight-dimensions-wellness.

Healthy People 2020 [Internet]. Washington, DC: U.S. Department of Health and Human Services, Office of Disease Prevention and Health Promotion. Retrieved from https://www.healthypeople.gov/2020/data/disparities/summary/chart/4759/2

Jebb, A. T., L. Tay, E. Diener, and S. Oishi. "Happiness, Income Satiation and Turning Points Around the World." *Nature Human Behaviour*, 2 (2018): 33–38.

McKenzie, J. F., B. L. Neiger, and R. Thackeray. *Planning, Implementing, & Evaluating Health Promotion Programs: A Primer*. 7th ed. New York, NY: Pearson, 2017.

National Recreation and Park Association. Role of Parks and Recreation on Health and Wellness. Retrieved from http://www.nrpa.org/our-work/Three-Pillars/role-of-parks-and-recreation-on-health-and-wellness/

Report of the 2011 Joint Committee on Health Education and Promotion Terminology. American Journal of Health Education, 43: (2): 1–19. doi:10.1080/19325037.2012.11008225

Rimer, B. K., K. Glanz, and National Cancer Institute (U.S.). *Theory at a Glance: A Guide for Health Promotion Practice*. Bethesda, MD: U.S. Dept. of Health and Human Services, National Institutes of Health, National Cancer Institute, 2005: 10–12.

Shared Use of School and Community Facilities: Addressing Childhood Obesity through Shared School Facilities. Retrieved from https://www.saferoutespartnership.org/state/bestpractices/shareduse

World Health Organization. Constitution of WHO: Principles. Retrieved from http://www.who.int/about/mission/en/

CHAPTER 10

Perspectives on Stress

Stress is what happens when nothing happens.

—MAYOR MARIE HUFF

Stress is the body's response to any demand placed upon it—real or imagined. It is a biological byproduct of millions of years of evolution in a world of uncertainty. In the rest of the animal kingdom and in our not too distant past (say up to as recent as a few thousand years ago) stress was usually the reaction to short-lived emergencies—threats that required immediate action. Consequently, the ability to survive was linked to the extent to which an individual was capable of a rapid response when faced with danger; success was measured in terms of a rapid escape or winning a fight. Thus, we often hear the body's response to stress referred to as the "flight or fight" response. In our discussion on stress, let us begin with a look at five case studies showing how one's response to stress is as automatic today as when wild prehistoric creatures lurked in the dark. These studies are little windows into the lives of people who, like all of us, find themselves coping with stress.

Case Study 1

Some days are colder than others, some are wetter, but this day was as cold and wet as I could remember. Not cold enough to freeze, but cold enough to pierce to the bone. A few degrees and the torrential rain would have turned into large soft flakes of snow, and instead of drowning the city in its flood, the heavens would have kissed the city with a cleansing blanket of white. I pushed myself closer to the damp building, pulled my trench coat a little tighter around my face and peered out into the neon darkness, wondering how it had come this far, and whether it could possibly reach completion. Success meant making contact, receiving the packet and getting back to the embassy. But where was Martin? He should have been here 7 minutes ago. Standing in the rain like this was no way to maintain a cover. I stood out like a penguin in Miami, and my autonomic nervous system knew it. I could either hear or feel my heart beating. Rapid and strong, it was pumping blood to my large muscles. Simultaneously the arterioles feeding my skin were constricting. Like an animal on the hunt or being hunted, I was primed to fight or flee. My eyes dilated to allow the maximum absorption of light, they even changed shape, flattening slightly to increase my distance vision. Where's Martin? He was 8 minutes late now! Two more minutes without contact and the mission would be aborted. With each passing second my sympathetic nervous system made further adjustments to cope with what seemed certain danger. My energy level rose as the pancreas stimulated glycogen which in turn lead to an increase in glucose and merged with the already increased levels of epinephrine. My stomach felt like a knot as sphincter contractions inhibited digestive secretions. I was freezing, but I could feel the sweat soaking my shirt. For a moment, I chuckled at the irony—I was sweating in a cold rain.

There was no one on the street that night, and with only one minute left, my natural instinct was to leave as quickly as possible. I felt like a race horse anxiously awaiting the starters call. But duty called, 30 seconds more to wait. It was then that I saw the car. It's lights were off, it was moving slowly down the quiet wet street. I knew it wasn't Martin. He would never come by car, and even if he had, he would have come directly to the pickup point; but Martin would never have come by car anyway. They were looking for something, for someone. There was no point in waiting. Martin wouldn't be coming tonight, or for that matter, any other night. And, if I didn't get out of there before I was sighted, this cold, wet night would be my last as well. The messages reaching my hypothalamus and surrounding limbic portions of the brain were intense and urgent. The adrenal cortex released another flood of epinephrine, my hair was standing erect now, my heart pumped faster and my bronchial muscle relaxed to allow the intake of a greater volume of oxygen. The car suddenly accelerated. I had been spotted, the starter's call was sounded and I bounded forward, feeling the great power unleashed by my fear. As I sprinted to the alley where my car was parked, a neon lighted snowflake drifted by my face and brushed my lips, and the whine of a bullet cried through the rain turned snow.

This case study is, of course, of a fictional experience. What is not fictional about the account is the physiological changes that occur when a person perceives him or herself at risk. When we find ourselves in threatening circumstances the body goes to work to increase the probability of survival. Adrenaline stimulates the body for flight, or for fight. Blood is directed into the large muscles, and glucose is made available for fuel. Interestingly enough, the body responds in this manner even if the threat is more of a perception than a reality. It responds even if the threat poses no direct threat to a person's physical well-being. You might experience this same response when you get an e-mail from your boss, and it only reads, "See me!"

The high country of Utah is a special place. The sky is still blue there, and the whispy stratocumulus clouds that live there are still white. The quaking aspens shimmer against those blue skies and the stately blue spruce stand at attention as though saluting Mother Nature's masterpiece. The streams that flow through those mountains are crystal clear and ice cold, and during the summer team with rainbow trout. High country meadows, luxuriantly green from daily afternoon showers, punctuated by a plethora of wildflowers, provide nourishment and shelter for a varied community of wildlife. It is a place where the stress of our smog covered cities and blighted suburbs is simply not allowed.

Fishing for those rainbow trout is a favorite summer recreational activity for a lot of people who have access to Utah high country. And, it is easy to understand why. There are few things more relaxing than casting your line into a crystal clear stream, on a sunny lazy day, in a high valley meadow. The sounds of the stream harmonize with the whisper of the aspens. Birds sing in the forest and the mixed sounds of cicada, crickets, and bees make for a concert that can never be adequately described, only felt. And, on such a day, in such a place the sympathetic nervous system takes some time off.

It was on such a day that Thelma and her family arrived at the little meadow known as Buttercup Flat. After a delicious picnic, the family spread out along Buttercup Stream for an afternoon of fishing. All was right with the world. The stress of city life was quickly forgotten. Thelma's pancreas was secreting pancreatic enzymes, her heart was beating slowly, her breath came in slow even inhalations, and she was keenly aware of the warmth of the sun on her skin.

Overall, Thelma was experiencing a parasympathetic mountain high—she was relaxed and happy. And, in her blissful state, she sought to catch the elusive rainbow trout, and failed to notice the approaching game warden.

The game warden was a kind man, a gentle man, and an intellectual man. He was also a former football player who stood 78 inches tall and weighed nearly 300 pounds. With his western boots on, and with his Smokey the Bear hat, he appeared to stand well over 7 feet. On this day he also wore his down filled ranger's jacket. Thelma didn't hear him coming, didn't know that he was there to check her fishing license, didn't know that her parasympathetic leisure was about to take a dramatic turn.

The ranger said, "Excuse me, Ma'am, may I see your fishing license." Thelma didn't hear him; all she heard was the lovely concert that Mother Nature was putting on. Gently the ranger tapped her on her shoulder. The ranger must have looked like a giant to Thelma that day, or perhaps a bear. The ranger who told me the story doesn't really know what went through Thelma's mind. He didn't stay to ask, for what happened next is a phenomenon that few of us ever will experience, and none of us want to. Most likely what happened was that Thelma's sympathetic nervous system was stimulated by the touch and sight of the ranger, a flood of epinephrine was released, her blood sugar was immediately elevated, her digestive secretions were shutoff, her heart rate increased and blood was shunted from other organs to the large muscles. All of this occurred unnoticed by the ranger, but he noticed one other sympathetic nervous system response: he noticed that Thelma's urinary bladder spontaneously emptied, altering the color of her powder blue slacks. The ranger suddenly at a loss for words heard himself say, "Have a nice day." With that he quickly returned to his truck.

This case study is a portrayal of an actual event. Again, it illustrates that when a person experiences a real or imaginary threat, the body responds. We don't have to think about the response, it happens automatically. It is an autonomic function associated with the sympathetic nervous system. That it is something we have little control over is clearly illustrated in the conclusion of the story. And, just as there are apparent changes in one's anatomy and physiology when experiencing stress, there are subtle changes occurring within the internal organs as well. For example, the endocrine system responds to stress quickly. The adrenal medulla releases adrenaline and the hypothalamus secretes corticotropin-releasing hormone. This causes the pituitary to secrete adrenocorticoptropic hormone (ACTH). This, in turn, takes us back to the adrenals where the ACTH stimulates the adrenal cortex to release glucocortcoids, principally cortisol, into the blood. Cortisol is very useful in helping the body activate the flight or fight response. But, if the stress runs unabated, this same hormone can have a devastating impact on one's health. More on this later.

CASE STUDY 3

Jeri felt as though she were going to explode. The children were driving her crazy. Jimmy wouldn't stop crying and Mary kept whining that she didn't want to go to school. The toast was burned again, and the school bus would be there any minute. Some routines don't ever improve with time and this was one of them. No matter how she tried to get Mary to the school bus stop on time, something would go wrong. This morning it was Jimmy. "Probably another earache," Jeri thought as she frantically tried to stuff peanut butter sandwiches into uncooperative plastic sandwich wrappers. The sitter wouldn't be there for another 15 minutes, and she couldn't really attend to Jimmy until Mary was on the bus, and she still had to ready herself for her own school.

Ever since her husband, Eric, had left them, her life had been a whirlwind of despair. Nothing ever seemed to come to completion. Her life was somewhat like Eric's child support checks—missing. She was doing the best she could, working afternoons and evenings, as a waitress, and in the mornings attending accounting courses at the university. Occasionally she would try to go on a date, but the men that were interested in her were rarely interested in her children or her problems. She felt torn in a dozen ways. Too many demands on her time, and resources, left her feeling unable to complete anything to her satisfaction. She felt she was a lousy mother, a poor student, and she hated her work.

Physiologically she was in a constant state of sympathetic arousal. Her autonomic nervous system remained in constant readiness for threatening situations. She was primed for flight or fight, but in reality there was no where to run and no one to fight. Her blood pressure slowly increased, unable to eat she lost weight and energy, she seemed to have constant health problems, as she put it, "If a person with a cold calls me on the phone, I'll catch it."

Through the kitchen window of her two bedroom apartment she could see the school bus approaching. Her head throbbing, she helped a reluctant Mary into her coat, and pushed her through the door. Down the stairs and across the lawn they half-walked, half-ran. As Jeri leaned over to kiss Mary good-bye, Mary quietly asked, "Mommy, where's my lunch box?"

In this case study, which although fictional, occurs daily in the lives of millions of people around the globe, the stress is unrelenting. It is a classical example of "chronic stress." Constant stress causes the body to continually prime itself for response. In normal situations, the energy required to respond to the stress is usually quickly expressed: the person runs from the danger or defeats. The human body is not designed for exposure to unrelenting stress. Part of the problem is associated with high levels of glucocorticoids. As you learned in the previous example, cortisol is essential to enabling the body to respond to stressful situations. Unfortunately, if the cortisol levels don't return to normal there are unhealthy consequences. It has long been known that prolonged exposure to high levels of glucocorticoids can result in hypertension. It can also lead to a suppressed immune system, which can be manifest in a wide array of illnesses.

Case Study 4

Trevor's autonomic nervous system switched to the sympathetic every time he thought about the coming weekend. But he liked the feeling. He conjured up a hundred different images. He visualized the drive to the coast, the winding mountain road leading to Stinson Beach, the first sight of the breakers and the little specks that were the surfers he would soon join. He even visualized the cold eyes and jagged smile of the Great White Sharks believed to breed in the waters off Stinson. It was the thought of the Great White that would push his level of arousal into the discomfort zone, otherwise, his body reacted favorably to the images of the perfect wave and the perfect ride.

What a place to live. Two hours to the beach and two hours to skiing. The best of both worlds within a radius of two hours. Thoughts of either sport would always "turn him on," for he thoroughly enjoyed both. Skiing was even more exciting than surfing. It was probably the speed factor that made the difference for him. On a good run, he could clock up to 60 miles an hour, do several jumps, many up to 30–40 feet, and scare the daylights out of more timid skiers.

Rarely did he feel bored when skiing. There was always a new approach to a run, a new trick to try, a different jump to take. In fact, to allow yourself to relax when skiing was dangerous. For your own good you had to stay optimally aroused. In skiing your fight is with the hill and if you win you get a good flight. It is much the same with surfing, although

while waiting for a wave, it's probably only thoughts of the Great White Shark that keep the sympathetic system functioning, and thus the body ready for the next great wave.

So perhaps, all stress isn't bad. In fact, there are times when we actively seek stress producing situations. This leads to an alternative way of speaking of stress. What we really want to avoid is "distress." The body is equipped to deal with a certain measure of stress. As long as we have the capacity to cope effectively with the stress, it doesn't necessarily have to be a bad thing. The rule here is: even if it produces high arousal, stress is not harmful as long as the body views the stress response as falling within what might be called the "optimal zone." When the response becomes uncomfortable, it is then that it becomes distress.

So, What Is Stress?

It is important to recognize that the danger need only be perceived in order for the body to produce a stress reaction. In the sketch about Trevor, by merely thinking about surfing and skiing, he would become excited. Of course, in Trevor's case, this was not harmful, nor was it so significant that it provoked a fight or flight response; it instead induced a rather pleasant feeling. And, this makes another important point regarding stress: In and of itself stress is not bad—it is when stress produces negative physiological and psychological outcomes that stress becomes undesirable, and thus should be reduced. It is when stress becomes distress that it becomes problematic. In the "Where's Martin" sketch, although intense, our hero's response to his stressful situation may have saved his life. This type of **short-term stress** is usually short-lived, but accounts for great bursts of energy. Most of us will experience this type of stress when frightened by a strange sound in the middle of the night, or when a police car pulls up behind us, or when engaged in "high risk" recreation.

The "Single Mom" sketch is an example of harmful stress. Jeri was clearly overburdened. Frustrated and angry she was easily annoyed, distracted, and sorrowful. In addition, unable to eat or rest effectively, her physical health was frequently compromised. Jeri was suffering from what is called **chronic stress**[1] and it is this stress that tends to do the greatest damage to a person. To understand why, we need to look at stress from a physiological point of view.

Hans Selye is a Canadian scientist who has devoted much of his professional career to the study of the body's reaction to stress.[2] He is known for a theoretical model referred to as the **general adaptation syndrome.** In this model stress is divided into three phases: (1) "The alarm reaction" phase, (2) the "resistance" phase, and (3) the "exhaustion" phase.

The Alarm Phase of Stress

When confronted by a perceived threat, the brain (principally the hypothalamus) immediately activates the body's defense system. The brain sends signals to the endocrine system which releases certain hormones into the bloodstream, which in turn regulate a great number of physiological functions. Activation of the endocrine system occurs along two pathways: (1) the sympathetic division of the autonomic nervous system, and (2) the activation of the so-called master gland of the endocrine system, the pituitary.

When the sympathetic nervous system is activated the central part of the adrenal medulla (the middle portion of the adrenal gland, a triangular shaped gland attached to the upper surface of each kidney) is stimulated to produce **dopamine, norepinepherine** and **epinephrine.** These hormones are transported throughout the body via the bloodstream increasing the body's ability to respond to emergency demands. Among the important changes stimulated by these hormones are: increased heart rate and pressure, increased blood flow, increased respiration rate and oxygen consumption, increased perspiration, inhibition of digestive juices, subtle but important changes in vision, and an increase in blood sugar.

In addition to the above, the hypothalamus activates the pituitary gland, which secretes **adrenocorticotropic hormone** (ACTH), which in turn stimulates the outer portion of the adrenal gland (the adrenal cortex) causing it to release into the bloodstream **corticosteriods.** These hormones permit many biochemical reactions to proceed at optimal rates, and therefore make an important contribution in emergency situations.

In the "Where's Martin" sketch the ominous sight of a car without lights, slowly approaching our hero, sounded an alarm. This alarm activated the

sympathetic nervous system as well as the pituitary gland. The sympathetic nervous system triggered the release of the catecholamines dopamine, epinephrine, and norepinepherine. These in turn elevated the body's available energy and our hero "felt like a race horse." In addition, the adrenal cortex was stimulated producing adrenal corticosteroids, which further helped bring his body to an optimal state of physical readiness. Thus stimulated, he was able to flee like the wind down rain soaked streets.

On a less dramatic level I recently experienced an alarm reaction while driving home from my work at the university. I was tired and anxious to get home. My foot was a little heavier than usual, and it was difficult to keep my high powered, foreign engineered, steel gray 1977 Toyota pickup at the speed limit. Suddenly, as if from out of nowhere, I saw the roof lamps of a California Highway Patrol unit. Panic. My heart leaped into action, perspiration filled my palms, and epinephrine stimulated my musculature. I slowed, taking a closer look at the patrol car which was now about to pass me. Inside were several young people, laughing and chatting. The car was filled with skiers headed for the Sierra, and the roof lamps were nothing more than skis. What did I say about real versus imagined threats. . . .

Resistance Phase

In cases of acute stress, once the immediate perceived danger has passed, the body returns to its normal state. We tend to relax and turn our attention to our daily tasks. But, there are some situations where the perceived threat to our well-being never completely abates. Take Jeri for example. Her lifestyle was filled with frustration. Too many demands on her time caused her to feel both helpless and hopeless. It was almost as if her very lifestyle was her enemy. Thus, for Jeri, stress was an ongoing experience. In situations such as this, the body attempts to adapt to the stress through continued autonomic and endocrine responses, but at slightly lower levels than in the initial phase. In addition, one's ability to perform cognitive tasks is usually taxed under stressful conditions. We don't know how Jeri was doing in school, but she obviously had difficulty remembering things such as Mary's lunch box. As the body struggles to resist the effects of stressful conditions, it slowly wears down, slowly deteriorates, ultimately leading to the final phase—exhaustion.

Exhaustion

If stress runs unabated for a long period of time, an individual may simply run out of his supply of certain important hormones. When this occurs, the sympathetic nervous system essentially shuts down, forcing the parasympathetic division of the autonomic nervous system to take over. Such a situation can be described as total exhaustion. During periods of long stress, prior to total collapse, the stress response may do serious harm to certain internal organs and contribute to the onset of disease. For example, chronic stress has been linked to coronary heart disease, hypertension, peptic ulcers, headaches, influenza, herpes, skin disorders, chronic back pain, rheumatoid arthritis, stroke, and even cancer.[3] In addition, people under stress may be more inclined toward alcohol, drug usage, and cigarette smoking—behaviors which can compound health liabilities produced by chronic stress.

Sources of Stress

You may be familiar with something called the Social Readjustment Rating Scale (SRRS). It is not uncommon for people interested in stress to use this instrument to estimate the amount of stress in their lives. It is frequently seen in articles and books dealing with stress. This scale was developed in the 1960s[4] and essentially consists of a list of life events (n=43) that are supposed to be correlated with stress. To use the scale you simply check off those events that have occurred to you within a recent time period, add up the values of the events checked and thereby derive a score that purportedly is an estimation of the stress in your life.

This approach to measuring stress has some serious deficiencies. First, it fails to take into account the difference in perception between people. Not everyone is going to view the 43 events on the SRRS in the same way. For example, an individual whose marriage has been a constant source of stress may find "marital separation" a blessing rather than stressful. Similarly, "fired at work" may not be stressful if it leads to a better situation, and a reduction of job related stress. Using average weights (which is what the SRRS does) fails to take into account the fact that people view "stressful situations" differently.

Another problem with the SRRS is that it presumes that the 43 events listed are an accurate reflection of the universe of stressful events. It is quite likely that this list is at best incomplete, and at worst, a misrepresentation of the types of stressful events that one is likely to experience. Similarly, the description of the stressful events listed are incomplete and subject to various interpretations, calling into question the reliability of this instrument.

In examining the extent to which you are personally afflicted by stress as well as identifying the sources of stress we think pencil and paper exercises may be useful, but need to be focused more toward the individual and less toward presumed relationships. Consequently, the "OH OH Scale" was developed to enable an individual to examine specific stressors in his or her personal life.

I am so accustomed to being stressed, that one day I woke feeling so relaxed that I knew something was wrong. This proved very stressful.

—Dawn Johnson

Ways of Dealing with Stress

We are not always effective in dealing with stress. Unfortunately many of our responses are negative. One method of rapidly expending stress generated energy is through **aggression.** Striking out at the perceived source of one's stress may temporarily reduce some stress, but it is quite likely that in the long run it will actually contribute to and compound the original stress. Misplaced aggression may also be a misguided attempt to reduce stress. I spoke to a clerk once who told me that she is often the victim of apparent misdirected aggression. Waiters and waitresses are another group who are often the recipients of stress related anger. Whether the aggression is physical or verbal (i.e., shame, ridicule, belittlement, etc.), the outcome is usually negative and thus leads to more stress.

Another common response to stress is **withdrawal.** This can take two forms: (1) physical, where you physically stay away from the perceived source of the stress, and (2) mental, where you attempt to escape from the source of the stress by daydreaming, sleeping, denial, or altering your state of mind through the use of alcohol and other drugs.

Clearly aggression and withdrawal are undesirable responses to stressful situations, both can detract from the overall quality of one's lifestyle and set the stage for further stress which in chronic conditions can lead to a total physical and emotional breakdown. Consequently, it is important that positive steps be taken when faced with stressful situations.

Coping with Acute Stress

In situations where stress is a unitary response to a single factor, the emphasis is on discharging the energy produced by the sympathetic nervous system interacting with the endocrine system. This is the kind of stress one might feel immediately before taking a test, going on a date, or playing a sport. Usually, once the source of stress is engaged the energy dissipates or is positively directed resulting in a decline in stress and an increase in positive responses. In some situations, it may be essential to redirect your attention, and pursue some activity which can yield a cathartic outcome. For example, when I experience acute stress I get excellent relief from an aerobic workout. The music, movement and endorphin secretions resulting from physical exertion usually leave me feeling relaxed and in good spirits.

Coping with Chronic Stress

Essential to successful coping with long term stress is the identification of the sources of stress that are compromising the quality of your life. The OH OH test is one way to do that. Obviously, there are other ways too. You can accomplish this through introspection, through counseling, and education. This step requires honest and objective self-analysis. Until you thoroughly understand why you experience stress, it will be difficult to develop a strategy to eliminate the sources of stress from your life. In terms of chronic stress, it is not enough to learn to live with it, rather it is essential that you eliminate it from your life.

Once you have a good idea as to the source of chronic stress in your life, it is essential that you determine whether or not it can be eliminated. There are certain situations and conditions which may be difficult or even impossible to change. If you determine that it is impossible to actually bring about a physical change in the situation, then you have only two options: (1) allow the situation to continue to affect you or (2) adapt to the situation by developing an attitude that allows you to view the situation as less serious or personal. Generally, we can identify things about a stress producing situation that we can change. For example in Jeri's case, she might benefit from working less or taking fewer

university classes. Perhaps a low interest loan might help relieve some of her stress. If these alternatives are unavailable then her only alternative is to adapt to her situation by altering her perception regarding the demands on her time, or alter her attitudes about the stress producing events in her life. If she is unsuccessful then the pressures in her life will continue unabated until her own biology forces her to withdraw physically through a physical collapse.

Bringing about changes in patterns that are producing chronic stress may take time, energy, and assistance. Sometimes, the changes that are required to reduce chronic stress require the assistance of a counselor, psychologist or physician. Sometimes, change can be facilitated through education. But rarely does it happen quickly. Usually it requires time and dedication. During the period of time during which life patterns are being changed, it is particularly important to practice coping skills. I like to call these Stress Skills.

Stress kills, unless you possess stress skills . . .

Stress Skills

Relaxation Skills

Progressive muscle relaxation and autogenic training are two popular forms of relaxation exercises. Progressive muscle relaxation involves systematically and sequentially relaxing each of the major muscle groups. This is accomplished by flexing each muscle group for a few seconds and then relaxing. This can be done under the direction of a facilitator or through self direction. A frequently used progression begins with the feet and concludes with the head and facial muscles. Progressive muscle relaxation is often accompanied by deep breathing. This allows you to increase the quantity of air and hence oxygen essential for cellular respiration. Typically one takes a deep cleansing breath through the nose and then slowly exhaling through the mouth. As you do this, try to focus on the movement of the air moving deep into the lungs and then dispersing throughout your body. Allow yourself at least 15 seconds per anatomical area. Try it.

Autogenic training is somewhat similar to self-hypnosis. It literally means self-generating or self moving. It is a process whereby you give yourself verbal cues. Cues are presented silently and direct your concentration to a feeling normally associated with relaxation. Such words as warm, gentle, relaxed, quiet, refreshed are good cues for autogenic exercises. Normally in an autogenic exercise you visualize relaxing scenes or pleasant memories. Many people combine the physical relaxation of progressive muscle relaxation with the visualization of autogenics. After about 15 minutes of relaxation you terminate the exercise with an energizer cue. This is a phrase that is associated with strength and energy. You might say, "Now you are about to awaken, and as you do you will feel happy, full of energy and very positive."

Everyone talks to himself, it's just that some of us have better conversations.

—Ernest Jones

Cognitive Restructuring

Self-talk is often at the heart of stressful responses. An event occurs, you have a little chat with yourself about it, and the nature of this conversation determines how you feel. It is your own thinking that produces most feelings, not the external event. Cognitive restructuring is a technique designed to assist you in changing the nature of the conversations that you have with yourself, in order that you become less inclined to talk yourself into a stressful response.[5]

Self-talk is largely based on what we believe about something. Unfortunately, not all of our beliefs are based on fact. Frequently, we view the world through the expectations of others, through religious belief systems (which call for perfection) and through inaccurate images of ourselves and significant others. These beliefs often fall into the irrational category and frequently contribute to our self-destructive conversations.

We learn a great deal through our conversations with others. Why then is it that we have such difficulty learning from the conversations we have with ourselves.

—Jones Williams

Assertiveness

One of the most common sources of stress is not being able to tell someone else what we are thinking or feeling.[6] Some people think that assertiveness is tantamount to being abrasive and egotistical. Not so. Aggressiveness and assertiveness are two entirely different things. One can be assertive without offending. One can be assertive without being angry.

A key word to remember in being assertive is "I." Take responsibility for your feelings, needs, and desires. State clearly, calmly, and objectively what it is that you desire or require. Be firm, be positive, keep your sentences short, maintain good posture, and eye contact. Avoid "you" statements. (You statements make a judgment about the other person, or demand a certain behavior from the other person.) For the most part they tend to put people on the defensive and often mask the true intent of your message. Tell it like it is, and see how less complicated your life can become.

Learn to Play

Stress and play are mutually exclusive terms. By learning how to play you can insure yourself little stress free islands to which you can periodically visit. Make recreation an important part of your life. Include time for jogging, music, art, hobbies, sports, etc. You can't be at stress when you are having fun. The word *recreation* can be thought of as meaning an activity which re-creates, which lifts up your spirits and fortifies you against life's daily stressors.

One Reason Why Play Helps Us Cope with Stress

Play has capacity to stimulate the production of very powerful substances which when diffused through the brain have the ability to lessen pain, increase arousal and produce a generally pleasant sensation. This class of chemicals is known as endorphins (literally inner morphine). Endorphins are sometimes subsumed under the name *euphorigens*.

When under stress, some people feel the need to seek relief through euphorigens. Unfortunately most artificial euphorigens are highly addictive and thus possess the potential of seriously compounding the problems that motivated the euphorigen user to get involved with drugs in the first place. A person addicted to a drug directs his or her life in service to the addiction. The acquisition and ingestion of the drug becomes an obsession affecting all aspects of the user's life. In addition, most drugs have serious side effects. For example, large quantities of alcohol can lead to severe brain damage, the injection of heroin is a leading cause of AIDS, cocaine and amphetamine use can lead to psychotic reactions and hallucinogenic drugs can seriously impair one's judgment. Although providing temporary relief from stress, artificial euphorigens possess too many liabilities to warrant their use. Perhaps the most significant problem associated with euphorigens is that they tend to mask the underlying problems, thus making it that much more difficult to eliminate the underlying source of stress.

Play, unlike "unnatural highs" has no serious side effects, does not impair judgment or produce psychotic reactions. The ability to think clearly is important when it comes to coping with sources of stress. Play stimulates us to effective thinking while simultaneously producing natural euphorigens which tend to produce feelings of well-being, pleasure, and self-confidence.

The only sure cure for anxiety or boredom is to play.
—Sara Louise Williams

Stay Physically Healthy

Your ability to cope with stressful situations is in part dependent upon your physical health. It is important that during times of stress that you eat a well balanced diet, allow for adequate sleep, and get sufficient exercise.

Have a Personal Support Group

During times of stress it is important that you have people to whom you can turn for comfort and support. Family, neighbors, church members, or organized support groups can be helpful during difficult times.

You can always tell a real friend; when you've made a fool of yourself he doesn't feel you have done a permanent job.
—J. Laurence Peter

Know When to Turn to Professional Help

In regard to seeking treatment, one of the biggest problems is the tendency of people to delay taking the first step. In cases of chronic stress, or severe occurrences of acute stress, professional counseling, or therapy may be the only logical approach to the problem. But for many people the social stigma associated with seeing a "shrink" makes seeking professional help a difficult course to take. If you feel that life is just too stressful, don't hesitate to call for help. When your car breaks down you call a mechanic, don't you?

Stress is a nasty thing, but the unfortunate thing about it is that when we feel like life is giving us a beating, a closer look will generally reveal that we are the ones holding the switch.
—Ed Clark

While You're Waiting for the Mechanic: Laugh

Of all the mechanisms available to help us cope with stress, humor stands near the top. One can look at the functions of the stress response as "flight or fight," but there is a third alternative, at least in this day's world. Quite often it is inappropriate to fight or flee when faced with stress, but it may not be inappropriate to laugh. A good hearty belly laugh can express excess energy almost as effectively as anything else. Laugh and the body calms down. Laugh and the adrenal cortex slows its production of glucocorticoids. Laugh and positive mood inducing chemicals are secreted. Laugh and the stress response shuts off. Humor as means of coping with stress is so important, the remainder of this chapter is devoted to this topic.

Humor has not always been a funny topic. At one time it had a very different and serious definition. During ancient times it was believed that the body was composed of four basic elements called **humors.** Hippocrates (460–370 B.C.) believed that an imbalance among these humors (blood, phlegm, black bile, and yellow bile) resulted in pain and disease, and that a cure could only be effected by bringing the humors back into balance. For centuries this idea was one of the fundamental foundations of medicine. Galen (130–200 A.D.), the personal physician of Marcus Aurelius, theorized that in addition to being related to physical health, these humors were also related to personality or temperament. Eventually, any personality trait came to be referred to as a humor. To this day you occasionally hear people refer to humor in this way. A person in a disagreeable mood may be described as being in a "black humor." By the 19th century and particularly following the discovery of cellular pathology, the idea that health and temperament were the function of bodily humors fell into disrepute. To understand today's meaning, you need to know that to the ancient Greeks the principal manifestation of an imbalance of an individual's humors was ludicrous behavior accompanied by laughter. Aristotle viewed laughter as a means of controlling inappropriate or excessive behavior. In fact, people who demonstrated silly or absurd behavior, or who laughed excessively came to be known as **humorists.** Once humor lost its credibility as a medical theory, all that remained was its connection to ludicrous behavior, and that is how it came to have its current meaning.

Modern Definitions of Humor

Defining and analyzing humor is a pastime of humorless people.

—Robert Benchley

The dictionary defines humor as a noun meaning "the capacity for perceiving the amusing or ludicrous" or "anything, as speech, writing, or action which stimulates laughter." Thus, in common parlance it has two distinct meanings: (1) a state of mind, and (2) an attribute capable of producing laughter. Paul McGhee, developmental psychologist and humor researcher, amplifies this idea. He states:

We may have difficulty defining humor, but we know it when we see it, and we know that we are more likely to see it in some moods than in others. Most dictionary definitions emphasize two distinct meanings of the more specific usage of the term. The basic one is the mental experience of discovering and appreciating ludicrous or absurdly incongruous events or situations. Humor is also defined as those attributes of an event that make us laugh; namely attributes that lead us to perceive the event as ludicrous or humorous. The problem is that this is a very circular definition. We must conclude then that humor is something that exists only in our minds and not in the real world.[7]

McGhee's point is that ultimately in order for something to be considered as possessing humor, it must first be perceived as humorous. Ultimately the decision as to whether something is funny rests with the perceiver. Therefore, argues McGhee, humor is ultimately a function of perception. he argues that it is not an emotion, an event, a situation, or a behavior. Rather, humor is described as a state of mind which follows exposure to something viewed as humorous. This condition is characterized by certain behavioral manifestations such as smiling and laughter; certain biological manifestations such as increased arousal, and certain psychological manifestations such as feelings of well-being. Thus, to McGhee, it is not the cartoon that is humor, but the state of mind invoked

by the stimulus of the cartoon interacting with the perceptual set of the receiver. Humor is not the situation or event, but the perceiver's cognitive and emotional response to it; not the behavior but the perceiver's reaction to it.

From a philosophical point of view, McGhee's idea that humor is a state of mind is logical and laudable; however, from a practical standpoint, it may be too limiting. In practical everyday usage, it is not uncommon for people to use the word humor in reference to the object of perception as opposed to a cognitive/emotional product. For example, you may have heard people say, "I don't understand *that type of humor*," or "I don't see the *humor in that.*" Implicit in these examples is the idea that people view humor as an attribute, something to be perceived and evaluated. In day-to-day conversation, this may be a more popular usage than the state of mind definition.

These two notions do not have to be viewed as mutually exclusive. Indeed, just the opposite is true. You cannot have one without the other. Something is only potentially humorous until it is perceived by someone who has the capacity to understand and appreciate the humorous attributes of the perceived object or phenomenon. For example, when a person is in a bad mood, it may be impossible for him or her to perceive the humor in something, even though that something is rife with potential humor. Try to make a depressed person laugh and the response might be something similar to this, "That's not funny; I'm not in the mood!" Later on, following a change in mood, the same stimulus might be perceived as very humorous. The object of perception has not changed, but the perception of it has. The person, no longer influenced by a negative mood, is able to perceive the humorous elements and experience the pleasant sensation of humor.

It is this capacity to selectively perceive humorous elements that we refer to as a **sense of humor,** and it is the sense of humor that brings together the two definitions of humor. The extent to which one possesses a sense of humor is the extent to which he or she is capable of perceiving the humorous elements in some object or phenomenon. The extent to which this is possible is also the extent to which one is capable of experiencing the "mental experience of discovering and appreciating ludicrous or absurdly incongruous ideas, events or situations."[8] Thus, it can be said that humor is both object and outcome, bound together by one's perceptual abilities. In the next section we will focus on humor as an object or phenomenon of one's perception—something holding the potential to produce laughter in a perceiver.

Laughter is the sensation of feeling good all over and showing it principally in one place.

—Josh Billings

If you are not allowed to laugh in heaven, then I don't want to go there.

—Martin Luther

Theories of Humor

Lefcourt and Martin contend that all humor theories can be categorized into three main types: arousal theories, incongruity theories and superiority theories (4). In addition to these, McGhee and Goldstein would have us add linguistic and brain psychophysiological theories.[9]

Arousal Theories

Central to the theories under this heading is the notion that humor is a function of an individual's need to release tension or excess energy. This notion may have grown out of early theorists' attempt to explain the physical manifestation of humor—laughter. An example of this theory can be found in Berylne (1969) where it is argued that laughter plays an important role in maintaining optimal arousal because it not only provides an important means of reducing arousal, but also is instrumental in arousal seeking.[10]

Incongruity Theories

Whereas arousal theories try to explain humor in terms of biological arousal, incongruity theories explain humor as a cognitive process which occurs when two or more unequal or incomparable ideas, concepts, or situations are brought together in an unexpected manner. As Paul McGhee states, ". . . the perception of an incongruous relationship (absurd, unexpected, inappropriate, and otherwise out of context) forms the basic foundation for all humor. . . ."[11] The notion is not particularly new. As early as 1560, in his "Treatise on Laughter," Laurent Jobert explained laughter in the following manner:

Now in all laughable matters there must be something new and unexpected, beyond what is hoped for very intensely. For the mind, suspended and in doubt,

reflects imaginatively on what will be coming, and in facetious things, the end is usually quite the opposite of what is expected, which causes us to laugh.[12]

The concept of incongruity can be illustrated by the following observation by Virginia Ostman:

If lawyers are disbarred and clergymen defrocked, doesn't it follow that electricians can be delighted; musicians denoted; cowboys deranged; tree surgeons debarked and dry cleaners depressed?[13]

In Paris they simply stared when I spoke to them in French: I never did succeed in making those idiots understand their own language.

—Mark Twain

Superiority Theories

Superiority theories argue that humor results when one perceives another as inferior. Humor that attacks others is referred to as **tendentious** humor. Through disparaging another, it is argued that one enhances his or her feelings of self-worth.

Linguistic Theory

In the study of humor linguists have been concerned with one specific type of humor—humor resulting from manipulating words, i.e., arranging words in such a manner as to create a humorous effect. Studies of this sort focus on the mechanical and structural aspects of humor, and "describe how phonological, morphological, and syntactic categories can be manipulated to produce ambiguities . . ."[14] Following is an example of linguistic humor:

Q. Why isn't a person's nose 12 inches long?

A. Because then it would be a foot.

How Humor Helps Mediate the Effects of Stress

Physical Benefits of Humor

We have all heard it said that "laughter is the best medicine." This is certainly not a new idea. It is a subject that has occupied writers and thinkers throughout recorded history. For example, the *Book of Proverbs* in the **Old Testament** addressed the topic thusly, "A merry heart doeth good like a medicine" (17:22). Plato and Aristotle addressed the subject. Galen, physician to gladiators and prominent philosopher, pondered the relationship of laughter to health. Joubert, a Renaissance philosopher, wrote extensively on the subject. Within recent years it has been the subject of formal scientific inquiry.[15]

The current interest in the healing power of humor can be traced back to Norman Cousins' book, *Anatomy of an Illness*.[16] In it he recounts his amazing story of his recovery from **ankylosing spondylitis.** His doctors only gave him one chance in 500 to recover. Rather than giving in to the prognosis, he undertook a radical form of self-treatment. He immersed himself in humorous films and books. He put to test the old axiom about laughter being the best medicine, and soon he was experiencing some pretty amazing results.

> *I made the joyous discovery that 10 minutes of genuine belly laughter had an anesthetic effect that gave me at least two hours of painfree sleep. . . . When the painkilling effect of the laughter wore off, we would switch on the motion picture projector again, and not infrequently it would lead to another painfree sleep interval.*
>
> (Cousins 39)

Dr. Laurence J. Peter believes that humor contributes to pain control in four ways: (1) it can cause a person to focus his attention away from the sources of pain; (2) laughter reduces muscle tension around the affected part of the body, thus decreasing pain; (3) it can contribute to a positive attitude which is associated with pain tolerance; and (4) humor may stimulate the brain to produce catecholamine, which in turn stimulates the production of endorphins—the body's natural pain killers.[17]

There is some evidence that not only does humor contribute to the healing process, but that it also is important to health maintenance. Several medical authorities that believe humor stimulates the immune system, thus helping an individual stave off the ravages of common viral infections. Furthermore, he cites physicians that view humor as having a positive effect on blood pressure and heart rate. This phenomenon is similar to the bodily changes that take place during aerobic exercise.

Illness and pain subject the body, mind, and spirit to a great deal of stress. Humor can help mediate the physical effects of stress and promote a healthier body and mind.

PSYCHOLOGICAL BENEFITS OF HUMOR

> *A person without a sense of humor is like a wagon without springs—jolted by every pebble in the road.*
> —Henry Ward Beecher

Although many claims are made regarding the psychological value of humor, a careful review of the literature reveals that most empirical studies have focused on two categories: (1) anxiety or stress reduction, and (2) overcoming depression.

There is considerable evidence to support the value of humor in controlling distress and anxiety. Following an extensive study on the relationship of humor in regards to stress and anxiety, Lefcourt and Martin report the following:

> *We have found that humor, measured in various ways serves to moderate stressful experiences, whether they are stressors peculiar to the plight of the physically handicapped or to university students encountering hardships during their studies. Similarly, we have found evidence that marriage partners with a good sense of humor seem to be more active and constructive in the resolution of potential conflicts. Further we found that crippled victims of accidents and birth defects, who revealed a greater sense of humor in our investigations, were characterized by greater activity and engagement in life pursuits than were those with lesser sense of humor.[18]*

Depressive disorder, or as it is more commonly called **depression,** is a relatively common problem. It is estimated that each year about 15 million Americans suffer depression, and this does not include the minor lows that most of us experience from time to time.[19] Depression can be viewed as a form of psychological distress marked by feelings of sadness, dejection and despair. *Taber's Cyclopedic Medical Dictionary* describes depression in these terms:

> *Mental depression is characterized by altered mood. There is loss of interest in all usually pleasurable outlets such as food, sex, work, friends, hobbies, or entertainment. Diagnostic criteria include presence of at least four of the following:*
>
> 1. *poor appetite or significant weight loss; or increased weight gain*
> 2. *insomnia or hypersomnia*
> 3. *psycholmotor agitation or retardation*
> 4. *loss of interest or pleasure in usual activities or decreased sex drive*
> 5. *loss of energy*

6. *feelings of worthlessness, self-reproach, or excessive or inappropriate guilt*

7. *complaints of or evidence of diminished ability to think or concentrate*

8. *recurrent thoughts of death, suicidal ideas*[20]

Serious depression is a disorder of such significant proportions as to justify professional treatment. Severe and persistent depression may have a physiological basis. Peter states:

Research with antidepressant medicines has shown how body chemistry affects the ability of the brain and nervous system to respond. If the body is low in chemical neurotransmitters, the whole system becomes sluggish, resulting in depression. . . . It is important therefore that the person suffering from a long-term severe depression be diagnosed and receive medical or psychiatric treatment.[21]

In the treatment of serious depression some therapists have had success with various applications of play and humor therapy; however, it is important to point out that humor is not universally used or advised in the treatment of the emotionally disturbed. McGhee cautions that in some cases humor therapy may be inappropriate and potentially dangerous to the patient who is unable to accurately interpret the object of the humor.[22] Naturally there is much that could be said regarding the therapeutic application of humor; however such a discussion goes beyond the purview of this text. On the other hand, the application of humor in helping cope with the normal dips in mood that most of us experience requires no special training and can easily be applied on a self-help basis. In reference to this, Dr. Peter suggests that we use humor to do the following:

1. Use humor to reduce tensions and to create a relaxed atmosphere.

2. Use humor as an outlet for unacceptable feelings, behaviors, or impulses.

3. Use humor to improve your frame of mind.

4. Use humor to facilitate conversation regarding sensitive matters.

5. Look for humor in seemingly serious situations.

6. Laugh at least 20 times a day.[23]

Even if you are unhappy, laughing 20 times a day will certainly give others the impression that you are doing just fine. Indeed, one of the surest ways for an outside observer to judge the mood of an individual is to look at his or her face. One's facial anatomy is closely connected to one's emotions. It is difficult to smile when you are unhappy, and even should you succeed odds are that it will be viewed as a sad smile. On the other hand, an individual who is happy is given to pleasant expressions; often punctuated by broad smiles and laughter. As Joubert said:

The face of man is most excellent in that it is not covered with hair, scales of feathers . . . and for this reason the face of man is appropriate for all its changes, like a chameleon to make manifest and put into evidence the passions and internal movements, a condition truly human and praiseworthy.[24]

The connection between one's internal state and facial expressions raises a provocative question. Does it work both ways? Can one influence his or her internal state by intentionally assuming the posture and expression of humor. Perhaps that is asking too much; future research will have to make that determination. What does seem probable, however, is the idea that exposure to appropriate amounts of humor can contribute to one's feeling of well-being, help minimize stress, and counter depression.

Leisure and Humor

The most fundamental, most important function of humor is its power to release us from the many inhibitions and restrictions under which we live our daily lives.

—Harvey Mindnes

All of us live within social environments consisting of social mores and values which combine into powerful social expectations possessing the potential for minimizing one's sense of individuality and freedom. When one's sense of freedom is diminished by social influences, one's capacity to experience leisure is greatly compromised. It is in situations where one feels least free, that humor demonstrates its strongest connection to leisure. In humor one is able to momentarily free himself or herself from the social (and even the physical) bonds that stifle perceived freedom and its concomitant emotion, intrinsic satisfaction. Indeed, during such times, humor may be the only representation of leisure to which one can aspire, or into which one can escape.

Leisure-oriented individuals are people possessing a high degree of internal locus of control and intrinsic motivation. They tend to possess both a sense of appreciation of and capacity for finding humor in diverse situations. Indeed, research has demonstrated a significant relationship between humor and healthy psychological adjustment.[25] Those individuals whose lives are largely directed by external factors often show little response to humor. These people, lacking in internal control, are as McGhee puts it, ". . . chained to the social expectations for reasonable behavior and thinking."[26] People whose lifestyles are marked by little freedom, and thus little leisure, tend to have limited capacities for humor. McGhee believes that such people could develop a greater feeling of freedom through learning to appreciate and demonstrate humor. The extent to which humor contributes to such feelings is the extent to which humor is connected to leisure. Although there is little research examining this connection, it is quite likely that subsequent research will eventually demonstrate that when one is at humor, one is also at leisure.

When Humor Causes Stress!

Unfortunately, humor is not always a manifestation of a well-adjusted individual. Even though, for most of us, play and laughter are associated with healthy personalities, there are times (and people) for whom laughter marks maladjustment. The laugh of a disturbed patient in a mental hospital is easy to discern from the laugh of a healthy person. The distorted smile of an emotionally disturbed individual is often a caricature of the pleasant smile of a normal person. Not only do we see a difference in the physical manifestations of humor among certain patients, but we also see such patients often laughing at inappropriate times or at inappropriate circumstances, situations, or events.

There is yet another side to humor that must be discussed, and that is the use of disparaging or tendentious humor. This is humor that comes at the expense of another. We have all heard the cruel laughter of people who find humor in the misfortune of others. Disparaging humor may take the form of sarcastic comments or jokes which focus on another's misfortune or immutable characteristics. People who make such jokes often do so from a personality foundation affected by instability, low self-esteem, and weak interpersonal skills. There is some evidence to suggest that the type of humor an individual uses or is sensitive to may be related to areas in which he or she is having emotional difficulty.[27]

A person reveals his character by nothing so clearly as the joke he reveals.

—G. C. Lichtenberg

Defuse Stress by Developing Humor Skill

Most of us could benefit from learning to take life a little more leisurely, and as pointed out above, that might mean taking life a little more humorously. Some of the benefits that one can expect from an expanded sense of humor are summarized by Dr. Peter:

A sense of humor gives you the ability to (1) relax so that your objectivity can help you see the inconsistencies in your own behavior and the incongruities in the human condition, (2) resolve problems, (3) laugh at illness and trouble, (4) create your own mirth, and (5) communicate effectively.[28]

These are all very attractive outcomes, but if one wants to increase his or her sense of humor, where does one start? Following are two steps that I think are important, if you want to expand your appreciation and capacity for humor.

1. **Develop a playful attitude.** An attitude is fundamentally a construct that refers to the extent to which you feel positive toward something; the extent to which you like something. To alter an attitude toward greater appreciation of play may not be an easy task, particularly in cases where there are underlying unresolved psychological issues that confound one's interest in learning to be more playful. In such cases, self-help may be an unrealistic solution; rather, professional counseling may be in order. For the majority of us however, a shift in attitude is not an unreasonable goal.

   It is theorized that an attitude can be changed by altering the basic beliefs about an object or by changing one's evaluation of the attributes or characteristics of the object of the attitude. What this implies is that if you want to change your attitude about playfulness, or humor or anything else, you need to alter the appropriate values. Inasmuch as most adult values are rooted in childhood socialization, a concerted effort may be required to not only learn about the object of the attitude but to also unlearn the concepts of early childhood.

To accomplish this, two strategies are suggested: (1) become thoroughly familiar with the literature regarding the value of play and humor; and (2) practice using humor in your daily life. By familiarizing yourself with the literature regarding the values of leisure, you begin to establish a cognitive basis for modifying your attitudes regarding humor. By actively trying to look at life a little less seriously, and by trying to find humor in events that are neither inherently funny nor serious, you can begin to experience some of the intrinsic value of the humor experience. This will reinforce the cognitive shift that is promoted by the information you are acquiring through your study. Practice makes perfect and changes attitudes.

Practice what? Dr. J. Laurence Peter has some suggestions worth noting:

1. Adopt an attitude of playfulness. This does not mean that you will do outrageous things, but that your mind is open to uncensored, iconoclastic, silly, or outrageous thoughts.

2. Think funny. See the funny side or flip side of every situation. Select and refine your outrageous thoughts that best expose our conceits, pomposities, and incongruities.

3. Laugh at the incongruities in situations involving yourself and others.

4. Laugh only with others for what they do rather than for what they are.

5. Laugh at yourself . . . with acceptance of self.

6. Take yourself lightly. Take your responsibility to yourself and others seriously.

7. Make others laugh.

8. Realize that a sense of humor is deeper than laughter and more satisfactory than comedy . . . a sense of humor sees the fun in everyday experience. It is more important to have fun than to be funny.

2. **Acquire some humor skills.** In addition to Dr. Peter's list, I have a few suggestions for you:

   i. **Read the comics.** The humorous perspective can't be better illustrated than in the daily comics. Succinct and to the point, they present the world from a humorous perspective.

   ii. **Collect humorous material.** There is a wealth of jokes, songs, poems, stories, novels, illustrations, and videos that are of a humorous nature. By using your free time to enjoy the creative efforts of others, your own creative juices will be stimulated.

   iii. **Try your hand at creating humor.** Try cartooning for example. You don't have to be an artist to be a cartoonist (James Thurber proved that). Try poetry, short stories, or even wacky inventions. Let your mind play with some ideas, and then try your hand at creating something humorous from them.

   iv. **Create a "humor stimuli" kit.** This is something I have been doing for years. When I find a toy or other humorous object that I like, I buy it and put it in a utility kit. Just opening the kit makes me smile. Lately I have been collecting magic tricks to include in it.

   v. **Having a sense of humor doesn't mean you have to be an entertainer.** It means that you have a sensitivity to humor; that you can recognize humor in the incongruities of life, and that you don't take things too seriously. But, I do believe that it is a good idea to have a few good stories, jokes, gimmicks, or gags that you can use now and then. It's not always enough to be someone else's appreciative audience. When you find something worth sharing—practice it a few times so that you will deliver it with good timing and you won't forget the punch line.

   vi. **Take every appropriate opportunity to be creative, playful and fun.** Sometimes that can take the form of a playful note to someone you care about; dressing in a creative and playful way; interjecting humor at a meeting; sharing a smile with a stranger.

Humor has an enormous half-life; once you start the process it goes on forever.
—Mildred Williams Olson

NOTES

1. Adams, J. D. *Understanding and Managing Stress.* (San Diego: University Association, Inc. 1980): 80.

2. Selye, Hans. *The Stress of Life.* (New York: McGraw-Hill, 1984).

3. For more on cancer and stress, the reader is referred to Cooper, C. L. "The social psychological precursors to cancer." *Journal of Human Stress* 10.1 (1984): 4–10.

4. The interested reader is referred to Holmes, T. H., and R. H. Rahe, "The Social Readjustment Rating Scale." *Journal of Psychosomatic Research,* 11 (1967): 213–218.

5. Steinmetz, Jenny, Jon Blankenship, Linda Brown, Deborah Hall, and Grace Miller. *Managing Stress Before It Manages You.* (Palo Alto, California: Bull Publishing Co., 1980): 37–55.

6. Steinmetz et al. 75.

7. McGhee, P. E. "The Role of Arousal and Hemispheric Lateralization in Humor." In P. E. McGhee and J. H. Goldstein (eds) *Handbook of Humor Research: Basic Issues.* (Vol. 1, New York: Springer Verlag, 1983): 4.

8. McGhee, 6.

9. McGhee, 29.

10. Berlyne, D. E. "Laugher, Humor, and Play." In G. Lindzey and E. Aronson (Eds). *Handbook of Social Psychology.* (Second Edition, Vol. 3, pp. 795–852. Reading, Mass: Addison and Wesley, 1969).

11. McGhee, 42.

12. McGhee, 26.

13. Peter, 496.

14. McGhee, 60.

15. The reader is encouraged to visit the *Handbook of Humor Research.*

16. Cousins, Norman. *Anatomy of an Illness as Perceived by the Patient: Reflections in Healing and Regeneration.* (NY: Bantam, 1981): 39.

17. Peter, J. Laurence, 6–9.

18. Lefcourt, H. and R. Martin. *Humor and Life Stress: Antidote to Adversity.* (NY: Springer-Verlag, 1986): 124.

19. Peter, p. 70.

20. Thomas, Clayton, Ed. *Tabers Cylopedic Medical Dictionary.* (Philadelphia: F. A. Davis, Co. 1990): 441.

21. Peter, 75.

22. McGhee, 204.

23. Peter, 76–77.

24. McGhee, 6.

25. McGhee, 236.

26. McGhee, 234.

27. McGhee, 238–239.

28. Peter, 186.

REFERENCES

Adams, J. D. *Understanding and Managing Stress.* San Diego: University Association Inc., 1980.

Apter, M. J. *The Experience of Motivation: The Theory of Psychological Motivations.* NY: Academic Press, 1982.

Barlyne, D. E. "Laughter, Humor and Play." In G. Lindzey and E. Aronson (Eds.) *Handbook of Social Psychology.* Second Edition, Vol. 3, pp. 795–852. Reading, Mass: Addison and Wesley, 1969.

Chapman, and H. C. Foot (Eds.) *It's A Funny Thing, Humor.* 1977. London: Pergamon Press.

Cooper, C. L. "The Social Psychological Precursors to Cancer." *Journal of Human Stress.* 10 (1): 4–1, 1984.

Cousins, Norman. *Anatomy of an Illness as Perceived by the Patient: Reflections on Healing and Regeneration.* Grand Rapids, MI: Zondervan Books, 1975.

Engstrom, T. W., and R. A. Mackenzie. *Managing Your Time.* Grand Rapids, MI: Zondervan Books, 1975.

Freud, S. *Jokes and Their Relation to the Unconscious.* Leipzig: Deutiche, 1905.

"Humor." *International Journal of Psychoanalysis.* 1928, 9: 1–6.

Hobbes, T. *Leviathan.* 1968 (originally published 1650). Hammondsworth: Penguin.

Holmes, T. H., and R. H. Rahe. "The Social Readjustment Rating Scale." *Journal of Psychometric Research.* 11: 213–218.

Koestler, A. *The Act of Creation.* London: Hutchinson, 1964.

LaFave, L., J. Haddad, and N. Marshal. "Superiority, Enhanced Self-Esteem, and Perceived Incongruity Humor Theory." In A. J. Chapman and H. C. Foot (Eds.) *Humor and Laughter—Theory, Research and Applications.* London: Wiley, 1976.

Lefcourt, H., and R. Martin. *Humor and Life Stress: Antidote to Adversity.* NY: Springer-Verlag, Inc. 1983.

Leventhal, H., and M. A. Safer. "Individual Differences, Personality and Humor Appreciation."

McDowell, C. Forest. *Leisure Wellness: Coping Strategies and Managing Stress.* Eugene, Oregon: Sun Moon Press, 1983.

McGhee, P. E. "The Role of Arousal and Hemispheric Lateralization in Humor." In P. E. McGhee and J. H. Goldstein (Eds.). *Handbook of Humor Research: Basic Issues.* Vol. 1, New York: Springer Verlag, 1983.

Pelletier, Kenneth R. *Mind as Healer, Mind as Slayer.* New York: Dell Publishing Co., 1977.

Pepicello, W. J., and P. W. Weisberg. "Linguistics and Humor." In P. E. McGhee and J. H. Goldstein (Eds.). *Handbook of Humor Research: Basic Issues.* Vol. 1, New York: Springer Verlag, Inc. 1983.

Robinson, Jerry W., Ropy Clifford, and Joke DeWalle. *Stress in Community Groups*. University of Illinois, Urbana, 1975.

Selye, Hans. *The Stress of Life*. New York: McGraw-Hill, 1984.

Spencer, H. "The Physiology of Laughter." *MacMillan's Magazine*. 860, 1: 395–402.

Steinmetz, Jenny, Jon Blankenship, Linda Brown, Deborah Hall, and Grace Miller. *Managing Stress Before It Manages You*. Palo Alto, California: Bull Publishing Co., 1980.

Suls, J. M. "Cognitive Processes in Humor Appreciation." In P. E. McGhee and J. H. Holdstein (Eds.). *Handbook of Humor Research*. Vol. 1: 39–58. New York: Springer Verlag.

Weiten, W. *Psychology Applied to Modern Life*. Monterey, California: Brooks/Cole Publishing Co., 1986.

Wolff, H. A., C. E. Smith, and H. A. Murray. "The Psychology of Humor: A Study of Responses to Race-Disparagement of Jokes." *Journal of Abnormal and Social Psychology*. 28, 1934: 341–365.

Zillman, D. "Disparagement Humor." In P. E. McGhee & J. H. Goldstein (Eds.). *Handbook of Humor Research*. (Vol. 1: 85–108). New York: Springer Verlag.

Zillman, D., and J. R. Canlor. "Affective Responses to the Emotions of a Protagonist." *Journal of Experimental and Social Psychology*. 13, 1977: 155–165.

CHAPTER 11

PERSPECTIVES ON AGING AND LEISURE

Sal Arrigo, Jr.

As we begin to let go of the responsibilities and demands of our middle age, opportunities arise to begin to tend to those qualities we possessed as children—curiosity, playfulness, and joy. In childhood these were just part of who we were; they can be part of who we are again. Later adulthood is when we can re-create ourselves to bloom from within. Planning for our aging is so much more than money—we need to plan to bloom into what we always could have been.

—BARBARA GILLOGLY, CHAIR, AMERICAN RIVER COLLEGE GERONTOLOGY DEPT.

A Look at Aging in America

Gerontology *is defined as the study of the field and process of aging.*

Just take a look around and ask yourself how many gray-haired people you see. Do you think you can begin to count the number of individuals who fit in this age category? More specifically, let's take a look at aging in America. In the *65+ in the United States: 2005* report from the U.S. Census Bureau, there are approximately 36 million people that fall into this demographic age segment. This represents 12 percent of our entire population![1]

If you want to delve even further into aging in America, consider some of these numbers. According to the New England Centenarian Study in July 2007, centenarians, (those individuals 100 years of age or more), are the fastest growing group of our population. The second fastest is the age group 85 and over. There are about 40,000 centenarians in the United States, with women representing around 85% and men 15%.[2] As you digest these numbers, consider the fact that the Baby Boom generation (people born between 1946 and 1964) begin to turn age 65 in 2011. When we reach the year 2030, the older population is expected to double from 35 million (in 2000) to 72 million as projected by the U.S. Census Bureau.

Senior citizens do represent a major segment of our world. You can take the aging situation global and discover, according to the U.S. Administration on Aging, that the world population 60 and over is estimated to be 605 million. This number is expected to grow to almost 2 billion by 2050.[3]

As we consider what senior citizens do on a daily basis, one cannot overlook the fact that due in part to improved health care technology and medicines, these seniors are active. This age group will touch every part of our lives for many years; they will have a major impact on business, economy, lifestyle, and more. We need to develop our attitudes and embrace our senior citizens—they deserve it.

They are active participants in many recreational programs. They enjoy their leisure time traveling, exercising, volunteering, and getting involved in activities they may have enjoyed as young people. However, responsibilities of marriage, going to war, and having a career forced them to temporarily postpone these leisure pursuits. To **take Dr. Gillogly's advice,** "We need to plan to bloom." Leisure and gerontology professionals find activities such as genealogy (searching for family history), arts and crafts, tap, and country line dancing to be popular among seniors. As one may participate in these activities without a partner, many seniors who have lost a spouse are involved in them. Seniors pursue a wide variety of activities, among them hobbies such as coin and stamp collecting.

Senior citizens are like living history books. They have plenty of wisdom that has been gained over the course of their years. I advise students to seek out this wisdom and use it to their advantage. When we get advice from an older person we may not always follow it. However, often this advice proves to have been correct. We may find ourselves asking the question, "How did he/she know that?" *Life experience* is the simple answer. One of the exercises that I like to have my students "experience" is to discover the choices that senior citizens make when it comes to their leisure.

DESIGN YOUR SENIOR ACTIVITY CALENDAR

1. Imagine yourself at age 65; what leisure programs do you want to experience? Draw up a calendar for one week (Sunday through Saturday) and schedule your activities from 6 AM until 8 PM each day of the week.

2. What did you come up with? Was it easy to design or did you struggle with your choices? Did you "give up" on a leisure activity that you currently participate in thinking you're too old at age 65 to continue?

3. Go back and re-examine your choices. Are there changes you would like to make?

You will discover that activities chosen by senior citizens relate directly to their life and leisure satisfaction. Ragheb and Griffith (1980) suggest leisure professionals must design, plan, and offer services that contribute not only to participants' leisure satisfaction, but also to life satisfaction, to the psychological well-being, and thus to the happiness of older persons.[4] Hoyer and Roodin[5] (2003) presented a report by Guinn[6] (1999) indicating that it really doesn't matter what leisure activity retired persons are involved in as long as they feel they are challenged and demonstrate some competence in the activity.

Understanding and appreciating the aging process is critical to an individual's ability to relate to older people. It is also essential if one is to approach one's personal experience with aging in an effective and productive manner. Fortunately, gerontologists, and other social scientists, have carefully examined aging from a scientific view. The studies done by social scientists on the aging process and experience have yield several important theories. In the section that follows, several of these theories are presented.

AGING: THE THEORETICAL PERSPECTIVE

Aging is the simplest consequence of life. With our first breath, we mark the beginning of a long path. We celebrate that first breath every year at the same time. Each year we are defined by a new number. Each year we acknowledge that we have aged.

Yet, when we speak of *aging,* we know that we are talking about something else, we are talking about the downturn in the aging process that heralds the approach of the older years. We are talking about the time in life when it is clear that the corner has been turned and the body is no longer growing and developing. In practice, we divide life into two very broad categories: the growth years and the aging years. And, in regard to the latter, several theories have been developed to explain the experiences and processes that generally typify that time.

Most noticeable in the aging process are the biological changes that occur as one approaches and engages the later years. Many theories have been derived to explain the physical changes that occur; however, none of the extant theories provide an adequate and comprehensive explanation. However, when viewed collectively they serve to provide a useful platform for viewing the aging process. One of the earliest theories was that the body, much like any machine, simply could not resist the effects of daily usage—over time everything wears down and wears out, and thus it was with the body. A more recent theory argued that aging results from increasing immune system disorders which resulted in the body's own immune system compromising the cellular structures of the body by preventing cellular replication. A related theory suggested that the inability of collagen to repair itself and grown new tissue resulted in the loss of elasticity in muscle tissue, skin, blood vessels, and other organs. Free radicals have been associated with the aging process. Free radicals are compounds possessing an unpaired electron. Thus they are highly reactive. It is their capacity to combine with other molecules that makes them problematical since they can produce mutations and other damage to cellular structures. Most recently, it has been theorized that aging occurs in response to a genetic clock that begins to shut down organ systems by making cellular metabolism less and less effective until it leads to death. Work now in mapping the human genome shows great promise in unraveling the mystery of physical aging.

Just as there are theories that attempt to explain why we age, there are theories that explore the social and personal aspects of aging. One of the first and most prominent theories is known as the "disengagement theory." This theory attributed to Cumming and Henry[7] (1961) argues that as people age they slowly and gradually separate themselves from society. It is further argued that this disengagement serves an important social function, both for society and the older individual. In essence, as the older individual disengages from society, fewer demands are put on the older person and similarly the older person feels fewer obligations to society. The net effect is that the older person is allowed to prepare for death while younger and more vital individuals are allowed to move into the social space vacated by the person who has withdrawn from society. Some people criticize this theory as reflecting the decreasing opportunities a highly evolving technologically based society offers older people rather than the result of a normal process common to aging.[8]

Another prominent theory is the "activity theory."[9] This theory can be viewed as contrary to disengagement theory. Here successful aging is viewed as dependent upon engaging in activity not withdrawing. It is assumed, in this theory, that one's

self-definition is largely dependent upon the roles that one fills in society. This theory argues that when one disengages it is natural to seek out new roles to compensate for the roles left behind. As long as such roles can be found and maintained, life satisfaction remains high. On the contrary, when one lacks a social role, life satisfaction diminishes. This theory provides an encouraging model for people entering into the senior years; however, it fails the test of a theory of aging. It does not adequately explain the dynamics that drive individuals to either engage or disengage, and it fails to answer the question of which come first—high levels of satisfaction or activity.

"Continuity theory" provides a rather reasonable explanation of what enables an individual to pass through later life successfully. In this theory it is argued that success in aging is dependent upon the extent to which the individual has developed a capacity to adapt to changes in his/her life. Neugarten, Havighurst, and Tobin (1968) were able to identify eight different patterns of aging, all of which represented variances in styles of adaptation. They demonstrated that the style that characterized a person's younger years persisted into retirement and later life. Those people who resisted change were those who had the most difficulty with later life. This is a useful explanation of why some people seem to engage in activity in later years while others prefer disengagement.

"Socialization theory" argues that society teaches people how to age. Social norms, roles, and behavior patterns are associated with each of the stages of life. As people age, there are both subtle and not so subtle socialization practices at work. For example, in the workplace, there are incentives given to encourage older people to retire and make way for younger workers. The message here is that no matter how much experience you have, you can't compete with youthful energy and new ideas. Television commercials sell products expressly designed for older people. The message these commercials communicate to the young is that when you get to this age, you can fully expect to be retired, living in a retirement community in Arizona, using Viagra to spice up your sex life, and adult diapers to preserve your dignity. Sitcoms and movies communicate caricature images of older people, but they also teach younger generations what is expected of people when they age. Senior discounts suggest that older people are to be pitied, and age restrictions for driving imply that physical impairment is inevitable. This theory coupled with continuity theory offers a reasonable explanation of the behaviors that characterize the later years. However, it important to recognize that as adults, people have a considerable amount of discretion in terms of accepting and selecting socialization experiences. This is particularly true in regard to one's leisure orientation.

Although the leisure socialization that occurs early in one's life has a tremendous impact on one's leisure values, attitudes, and behaviors in later life, social learning is not limited to these "formative" years. It is also important to remember that socialization does not always produce immutable expectations in the older mind. The relative impact of later-life socialization on leisure (and the socializing role of leisure) may be less than during earlier years, but to assume that "you can't teach an old dog new tricks" may be an overstatement of the facts.

Nevertheless, as one ages, there are factors which might conspire to make it difficult for a person to learn those new tricks, and it is important that these be recognized. The best time of course to develop attitudes and values that tend one to activity and engagement is during one's formative years. As one gets older limitations begin to emerge which render socialization less effective in later life. These limitations of later-life socialization are summarized as follows:

1. As one gets older, one's physical abilities diminish, predisposing an individual to certain activities.

2. Some physical skills are best acquired in childhood, otherwise their development in adult life is doubtful.

3. The acquisition of favorable attitudes toward leisure during formative years lays the foundation for satisfactory socialization in later life (Iso-Ahola 175–182).[10]

Even though socialization limits may be very real and pose a challenge for leisure socialization in later life, we have all seen examples of people who have, as adults, made remarkable changes, who have continued to grow and develop. People may not learn as quickly during adulthood and later years, but change is always possible. Nevertheless, it must be stressed that the most important thing a person can do to ensure a continuation of new experiences during adulthood is to develop a positive attitude about leisure during one's youth. If such an attitude fails to develop, then the adult interested in maintaining a rich repertoire of leisure activities is faced with a double burden. Not only will he or she have to deal with the limitations inherent in the aging process, but also the limitations associated with early socialization.

The Life Cycle and Leisure Activities

As the genetic and environmental clocks alter one's physical characteristics, and as cognitive, personality and social changes occur, it follows that one's leisure activities should also change. Bammel and Bammel (1982)[11] in their book, *Leisure and Human Behavior*, examine this question using essentially the same life cycle divisions as presented in this unit. As one might hypothesize, active participation in physical recreation decreases with age. Spectator activities, television, and recreational reading tends to increase with age. As one gets older, family recreation tends to become more important. (See chart, "Changes in Recreational Activities by Age," page 133).

In this overview, it is important to recognize that this portrait of recreation patterns is a generic picture. It may not be applicable to all people or to all cultures. It does, however, illustrate the effect aging has on leisure behavior. In most cases, people slow down and become less physically active. Their recreation becomes less physical and more cerebral. That this is true for most people doesn't mean that it has to be true for everyone.

Social psychologists argue that the *self-perception* is highly influenced by the perception of others. This notion can be stated in this way: what we think about a person influences how we will perceive him/ her; how we perceive a person influences how we will act toward the person; and how we behave toward a person ultimately influences that person's self-perception. In looking at the leisure behavior normative to a certain age group, it is assumed that these norms have some predictive validity. That is to say, society, in general expects older people to behave in accordance with the normative expectations. Consequently, there is significant social pressure put on older people to act old, think old, and be old—to conform to what society views as correct behavior for the old. Similarly many older people assume that societal expectations are valid, and slip into stereotypical roles. Perceiving older people acting out these stereotypical roles then further reinforces society's ideas about the aging process.

Stereotyping the Senior Citizen

In our society, we continue to strive to find a "fountain of youth." Look at television and print advertisements and the amount of money spent on age-defying products. The focus on youth becomes almost ridiculous! If you're someone who can afford a facelift when you see the first sign of a wrinkle and want to keep that young look, then go ahead. The only problem is that you are still growing older.

I'm sorry to say that everyone gets a wrinkle or two, some aches and pains, and may even have to wear a hearing aid. Our society's over-emphasis on youth serves to create a negative stereotype of older people or "senior" citizens. However, this is simply the term used to identify people who have reached age 50 and over. Age 50 is used as a beginning point of reference for eligibility for services by a number of senior organizations and some government agencies. (Other agencies, such as Medicare, use age 65 as a reference point.) For those who question the use of the term "senior" citizen, consider this. When you are a freshman in high school or college, you're at the bottom of the totem pole. You move up the pole as you proceed through the school and when you reach

Changes in Recreation Activities by Age

Stage	Activity Profile
Teens	Socializing seems to be a central-life interest, peer recreation is very important. Movies and music characterize this period. Physical activity, team and individual sports is high.
Twenties	Socializing becomes more important as the search for that right person picks up speed. Dancing, socializing, night-clubbing, dinners out, etc., are all important. Once married, this pattern changes and spectating becomes more the order of the day (or night). Outdoor recreation and fitness activities are important.
Thirties	Social involvement centers around home and friends. Family get-togethers provide recreation and family contact. Outdoor recreation and physical recreation give way to cultural arts. Women show particular interest in competence and mastery.
Forties	Social recreation tends to revolve around the family, until the nest empties; then travel and social involvement increases. Camping and outdoor activities continue to show a decrease; for a minority there may be a renewed interest in physical conditioning.
Fifties	Social recreation tends to become more home oriented with an emphasis being placed on family get-togethers and visits with old friends. Travel interests may diminish. Television may be major source of entertainment. Spectator sports are high on our list of activities, but the over 50 sports leagues have seen an increase thanks to the Baby Boomers.
Sixties	Grandchildren provide a source of pleasure for many people during this period. For some, retirement provides an opportunity to start new hobbies and participate in civic affairs. Television provides much of the entertainment. Gardening and home based activities fill a large portion of time. Walking has become extremely popular in this age category and provides a social outlet as well. There is also a renewed interest in travel.
Seventies	Social involvement may revolve around newly retired friends. Card playing and social activities are popular. For some, interest in church activities increases. Other people move to retirement communities where a wide array of planned recreation is available.
Eighties Nineties Centerarian	At these ages there is a tendency to slow down our leisure pursuits. We will maintain some physical activities as our bodies allow, but we do try to maintain our social network. Family occupies a good deal of our time.

senior level, you're at the top. You have earned the respect of others and you have the experience that goes along with this status. It's the same with "senior" citizens. They have earned their status in society and should be afforded respect.

Senior citizens resent stereotyping! Gerontologists continue to counter the ill-founded notion that reaching a certain age automatically disqualifies older people from contributing to society. One sees only a few token senior citizens in the spotlight in the occasional movie or advertisement. This may change when the current generation of "baby boomers" reach senior status, about 2011! Today, even though age discrimination is illegal, stories abound in the workforce about employers who hire an inexperienced person right out of college and, in the process, nudge the older worker into retirement. There are still misconceptions regarding senior citizens in the workforce—that they're too old to be productive, they can't keep up with new technology, they will call in sick often. However, this is changing. Some companies are asking for help—and hiring back older workers as consultants, realizing that older workers have much to contribute in terms of professional expertise and life experience. If we look around we will discover that senior citizens are a vital "ingredient" in our society and contribute positively to our lives and leisure.

PERSONAL NOTE

My dad at 85 knew the importance of leisure. Even though he was dealing with a physical disability he knew it was important to maintain an active lifestyle. Dad kept mentally active by doing something he always loved—coin collecting and playing his favorite card game, solitaire. There were many times when he was not having a good day, but when he changed the focus to these two hobbies, the day got brighter. Right up until his death, leisure activities played an important role in his life.

My mom, who lived to the age of 83, was a great dancer in her day, but as she aged she became frail and needed assistance. Two activities she needed no help with were reading and listening to those dance records. She often remarked that if she could, she would have loved to hit the dance floor one more time.

People who approach retirement are quite concerned about a number of areas in their lives. These include, but are not limited to, health care, housing, transportation, socialization, and financial worries. It is also worth mentioning that becoming a burden to adult children is a concern, too. Many senior citizens do not want to become a burden to their children who may have children of their own to care for. The "sandwich generation" refers to adults who have responsibilities for both their children and their aging, frail, or unwell parents.

Let's look at concerns around health and health care. You can well imagine the scope of issues involved. To acquaint you further, I'd like to list a few:

- Affordable health plans and what plan is best for each individual senior citizen
- Cost of prescription medicine
- Assisted living
- Skilled nursing facilities
- Medicare or Medi-Cal
- Long-term care insurance
- Diet and nutrition
- Exercise
- Living Longer/Outliving your family
- Caregiving
- Consider these issues and realize that it costs 3 to 5 times more to care for someone over 65 than for someone younger.

This is a very short list, but it does give you a sense of what a senior citizen must address and then determine how to cope with getting the necessary and proper care. It is a major goal of senior citizens to "age in place." Gerontologists define "aging in place" as seniors remaining in their own homes and healthy for as long as possible. Consider designing a plan of action, both short and long term, to assist senior citizens with situations that may arise in their lives, and try to do this with the least amount of stress on them and their families. In other words, we have life insurance, car and house insurance designed to take care of specific concerns, so why not have an "aging in place" plan?

When it is no longer possible to maintain a comfortable standard of living at home, senior citizens may sell their homes and move into retirement communities or assisted living arrangements so that others may help care for their needs. This is often quite a traumatic experience as it means giving up familiar surroundings and admitting that part of one's independence is slipping away. As with housing, transportation (the means of independence for senior citizens) is a major issue. This area of concern is a hotly debated topic among Department of Motor Vehicle professionals, gerontologists, law enforcement, politicians, and senior citizen organizations. When is a person too old to drive a motor vehicle? How safe is the older driver? When one's eyesight, hearing, and reaction time start diminishing, this may seem the time to "pull" someone's driver's license. However, for the senior citizen driver having a driver's license represents the difference between getting around the community and depending upon others for transportation. A number of companies specialize in senior and disabled transportation, but many seniors avoid this service, rather than admitting that they need help getting around.

Socializing is just as important as transportation. The two go hand-in-hand. Maintaining social contact and avoiding isolation is an area in which leisure professionals play a vital role. For instance, senior citizen centers provide a wide-range of activities. It's nice for such services to promote these activities, but if the senior cannot get there, programs will only look good on paper. For this reason programs for seniors work closely with transportation companies serving senior citizens.

Successful Aging

In 1997, Rowe and Kahn referred to successful aging as having three components—the avoidance of disease and disability, the maintenance of high physical and cognitive capacity in later years, and continued active engagement in life.[12] We all wish to achieve these three goals, but we do know that genetics and the wear and tear of life can alter one or more of these components. A major contributor to compensate for some physical or mental shortcoming is leisure. There is a wonderful video titled, "Surfing for Life."[13] It shows the lifespan of several senior citizens who first enjoyed the sport of surfing at a young age and continued this leisure pursuit into their 70's, 80's and 90's! You may not be

a surfer, but your own particular leisure interest can be adapted as you grow older.

"Surfing for Life" shows how people can engage in a leisure activity without worry, fear or regard for their bodies. As they grew older, they acknowledged that their physical abilities were diminishing, so instead of giving up surfing, they adapted. This is a lesson for all to recognize—there comes a point in our lives when our bodies start "telling" us to adjust our physical routines. It is interesting that by recognizing *mentally* that we need to change *physically*, it provides us with the impetus to continue positively with our leisure activities. We feel a renewed motivation ultimately leading to our satisfaction. We can say that during our lives we want continued stimulation. Sepp Iso-Ahola explains our leisure behaviors as our means to achieve "optimal arousal." People need optimal arousal in order to benefit both physiologically and psychologically.[14] Think about this theory for a moment—are you optimally aroused before, during and after your leisure activity? What stimulation did your leisure interest provide? In essence, your leisure choices must provide you with some level of optimal arousal; otherwise you may develop negative feelings for the leisure activity because it provides you with few positive benefits.

In addition, as the world grows older, industries will need to hire older workers because they will be unable to find enough younger workers to fill the demand, and also many people will need to work because of pension and budget cuts and lack of retirement funds. Even though industry in general is still lukewarm about hiring older workers, they cannot deny the experience an older person can bring to the jobsite. If you're still productive in your industry in your later years and it brings you happiness, consider work as part of your successful aging.

Activities and Recommendations for Your Personal Successful Aging

1. Manage your stress. Being able to bounce back from life's crises and manage well through tough times is vital to a longer life.

2. If you believe you have no time for leisure activities while you are young, start making

time, even for a passive activity like reading for pleasure. You not only carry this over into an older age, but it will provide you with some great mental stimulation.

3. Stay involved—socialize until your dying day. A phone call is one small example of being social. Senior citizens, as noted before, may not be able to transport themselves to a friend's house, but picking up the phone for a chat will act as a viable social substitute.

PERSONAL NOTE

There was a gentleman who one day walked into my office at a local senior citizen center looking rather "down-in-the-dumps." He explained how his wife died six months earlier and how he was moping around the house. I'll call this person Ralph. Ralph just wanted to do something, to volunteer like he told me his wife would like him to do. The senior center offered many leisure choices, and Ralph slowly took advantage of his opportunities. Ralph even met a friend who loved to go to the horse track—one of Ralph's passions. As it turned out, Ralph continued to volunteer for more than six years, became the center's Advisory Board President, organized dances and special event dinners and began to once again enjoy life. Ralph proved that if you give yourself a chance to live again, life as a senior can be a positive experience.

---

4. Educate yourself regarding your diet and exercise. Due to health problems senior citizens need to alter the "meat and potatoes" diet many grew up with. Watching salt and sugar intake is important; a registered dietician can be very helpful in directing you toward tasty and nutritious meal plans in later life. You can still eat healthy food, especially now with so many options available. Organic foods may be another option.

5. If applicable, get involved, or stay involved in your grandchildren's lives. Going to a soccer or basketball game, piano recital, or school play is both stimulating and supportive.

6. Try activities that you have always wanted to try. Senior citizens may have wanted to dance, travel for pleasure, or learn how to play bridge at a young age, but circumstances dictated otherwise. Now, later in life, seniors can pursue these lifelong leisure ambitions.

7. Volunteer. After many years on this earth, we acquire a number of skills. Why not use your talents to help others? It's a great way to get out of the house and participate in your community. If you're unable to easily leave your home, try being a phone volunteer for your favorite organization. Volunteerism keeps senior citizens active and provides an outlet for them to contribute to society, just as they did when working for pay.

Traditional and Non-Traditional Leisure Activities for Successful Aging

In *Beyond Bingo 2* (1998), the following services and leisure activities are recommended to keep the senior citizen involved in aging successfully:

- Write a newspaper column or contribute your writing talents to a senior citizen newsletter or church bulletin.

- Be a poet—share your rhyming skills with others.

- Form a Band—if you have the skills to play a musical instrument, why not make this into an intergenerational project? There are many younger people who would like to gain knowledge from an experienced musician.

- Go-Cart Racing—okay, maybe the seniors don't actually want to drive the carts, but making them and displaying the carts is a great activity. A little crazy, but don't knock it!

- Off Season Luncheon or Dinner—seniors may be "old" as related to a number, but they are active. Getting a little off-the-wall is fine. If you live in a snowy climate, who says you can't invite some of your friends to your house or senior center for a summer barbecue? You can do a lot with this activity as long as you allow your imagination to run wild.[14]

More Activities to Think About

- Armchair travel
- Book club
- Clothing boutique
- Calligraphy
- Chess and checkers
- Computer classes
- Cribbage
- Crochet and knitting
- Golf
- Jigsaw puzzles
- Martial arts classes
- Memoir writing
- Painting (drawing, oils, watercolor)
- Photography club
- Tai Chi
- Water aerobics
- Woodworking
- Yoga

A Final Note

As you read this, if it is possible, get up out of your seat and change perspectives. This is how you must treat your leisure, to view it from another angle. We must never get in a rut; we must always be looking out for new adventures, or to just slightly alter our existing leisure activities. When aging, we will gain the experience and knowledge necessary to enjoy our leisure to the fullest. We must maintain our enthusiasm for leisure and never forget the "rush" of simply engaging in our favorite pursuits.

NOTES

1. "65+ in the United States: 2005." U.S. Census Bureau. (*http://www:census.gov/servlet*)
2. www.bumc.bu.edu
3. www.aoa.gov/press/fact/alpha/fact global agmg.asp
4. Ragheb, M. G., and C. A. Griffith. "The Contribution of Leisure Participation and Leisure Satisfaction of Older Persons." SPRE Research Symposium. (Phoenix: NRPA, 1980).
5. Hoyer, W. J., and P. A. Roodin. *Adult Development and Aging, 5th ed.* (New York: McGraw Hill, 2003).
6. Guinn, B. "Leisure Behavior Motivation and the Life Satisfaction of Retired Persons." *Activities, Adaptation and Aging.* 23 (1999):13–20.
7. Cumming, E., and W. E. Henry. *Growing Old: The Process of Disengagement.* New York: Basic Books, 1961.
8. McGuire, Francis, Rosangela K. Boyd, and Raymond Tedrick. Champaign, Illinois: Sagamore. 1996. (21).
9. Iso-Ahola, S. *The Social Psychology of Leisure and Recreation.* (Dubuque, Iowa: Wm. C. Brown Publishers. 1980).
10. Bammel, G., and L. L. Burris-Bammel. *Leisure and Human Behavior.* (Dubuque, Iowa: Wm. C. Brown Publishers, 1982).
11. Rowe, J. W., and R. L. Kahn. "Successful Aging." *The Gerontologist.* 37 (1997):433–440.
12. *Surfing for Life.* Director: D. L. Brown. Surf Video Network. (1999).
13. Arrigo, Jr. S. *Beyond Bingo 2.* State College: Venture Publishing, 1998).

REFERENCES

Arrigo, Jr., S. *Beyond Bingo 2.* State College: Venture Publishing: 1998.

Baltes, P. B., and M. M. Baltes. "Selective Optimization with Compensation." In P. B. Baltes and M. M. Baltes (eds.) *Successful Aging: Perspectives from the Behavioral Sciences.* New York: Cambridge University Press. 1990. 118–163.

Bammel, G., and L. L. Burrus-Bammel. *Leisure and Human Behavior*. Dubuque: Wm. C. Brown Publishers.

Bammel, G., and L. L. Burrus-Bammel, *Leisure and Human Behavior*. Dubuque, Iowa: Wm. C. Brown Publishers.

Beck, SH in the Journal of Gerontology (Sep; 37 (5): 616–24 Brown, 1980. C. Brown, 1982.

Ellis, M. *Why People Play*. New York: Prentice Hall, 1973.

Gleitman, H., *Psychology*. New York: W.W. Norton and Company, 1981.

Gould, R. "Adult Life Stages: Growth Toward Self-Tolerance," *Psychology Today*. 1975, 8, February, 74–78.

Guinn, B. "Leisure Behavior Motivation and the Life Satisfaction of Retired Persons."

Hoyer, W. J., and Roodin, P. A. *Adult Development and Aging, 5th ed.* New York: McGraw-Hill, 2003.

Iso-Ahola, S. *The Social Psychology of Leisure and Recreation*. Dubuque, Iowa: Wm. C. Brown, Publishers.

Iso-Ahola, S. E. *The Social Psychology of Leisure and Recreation*. Dubuque, Iowa: Wm. C. Brown, Publishers, 1980.

Levinson, D. J. (with C. N. Darrow, E. B. Klein, M. H. Levinson and B. McKee), The McGraw Hill, 2003.

Ragheb, M. G., and Griffith, C. A. "The Contribution of Leisure Participation and Leisure."

Rowe, J. W., and Kahn, R. L. "Successful Aging." *The Gerontologist*. 37 (1997): 433

"Satisfaction to the Life Satisfaction of Older Persons." SPRE Research

Symposium, Phoenix: NRPA. 1980.

Seasons of a Man's Life. New York: Alfred A. Knopf, 1978.

Sheehy, G. *Passages*. New York: Dell Books, 1976.

Surfing for Life. Dir. David L. Brown. Surf Video Network, 1999.

CHAPTER 12

PERSPECTIVES ON THE FEDERAL GOVERNMENT'S ROLE IN RECREATION AND LEISURE SERVICES

Government is too big and important to leave to the politicians.

—CHESTER BOWLES

THE FUNDAMENTAL ELEMENTS OF AMERICAN GOVERNMENT

"Legal system?" you ask. It may be hard to see the relationship between leisure and the legal system, but it is there and it is very important. Our "Founding Fathers" were very concerned about ensuring the well-being and happiness of the citizens of the United States. They wanted to ensure that personal rights and freedoms would be protected. They wanted to protect against government excess, and they wanted to make certain that authority was distributed throughout the various levels of government. To accomplish these goals, the Second Continental Congress in 1776 began a series of deliberations, which eventually led to the adoption of the *Articles of Confederation* five years later. Under the Articles of Confederation, the nation was to consist of a federation of relatively sovereign states. The central government consisted of a congress, which had power to handle foreign affairs, make treaties, maintain armed forces, coin money, and operate a postal service. However, it had no powers to tax or control foreign commerce. It also lacked power to force the states to obey federal laws.

Recognizing that a stronger central government was essential for the continued success of the developing nation, leaders such as Thomas Jefferson proposed a new set of laws, which provided for a stronger central government. In 1787 the Constitutional Convention was held and a new constitution was created. It was adopted in 1787. To further protect the rights of the citizenry, in 1791 ten amendments were added. These ten amendments are collectively referred to as the Bill of Rights.

The Constitution strove to protect the rights of the states, but at the same time provide for a strong central government. The rights not reserved for the states resorted to the federal government, and the states in turn enabled local governments to carry out certain duties and responsibilities. The Constitution established three different branches of government. One of the principal features of this new government was a system of "checks and balances" that prevented any one branch from becoming overly powerful. The Declaration of Independence set forth a philosophy, which supports many of premises upon which the Recreation Movement is based.[1]

The Three Systems of Government in the United States

- Three systems interconnected but independent. These are the **federal** government, the **state** governments, and **local** governments (city, district, or county).

- Each level of government has **three interconnected but independent branches:** the legislative (makes the laws), the executive (the one that carries out the laws) and the judicial (interprets the laws).[2]

EXPLORE

We think of the phone book as a valuable learning tool. To familiarize yourself with the extent to which these three divisions affect your life, take a moment and look at the phone book under "Government." Note down governmental agencies found in your area. What did you learn about government from this exercise?

Do you have an interest in working for the federal or state government? Give a call to a local agency and explore the possibilities.

Examples:

- **Federal Government**
  - **Congress:** House of Representatives and the Senate
  - **Executive Branch:** the President and the federal administrative agencies
  - **Judicial Branch:** the U.S. Supreme Court, the U.S. Court of Appeal, the U.S. District Courts, and other federal courts
- **State Government**
  - **Legislative Branch:** the state legislature
  - **Executive Branch:** the governor and the state agencies
  - **Judicial Branch:** state courts
- **Local Government**
  - **Legislative:** city council or county or district
  - **Executive:** mayor or commissioner and the local administrative agencies

- **Judicial:** courts of limited jurisdiction (county court, small claims, municipal court, etc.)

The Supreme Law of the Land

The **United States Constitution,** ratified in 1789, is the foundation upon which all government in the United States is based. In addition to the Bill of Rights, 17 different amendments were added to the Constitution between 1795 and 1992. Furthermore, the Constitution clarifies the powers of the national government, and establishes the relationship between the national government and the states, a political doctrine known as "federalism." The rights of the people are clearly defined in *the Bill of Rights* as is the right of citizens to participate in the political process through their right to vote. In addition to the powers of government, the Constitution also establishes limits on the scope and power of both the federal and state governments. Each branch of government finds its operational powers rooted in some aspect of this important document. In summary, the Constitution can best be described as **the supreme law of the United States.**[3]

EXERCISE IN A BOX

Take a few minutes and read the Constitution. Is anything said that directly relates to leisure or recreation? What do you find in the Constitution that suggests that the authors of the Constitution were sensitive to the value of free-time activity and personal leisure pursuits?

The first three articles of the Constitution provide the basis for the organization of the federal government, and provides a model for the organization of state governments as well. Article I establishes a two-house legislature (called *bicameral*). Article I also contains the rules of impeachment for government officials. As most people know, thanks to the Bill Clinton-Monica Lewinsky scandal, it is in the Congress that impeachment proceedings are conducted. Article II outlines the nature of the office of chief executive, establishing the powers and duties of the president and vice-president. It also provides the basis for the creation of executive departments although it does not specify what they are to be. Article III outlines the nature of the Judicial Branch. It refers to the Supreme Court and the manner in which cases may be brought there. It describes the scope and jurisdiction of the court, but it does not clearly define the authority of the Court.

The framers of the Constitution were concerned with the delicate balance between these three branches. Although, most people think of the President as the head of government, the fact is that no one branch of government can operate without the other two. The balance of power is relatively equal between the three major branches of government. Even though each branch has fundamentally different responsibilities, because of the system of "checks and balances" that define their relationship, it is accurate to say that no one branch can be considered the lead player in governmental affairs.

CAN YOU GROW UP TO BE PRESIDENT?

The Constitution requires that you meet the following criteria:

- Be 35 years of age.
- Be a resident of the U.S. for at least 14 years.
- Be a natural born citizen.

If you meet the above requirements you can be President, provided you are elected by a majority of the people.

Laws originate with the Congress, but the President has the power to veto legislation that he opposes. Even when a law is passed, the Supreme Court can rule a law unconstitutional and therefore render it void. Presidents are elected for no more than two terms, but to free Supreme Court Justices from political concerns, Justices are appointed for life. Members of the Senate are elected, but it is the Senate that confirms the appointment of a Justice. Even though the President is designated Commander in Chief, it is the Congress that must declare war. When the people are dissatisfied with members of the legislative branch or the President and Vice-President, they can vote them out of office. To encourage objectivity among members of the Supreme Court and free them from political

concerns, Justices of the Supreme Court have no direct accountability to the voters.

Executive Departments and Governments and Government Corporations

Much of the President's authority can be traced to his ability to establish executive departments. In meeting the mandate to execute the laws of the nation, presidents have developed and organized the executive department into the following areas: the cabinet, executive agencies, regulatory agencies, and the executive office.

The Executive Office consists of advisers and administrative personnel to assist the President in administering the federal bureaucracy. Today the executive office consists of about 1,400 people and eight agencies. Included in these agencies are powerful agencies such as the National Security Council, the Office of Management and Budget, and the Council of Economic Advisers.[4] Perhaps, closest to the president is that branch of the Executive Office referred to as the "**White House Staff.**" The investigation of Bill Clinton focused attention on many members of his White House advisers and personnel.

The cabinet consists of governmental agencies called **cabinet departments.** These agencies are responsible for a particular area of national concern. Each cabinet (except for the Justice Department which is headed by the Attorney General) is headed by a *secretary* who is appointed by the President with the approval of the Senate. Many of these departments offer services or fund programs that in one way or another relate to recreation and leisure.

Cabinet departments can be added or deleted, but even in government, tradition holds sway, and for the most part cabinet departments are fairly stable. Currently the president's cabinet includes the following departments on the next page.

A quick visit to any cabinet department will show you that each of these agencies operate a variety of programs and departments. In subsequent portions of this chapter we will look at some of the cabinet agencies and also some of their programs. The federal government and its relation to recreation and leisure is so immense that we can only give you an overview here. If you want more information, you are encouraged to visit the Web sites recommended.[5]

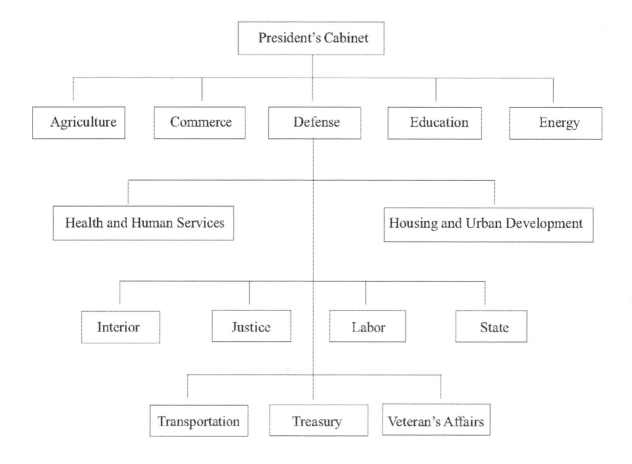

Executive agencies are sort of like cabinet departments, but they are not considered major enough to be included in the cabinet. The Environmental Protection Agency is an example of an "agency level" department that provides services that often indirectly relate to recreation and leisure. *Government corporations* differ from executive agencies in one important way, they function more like private corporations than government agencies. That is, they have more independence than other governmental entities. They are usually governed by a board of directors and perform more business-like activities than other agencies. A good example of a government corporation is the Tennessee Valley Authority which was established in the 1930s to provide flood control, recreation, and electrical power for the Tennessee Valley. The U.S. Postal Service is another example. There are many such agencies that are indirectly related to recreation and leisure services. We will look at examples of both executive agencies and governmental corporations in the pages to follow.

Because certain areas of the economy and government require oversight, the Congress has established *regulatory commissions.* These commissions are charged with making rules (codes) and seeing that these regulations are enforced. Examples include the Interstate Commerce Commission, the Food and Drug Commission, the Federal Communications Commission, and the Federal Reserve Board.

Governmental Authority to Provide Recreation

It is interesting to note that even though the Constitution doesn't specify recreation as one of our inalienable rights or one of the principal functions of government, the government offers numerous programs that are clearly of recreational value. Where does this authority originate? Ron Kaiser answers this question.

Ronald Kaiser, J.D., Ph.D. is an expert in legal matters relating to parks and recreation. In his book, *Liability & Law in Recreation, Parks and Sports*, Dr. Kaiser nicely summarizes the legal foundation upon which public recreation and leisure services are founded.[6]

> *The federal framework in parks and recreation emanates from the "property," "general welfare," and provision of the Constitution and civil rights "commerce" clauses of the Constitution. Federal regulatory authority stems from the civil liberties legislation. In a variety of cases the United States Supreme Court has upheld all rights guaranteed by the Constitution and federal statutes regardless of the services involved.*

> *States have the plenary legislative power to authorize and regulate state, local, and school park, recreation, and sports programs. Under the police powers, state agencies may be established to acquire, develop, and operate park and recreation facilities. The pattern of organizational structure is varied but all states provide some level of park and recreation services.[7]*

> *Authorization to provide park, recreation, and sports services may be delegated to municipalities and local schools. This power must be found in constitutional and statutory enactment [enabling legislation] and these units of government have no authority beyond that extended by these documents. Administrators should ascertain their legal authorization before undertaking new services.[8]*

> *School sponsored recreation and sports programs that are part of the school curriculum are generally held to be stated endorsed functions, whereas municipal services are local in nature and are discretionary to the unit of government. When school recreation sports programs are mandated in the state school code the local school district must strictly adhere to its provisions.[9]*

The Federal Government's Role in Recreation

The government didn't set out to get into the recreation and leisure business. Early recreational activities were of an indirect nature—the provision of federal land and water areas for multipurpose uses, including recreation. But, with the passage of time, government became increasingly involved in providing resources and services related to the public's need for recreation and leisure services.

Don Weiskopf points out that government involvement in recreation and leisure has steadily increased, and that now the government's involvement in leisure services cuts a very wide swath.

> *Federal involvement in outdoor recreation and conservation programs is well-recognized, but the increasing impact of federal revenue sharing, community development, public employment, and public works programs on behalf of city recreation efforts is not as well-known. The ability of local governments to meet recreation needs is strongly affected by federal programs in social welfare, housing, transportation, environmental education, arts and other recreation-related activities.[10]*

Overall, the federal government has developed a multitude of programs related to recreation—more than 90 separate departments, bureaus, commissions, or councils and 300 different operations. As of the present, the federal government has developed a plethora of agencies and departments that are involved, to some degree, with recreation. It is interesting to note that initially many of these programs were not at all interested in the provision of leisure services. Flood control, for example, was more important. But as with the case of the Tennessee Valley Authority, it soon became clear, that while preventing floods was important, so were the recreational opportunities that the resource made available to the public. Consequently, although the primary purpose of a governmental agency might have nothing directly to do with recreation, recreational application often became an important secondary objective.[11]

Although, the federal government has become an active player in the provision of leisure services, there is nothing in the constitution that requires the government to provide the public with recreational resources and leisure services, rather, government involvement in the provision of recreation resources is based on court interpretations of government's responsibility to care for the general welfare of the people.

Types of Federal Programs Associated with Recreation and Leisure[12]

The federal government provides the public with both direct and indirect recreation services. Following are eight different ways in which the government in one way or another enhances recreational opportunities for the public:

1. **Management of Outdoor Recreation Resources.** The federal government, and to a lesser degree the states, have both had an abiding interest in protecting and acquiring important national land and water recreational resources. The federal government operates numerous programs associated with the management of outdoor natural resources for recreational use. Perhaps the best known of these is the National Park Service. States often model their management of resources after the federal government.

2. **Conservation and Resource Reclamation.** When natural resources are damaged or destroyed, the government often initiates reclamation efforts. Similarly, when a valued resource (including air and water) is in danger, the government often institutes conservation programs. These types of programs have important implications for recreation and leisure service. Reclamation may provide the public with more public land. Conservation programs may encourage people to ride bicycles or participate in recreation that promotes clean air and water. This is particularly important in the more densely populated areas and inner cities.

3. **Open-Space and Park Development Programs.** Authorized by Congress in 1965 under the Land and Water Conservation Act, the federal government has encouraged the development of open-space by providing financial assistance to local governments for the development of parks, playgrounds, and outdoor areas.

4. **Direct Programs of Recreation Participation.** Through military recreation programs, therapeutic recreation in veteran administration hospitals, and through other federal programs, the federal government offers a variety of recreational programs. For example, 4-H is a federally sponsored youth program which includes both an educational and recreational aspect.

5. **Advisory and Financial Assistance.** Departments of Health, Education and Welfare, Housing and Urban Development, Labor, and others often provide financial and advisory assistance to public and volunteer agencies providing services to disadvantaged populations.

The legitimate object of government is to do for a community whatever they need to have done, but cannot do at all in their separate and individual capacities.

—Abraham Lincoln

6. **Aid to Professional Education and Research.** Since the early 1960s the government has taken an active interest in providing universities and colleges with financial assistance for special training programs. In addition to offering education grants, the government offers financial support for research in recreation related areas such as forest recreation, crime reduction, wildlife preservation, and conservation. Similarly, state governments often provide financial grants to colleges and universities.

7. **Promotion of Recreation as an Economic Function.** The economic value of recreation and leisure has not gone unnoticed by the government. The government actively promotes such recreational related activities as travel and tourism. States like California, Florida, and Hawaii are heavily involved in promoting their states as tourist destinations.

8. **Regulation and Standards.** As was pointed out earlier, state and federal governments not only institute laws, but also develop codes, regulations and standards that enable the laws to be enforced. Such regulations include policies regarding service to the disabled, the preservation of natural resources and historical sites, protection of endangered species, and equal opportunities for all citizens.

Let's take a closer now at some of the federal agencies providing, either directly or indirectly, recreational services in the United States today. The information regarding the various agencies of government was derived generally from agency web sites. For even more current information, you are encouraged to visit these sites yourself.

Federal Agencies and Departments and Their Relationship to Recreation and Leisure Services

State Department

The Secretary of State is the highest-ranking member of the cabinet. The "State Department" promotes foreign trade, protects the interests of Americans traveling and working in foreign countries, conducts studies on foreign affairs, enforces immigration laws, and proposes policies relating to global issues. It is also the agency that oversees protocol involving other countries. Although not specifically concerned with recreation and leisure issues, the Department of State indirectly influences recreation through promoting and developing trade agreements with countries that produce products used for recreational purposes. The Department of State also has an influence on tourism to foreign countries through treaties and agreements with such countries. Furthermore, it is not uncommon for the State Department to issue travel warnings for those Americans planning to travel into areas experiencing situations that might put American travelers at risk.[13]

The Department of Agriculture

The Department of Agriculture (USDA) is charged with ensuring a safe, affordable, nutritious, and accessible food supply; caring for agricultural, forest, and range lands; supporting sound development of rural communities; providing economic opportunities for farm and rural residents; expanding global markets for agricultural and forest products and services; and working to reduce hunger in America and throughout the world. Of particular interest to the recreation profession is that branch of the USDA which focuses on education and community development.

One program operated under the auspices of the USDA that clearly reflects recreation and leisure values is 4-H. The goal of 4-H is to help youngsters develop in "head, heart, hands, and health." In recent years the 4-H program has been experiencing two significant trends. One involves a more precise recognition that the basic purpose of 4-H centers on individual personal growth. By using 4-H projects as important vehicles for achievements and growth, participants are able to build lifetime skills. These skills are built into 4-H activities. They are designed to help participants become contributing, productive, self-directed members of a forward-moving society; they are centered on self-esteem, communication, and decision making. A second trend stresses citizenship and leadership. The program is designed to making American communities better places to live and work.[14]

The Department of Commerce

Created in 1913, the Department of Commerce has as its primary function the promotion of domestic and foreign trade to promote the nation's economic and technological advancement. A primary agency within the department is the International Trade Administration, which is charged with developing international trade. Undoubtedly some of this trade involves recreational products. Travel and tourism is promoted through the United States Travel and Tourism Administration. This branch of the Department of Commerce promotes the United States as a travel destination.[15]

The Department of Defense[16]

As the name implies, the Department of Defense (DOD) is the governmental department responsible for military affairs and the security of the country. The major divisions of the department are the Office of the Secretary, the Joint Chiefs of Staff, the military departments (Department of Army, Navy, and Air Force) and the Armed Forces Policy Council. There are two agencies within the DOD that have duties that relate specifically to recreation and leisure: (1) The U.S. Army Corps of Engineers, and (2) Morale, Welfare and Recreation Programs.

U.S. Army Corps of Engineers Recreation Program and Facilities

The Corps currently administers approximately 11.7 million acres of land and water. Corps projects provide over 30 percent of the recreational opportunities on Federal lands, with only nine percent of the Federal funds expended for recreational resources, and on less than two percent of the Federal land base. The Corps is the largest provider of water-based recreation with over 25 million people visiting a Corps project at least once each year. The U.S. Army Corps of Engineers records the second largest visitation figure among all Federal agencies.

Morale, Welfare, and Recreation Programs in the U.S. Military

Recreation for military personnel was first recognized as having value during WWI, since that time military recreation has become an important aspect of military life. Today recreational programs are offered to all military personnel and their dependents through the Morale, Welfare, and Recreation Program, which is administered by the office of the Assistant Secretary of Defense for Manpower, Reserve Affairs and Logistics. To give you an idea as to the scope of this program, the 1998 MWR budget was $135 billion. MWR programs generally include:[17]

- fitness and wellness oriented programs
- outdoor related recreation
- family and community recreation
- recreation facilities of all sorts

The Armed Forces Sports Programs Office

The military has an extensive sports and athletics program. Military sports programs include 12 Armed Forces Championships, 7 National Championships and 17 International Championships within *Conseil International du Sports Militaire* (CISM). It's open to all Active Duty personnel, to include Reservists and National Guard on active duty status. These championships feature 550 U.S. military athletes from the four branches of the service and approximately 7,000 other international athletes. CISM, which is headquartered in Belgium, is the second largest sporting organization in the world with 115 military member nations to include the U.S. Its motto of "Friendship Through Sport" establishes a common unity amongst its members. Our military athletes compete against their counterparts from other nations at venues around the world. The CISM and the National Championships are key preliminary competitions for our military athletes who qualify to compete at the Pan American and Olympic games.

The Department of Education

Created by Congress in 1979, the Department of Education is charged with ensuring educational opportunity for the nation's students. This is to be accomplished through three primary means: (1) federal financial support, (2) research programs, and (3) resource/information sharing. The history of the department dates back to 1867 when the Office of Education was first organized. In its early days, it recognized the significance of recreation in the educational process. It encouraged schools to provide recreational opportunities for both the students and the community in general.[18] It also encouraged the inclusion of leisure arts in the education program. Today, the emphasis on recreation is relatively limited. In the late 1990s, poor performance on standardized academic examinations by American students caused a great deal of concern about the quality of American education. Consequently, the current emphasis in the Department of Education is on increasing student performance in reading, writing, and mathematics.

History demonstrates that education and recreation are closely related. The schools have a history of providing recreational services not only for their students, but also for the public. In fact, the founders of the National Education Association considered education for leisure to be sufficiently important to include it as one of the seven fundamental functions of the professional education. Although the focus of the U.S. Department of Education is strictly on improving educational opportunities for America's students, recreation and leisure values are not entirely ignored and many of the programs sponsored by the Department of Education possess recreation and leisure values. For example, the Safe and Drug-Free Schools Program is one such program.

The Department of Energy

The Department of Energy was created in 1977. It's primary purpose was to deal with what Congress perceived as dwindling supplies of oil and natural gas. Today the "DOE" is involved with promoting and developing technologies that allow for the more efficient use of the nation's fuel resources. It works closely with other government agencies such as the Environmental Protection Agency, the Bureau of Mines and the Department of Defense, the Department of Transportation, the State Department, and Department of Interior. The availability of inexpensive and clean energy has a had a profound impact on recreational opportunities in this country. For example, travel and tourism in the United States is dependent upon fuel for transportation.[19]

Department of Health and Human Services[20]

Established in 1979, the Department of HHS, is the successor to the Department of Health, Education, and Welfare. Because of increasing concerns regarding education, the education component was transferred to a new cabinet level department, the Department of Education, also in 1979. The remainder of HEW was retained as the Department of Health and Human Services.

The department of HHS is the nation's principal governmental agency concerned with protecting the health of Americans and providing health related services for those unable to help themselves. Today HHS is the executive branch of government most concerned with social and health problems of the general population.

Among these programs are two, which indirectly affect recreation and leisure opportunities of those who participate. This is accomplished by providing parents with child-care assistance, and children with the opportunities of organized recreation through such programs as Head Start.

Administration for Children and Families[21]

This agency is responsible for over 60 different programs providing assistance to needy children and families. Among other services, it administers the Head Start program which serves nearly one million pre-school children. In addition, it provides funds to assist low-income families in paying for child care; it supports state programs providing for foster care; it also funds programs designed to prevent child abuse and domestic violence.

The Administration on Aging[22]

This program provides a nationwide aging network, which supports services to the elderly. The principal goal of these services is to assist older persons to remain active and independent. It helps the elderly by providing transportation, at home services, and ombudsman services. One of the well known programs offered this agency is the "meals on wheels" program.

President's Council on Physical Fitness and Sports[23]

Under the auspices of the Department of Health and Human Services, created by Executive Order 12345, is the President's Council on Physical Fitness and Sports. The main mission of the President's Council on Physical Fitness and Sports is to coordinate and promote opportunities in physical activity, fitness, and sports for all Americans, as directed and amended.[24]

The major functions can be described as, the promotion of community and school physical activity and fitness programs, and information dissemination and public awareness about the importance of physical activity and fitness. The President's Council on Physical Fitness is charged with following functions:

1. leadership of *Healthy People 2000,* a program designed to encourage health and physical fitness among the general population

2. preparation and dissemination of the first *Surgeon General's Report on Physical Activity and Health* (in collaboration with the Centers for Disease Control and Prevention)

3. development of a major Youth Fitness Campaign with the Advertising Council. Conduct of the school-based President's Challenge Physical Fitness Awards Program, the President's Fitness Awards Program, and the President's Sports Award Program

4. management of a traveling exhibition of 20th Century Presidents' involvement in fitness and sports to eight presidential libraries

5. conduct of Healthy American Fitness Leaders recognition program and *the Silver Eagle Corp* program for older Americans

The Department of Housing and Urban Development

This department, created in 1965, is responsible for two areas: (1) to ensure adequate housing, and (2) to promote urban development. HUD carries out programs to provide public housing improvement, housing finance, and neighborhood rehabilitation. Community development "Block Grants" allow for funding of a wide range of community development activities. Urban beautification is one of the goals of this department and as such development can include open-space, and recreation facilities.

Department of Interior

The Department of Interior's mission can be summarized as (1) to encourage and provide for the appropriate management, preservation, and operation of the Nation's public lands and natural resources for use and enjoyment both now and in the future; (2) to carry out related scientific research and investigations in support of these objectives; (3) to develop and use resources in an environmentally sound manner and provide an equitable return on these resources to the American taxpayer; and (4) to carry out trust responsibilities of the U.S. Government with respect to American Indians and Alaska Natives. The Department collects revenues from the leasing of natural gas and oil resources, both offshore and onshore; from coal, timber, and grazing on Federal lands, and from numerous other sources, such as recreation fees.[25] Funding, however, is largely through the Congress. The appropriations bill for the Department of Interior's programs for the fiscal year 2000 is estimated to be about $7,000,000,000 with additional monies budgeted for specific bureaus in the department amounting to an additional $800,000,000.[26]

Among the agencies falling under the auspices of the DOI are the Bureau of Indian Affairs, the U.S. Fish and Wildlife Service, the Bureau of Land Management, the Bureau of Reclamation, and the National Park Service.

The National Park Service

For those of us in recreation and leisure services, the National Park System has a special place in our hearts. This agency has the unique responsibility of making certain that wild areas are preserved for the enjoyment of the public. Similarly, state park systems manage programs that on a smaller scope emulate the charge of the NPS.

The mission of the National Park Service is ". . . to promote and regulate the use of the national park . . . which purpose is to conserve the scenery and the natural and historic objects and the wild life therein and to provide for the enjoyment of the same in such manner and by such means as will leave them unimpaired for the enjoyment of future generations."[27]

On August 25, 1916, President Woodrow Wilson signed the act creating the National Park Service. The NPS was to be a federal bureau in the Department of the Interior responsible for protecting the 40 national parks and monuments then in existence and those yet to be established. It was charged with promoting and regulating the use of Federal areas known as national parks, monuments and reservations . . . "by such means and measures as conform to the fundamental purpose of the said parks, monuments and reservations, which purpose is to conserve the scenery and the natural and historic therein and to provide for the enjoyment of the same in such manner and by such means as will leave them unimpaired for the enjoyment of future generations."

The National Park System of the United States, as of this writing, includes 376 areas covering more than 83 million acres in 49 States, the District of Columbia, American Samoa, Guam, Puerto Rico, Saipan, and the Virgin Islands. These areas are of such national significance as to justify special recognition and protection in accordance with various acts of Congress. The NPS has become a model for a worldwide national park movement. Today more than 100 nations contain some 1,200 national parks. Similarly, state parks can be found throughout the U.S.

By the Act of March 1, 1872, Congress established Yellowstone National Park in the Territories of Montana and Wyoming "as a public park or pleasuring ground for the benefit and enjoyment of the people" and placed it "under exclusive control of the Secretary of the Interior." The founding of Yellowstone National Park began parks or equivalent preserves.[28]

In the years following the establishment of Yellowstone, the United States authorized additional national parks and monuments, most of them carved from the federal lands of the West.[29] These are primarily administered by the Department of the Interior, but not all. Other monuments and natural and historical areas were administered as separate units by the War Department and the Forest Service of the Department of Agriculture. At that time, no single agency provided unified management of the varied federal parklands.[30]

An Executive Order in 1933 transferred 63 national monuments and military sites from the Forest service and the War Department to the

National Park Service. This action was a major step in the development of today's national system of parks, which today includes areas of historical as well as scenic and scientific importance.

Congress declared in the General Authorities Act of 1970 "that the National Park System, which began with the establishment of Yellowstone National Park in 1872, has since grown to include superlative natural, historic, and recreation areas in every region . . . and that it is the purpose of this Act to include all such areas in the System. . . ."

Additions to the National Park System are now generally made through acts of Congress, and national parks can be created only through such acts. But the President has authority, under the Antiquities Act of 1906, to proclaim national monuments on lands already under federal jurisdiction. For example, in 1998 President Clinton exercised this authority in developing more recreational land in Southern Utah.

The Bureau of Land Management

Another agency that controls a large number of resources used for recreation is the Bureau of Land Management. Although not its primary directive the DLM provides the public with extensive recreational opportunities. The Bureau of Land Management (BLM) is responsible for managing 264 million acres of land—about one-eighth of the land in the United States—and about 300 million additional acres of subsurface mineral resources. The Bureau is also responsible for wildfire management and suppression on 388 million acres.

Most of the lands the BLM manages are located in the western United States, including Alaska, and are dominated by extensive grasslands, forest, high mountains, arctic tundra, and deserts. The BLM manages a wide variety of resources and uses, including energy and minerals; timber; forage; wild horse and burro population; fish and wildlife habitat; wilderness areas; archaeological, paleontological, and historical sites; and other natural heritage values.

The BLM makes an effort to maximize the utility of the land under its control. This is done through application of multiple use and sustained yield principles. When it comes to recreation, the BLM essentially provides natural resources for resource-dependent recreation. The BLM's commitment to meeting the public's demand for recreational

resources is documented in *Recreation 2000: A Strategic Plan.*

The Bureau of Reclamation

The mission of the Bureau of Reclamation is to manage, develop, and protect water and related resources in an environmental and economically sound manner in the interest of the American public. It manages, develops, and protects water and related resources in an environmentally and economically sound manner in the interest of the American public. It serves as the fifth largest electric utility in the 17 Western States and the nation's second largest wholesale water supplier, administering 348 reservoirs with a total storage capacity of 245 million acre-feet (an acre-foot, 325,851 gallons of water, supplies enough water for a family of four for one year). It operates 58 hydroelectric power plants averaging 42 billion kilowatt-hours annually, delivers 10 trillion gallons of water delivered to more than 31 million people each year. It also provides 1 out of 5 Western farmers (140,000) with irrigation water for 10 million farmland acres that produce 60 percent of the nation's vegetables and 25 percent of the its fruits and nuts. The BLM manages in partnership 308 recreation sites which are visited by 90 million people a year.

U.S. Fish and Wildlife Service

The U.S. Fish and Wildlife Service's mission is, working with others, to conserve, protect and enhance fish and wildlife and their habitats for the continuing benefit of the American People.

The Service's origins date back to 1871 when Congress established the U.S. Fish Commission to study the decrease in the nation's food fish and recommend ways to reverse the decline. Placed under the Department of Commerce in 1903, it was renamed the Bureau of Fisheries. Meanwhile Congress created an Office of Economic Ornithology in the Department of Agriculture in 1885 to study the food habits and migratory patterns of birds, especially those that had an effect on agriculture. After several more name changes, The Bureau of Fisheries and Biological Survey was renamed the Bureau of Biological Survey in 1905 and transferred to the Department of the Interior in 1939, which in 1940 became the Fish and Wildlife Service. Further reorganization came in 1956 when the Fish and wildlife act created the United States Fish and

Wildlife Service and established within the agency two separate bureaus—Commercial Fisheries and Sport Fisheries and Wildlife.

The Bureau of Commercial Fisheries was transferred to the Department of Commerce in 1970 and is now known as the National Marine Fisheries Service. The Bureau of Sport Fisheries and Wildlife remained in the Interior. In 1974 the "Bureau" name was dropped and the agency is now simply called the U.S. Fish and Wildlife Service. In 1993 the Service's research activities were transferred to the U.S. Geological Survey.

Today the Service employees approximately 7,500 individuals at facilities across the country. These include the headquarters office in Washington, DC, seven regional offices, and nearly 700 field units with 500 national wildlife refuges and 65 national fish hatcheries.

The Bureau of Indian Affairs

The Bureau of Indian Affairs (BIA) mission is to enhance the quality of life, promote economic opportunity and protect and improve the trust assets of American Indians, Indian Tribes, and Alaskan Natives. This is accomplished through the delivery of quality services and maintenance of government relationships within the spirit of the *Indian Self Determination Act.* It is under the authority of this act that many Native American Tribes have established commercial recreation programs. Most of these programs take the form of outdoor recreation programs such as guided treks, hunting and fishing, and skiing. Tourism is a major source of income for some tribes, while other tribes have developed sophisticated gaming casinos.

Services provided to Native Americans by the **Bureau of Indian Affairs** often focus on managing tribal controlled outdoors-recreational resources. Within the Bureau, the Office of Trust Responsibilities (OTR) provides the services that are required to prudently manage all properties that are held in trust by the US government for Native Americans. And within OTR, the Division of Forestry offers direction relative to the management of forest/range lands, including management plan preparation, forest health assessment, timber sale administration, reforestation/rehabilitation, and wild land fire protection.[32]

The Department of Justice

Established in 1870, this department was created to see to the enforcement of federal laws, supervise federal prisons, provide legal counsel in cases involving the federal government, and provide legal advice for the president and the executive agencies. Although not directly charged with providing recreation or leisure services, the Justice Department's Civil Rights Division enforces federal laws pertaining to the Civil Rights Acts, the Americans with Disabilities Act and Equal Opportunities Act.[33]

The Labor Department

Initially given the task of ensuring the welfare of wage earners, the Department of Labor is charged with preparing the American workforce for new and better jobs, and ensuring the adequacy of America's workplaces. It is responsible for the administration and enforcement of over 180 federal statutes. These legislative mandates and the regulations produced to implement them cover a wide variety of workplace activities for nearly 10 million employers and well over 100 million workers, including protecting workers' wages, health and safety, employment and pension rights; promoting equal employment opportunity; administering job training, unemployment insurance and workers' compensation programs; strengthening free collective bargaining and collecting, analyzing and publishing labor and economic statistics.

The Department of Transportation

The Department of Transportation (DOT) was created in 1966 through the combination of transportation agencies or functions formerly dispersed throughout the government. Its primary charge is to promote and develop safe, rapid, and convenient transportation in the U.S. Currently the department has nine major branches. One of these divisions, the Federal Highway Administration (FHWA) coordinates highway transportation programs in cooperation with states and other partners to enhance the country's safety, economic vitality, quality of life, and the environment. Major program areas include the Federal-Aid Highway Program, which provides federal financial assistance to the states to construct and improve the **National Highway System,** urban and rural roads, and bridges. This program provides funds for general improvements and development of safe highways and roads. The Motor Carrier Safety Program develops regulations and enforces federal requirements for the safety of trucks and buses to reduce commercial vehicle accidents. It also governs the movement of hazardous cargos on America's highways. Safe and efficient highways play an important role in the recreational interests of many Americans. The **Federal Lands Highway Program** relates directly to recreation in that it provides access to and within national forests, national parks, Indian reservations, and other public recreation resources.[34]

The Treasury Department

One of the first departments, the Department of Treasury was established in 1789. It performs four functions: (1) it formulates financial policies (including tax policy), (2) it produces coin and currency, (3) it serves as the government's financial agency, and (4) it is charged with certain law enforcement responsibilities. The treasury department plays an important role in maintaining order in society. Not only does it work to ensure economic stability, it also works to suppress crime. For example, the Bureau of Alcohol, Tobacco and Firearms (ATF) is dedicated to reducing violent crime, collecting revenue, and protecting the public. ATF enforces the Federal laws and regulations relating to alcohol, tobacco, firearms, explosives, and arson by working directly and in cooperation with others. In order for a society to enjoy leisure and recreation, economic and social stability must first be attained.[35]

Veterans' Administration

The Veterans' Administration, established by Executive Order in 1930, operates 172 medical centers, 16 domiciliaries, 228 clinics, and 116 nursing home care units. The Veterans' Administration initiated the idea of recreation therapists in the federal government. Recreation therapists in Veterans' Administration hospitals use a variety of ways to treat individuals who are physically, mentally, emotionally or socially ill, or disabled. The Veterans' Administration uses recreation therapy as a means to improve the quality of participants' lives and to help facilitate their reentry into the community.[36]

Independent Agencies and Government Corporations

National Endowment of the Arts

The government has an interest in promoting an appreciation for the arts by encouraging artists to develop and share their talents as well as helping the general public gain access to fine art. The National Council on the Arts advises the Chairman of the National Endowment for the Arts (who also chairs the Council) on agency policy and programs, and reviews and makes recommendations to the Chairman on applications for grants.[37]

The mission of the National Endowment for the Arts is essentially to foster excellence, diversity and vitality of the arts in the United States, and to broaden public access to the arts.

The following are areas about which the Council advises the Arts Endowment:

- applications for federal grant funds recommended by advisory panels

- guidelines stating Arts Endowment grants-making policy, application review criteria, and procedures

- programming initiatives

- agency budget levels, allocations, and funding priorities

- policy involving Congressional legislation and other issues of import to arts in America.

The Council also recommends to the President individuals and organizations who might receive the National Medal of Arts for outstanding contributions to the arts in America. But, the Council's primary responsibility is to adjudicate applications for grant assistance as recommended by the advisory panels. Renamed the Heritage Conservation and Recreation Service in 1978, this agency was absorbed by the National Park Service three years later as a cost-cutting measure.

The Land and Water Conservation Fund

In 1965 Congress created the Land and Water Conservation Fund (LWCF) to preserve habitat and assure that all Americans have access to quality outdoor recreation. It utilizes a "pay as you go" program using revenues from resource use to support the creation of parks, forests, clean water, and open spaces and to guarantee outdoor opportunities and a clean environment for all Americans.

The Land and Water Conservation Fund receives $900 million each year, primarily from fees paid by companies drilling off-shore for oil and gas. Congress intended for this money to be used in two ways.

- The purchase of land and water areas for recreation and conservation and development of recreational resources open to all Americans.

- Provide federal funds to states to assist in planning, acquisition, and development of needed land and water areas and recreation facilities.[38]

At least 40 percent of LWCF dollars must be used for the federal purchases in a given year. Monies appropriated from the fund for federal purposes are used for the following:

- public acquisition of land and water by the National Parks System, or are authorized by the Secretary of the Interior for outdoor recreation purposes

- public purchase of private holdings within national forests and wilderness areas

- public acquisition of areas for the preservation of species of fish or wildlife that are threatened with extinction

- other acquisitions as authorized by law (e.g., In 1996 Congress authorized and appropriated $9 million to the Palisades Interstate Park Commission for the public purchase of Sterling Forest.)

Roughly 40 percent of funds for the state program are divided equally among the states. The National Park Service then takes into account other factors in distributing the rest of the state-side money, including total population of the state and total population of the state living in urban areas. State-side LWCF funds can generally be used to acquire land, build or repair recreation or park facilities, and provide riding and hiking areas for states or localities. Fund recipients since its creation enhance recreational access and provide wildlife and hunting areas. The LWCF state grant program matches up to 50 percent of the cost of the project, with the balance of project funds limited to state agencies and municipalities.

In the 30 years since its creation, LWCF has been responsible for the acquisition of nearly seven million acres of parkland and open space and the development of more than 37,000 parks and recreation projects. From playgrounds and ball fields to national historical sites, scenic trails, and nature reserves, LWCF has been the key to providing places for all Americans to recreate, relax, and get outdoors.[39]

The Federal Trade Commission

The Commission works to enhance the smooth operation of the marketplace by eliminating acts or practices that are unfair or deceptive. In general, the Commission's efforts are directed toward stopping actions that threaten consumers' opportunities to exercise informed choice. In addition to carrying out its statutory enforcement responsibilities, the Commission advances the policies underlying Congressional mandates through cost-effective non-enforcement activities, such as consumer education.[40]

Tennessee Valley Authority

The "TVA" is a federal corporation, created by the Congress of the United States in 1933 to operate Wilson Dam and to develop the *Tennessee River* and its tributaries in the interest of *navigation, flood control,* as well as the production and distribution of *electricity.* An independent agency of the executive branch, the TVA is administered by a board of three officials appointed by the president. TVA plants generate electricity for over 7 million people living in the southern part of the United States. In addition to providing energy and flood protection, the TVA provides a rich array of recreational opportunities. There are over 100 public recreation areas offering such recreational activities as boating, hunting, fishing, hiking, swimming, and camping. Recreation visitors contribute a significant amount of money to the economy of the Tennessee valley.[41]

Land Between the Lakes National Recreation Area

This is 170,000-acre national recreation and environmental education area located in western Kentucky and Tennessee. LBL's forests, lakes, and rolling meadows provide an ideal setting for camping, wildlife viewing, hiking, horseback riding, and other family activities. Land Between the Lakes attracts more than two million visits a year and is the centerpiece of a $600 million regional tourism industry. It serves as a demonstration in public land management to optimize outdoor recreation and environmental education for the American people.[42]

Boards, Commissions, and Committees

Advisory Council on Historic Preservation

This is an independent federal agency created by the *National Historic Preservation Act of 1966* (NHPA), and is the major policy advisor to the Government in the field of historic preservation. The Council is composed of 20 *members* who are private citizens and experts in the field appointed by the President, along with Federal agency heads and representatives of State, local, and tribal government. The Council provides a forum for influencing Federal policy, programs, and decisions as they affect historic resources in communities and on public lands nationwide, and administers *Section 106* of NHPA. It is served by a small *professional staff* with offices in Washington, DC, and Denver, Colorado.

The council is charged with doing the following:

- advise the President and Congress on matters relating to historic preservation and recommend measures to coordinate historic preservation activities [Section 202(a)(1)]

- comment to Federal agencies on the effects of their undertakings on historic properties [Sections *106, 110(f), 110(k),* and *111*]

- review and make recommendations regarding the historic preservation policies and programs of Federal agencies [Section 202(a)(6)]

- encourage public interest and training in historic preservation and educate parties regarding the Council's activities [Section 202(a)(2), (5), and (7)]

- recommend studies regarding historic preservation implications of tax policy and state and local legislation and assist as to guidelines for such legislation [Section 202(a)(3) and (4)][43]

U.S. Consumer Product Safety Commission (CPSC)

This is an independent federal regulatory agency that was created in 1972 by Congress in the Consumer Product Safety Act. In that law, Congress directed the Commission to "protect the public against unreasonable risks of injuries and deaths associated with consumer products." The CPSC works to reduce the risk of injuries and deaths from consumer products by: developing voluntary standards within the industry; issuing and enforcing mandatory standards; banning consumer products if no feasible standard would adequately protect the public; obtaining the recall of products or arranging for their repair; and conducting research on potential product hazards. In addition the CPSC is charged with informing and educating consumers through the media, state and local governments, private organizations, and by responding to consumer inquiries. Of particular importance to the field of recreation is the work done by the CPSC in the area of playground safety.[44]

The National Park Foundation

This agency can be thought of as the nonprofit partner to the National Park Service. Its primary mission is to do the following:

- help conserve, preserve, and enhance our National Parks for the benefit of the American people

- support programs primarily for education and outreach, visitor information and interpretive facilities, volunteer activities and National Park Service employees

- generate funds for grant making and assistance programs through gifts from private individuals, organizations, and a range of fundraising and marketing activities.[45]

Let's Take Recess. . . .

The federal government plays an important role in ensuring freedoms fundamental to a leisure lifestyle. Furthermore, the government plays an important role in the provision of recreation and leisure resources and programs. Perhaps most visible is the government's involvement in protecting our outdoor resources, but as has been shown, the government is also either directly or indirectly involved in numerous programs that affect the recreation and leisure opportunities of the general public. This high level of involvement is good, but as has been pointed out by many critics and thinkers, there is little coordination and articulation between the various governmental agencies providing recreation and leisure related services. As leisure becomes more of a national issue, it is likely that the importance of an articulating agency will be realized and a cabinet level agency with jurisdiction over recreation and leisure related matters will be established. Such a development would serve to further both the needs of the public and the recreation profession.

NOTES

1. The Constitution of the U.S. is the legal foundation for all laws pertaining to recreation and leisure services.

2. Visit http://www.USGov.edu/ for a directory of U.S. government services.

3. For a copy of the Constitution, visit this website: *http://www.u.s.constitution.*

4. Wasserman, Gary. *The Basics of American Politics.* (NY: Addison Wesley, 1997): 76.

5. To get a sense of the scope of the federal government visit *http://www.lib.lsu.edu/gov/fedgov.html.*

6. Kaiser, Ronald A. *Liability and Law in Recreation, Parks, and Sports* (Englewood Cliffs, NJ: Prentice-Hall, 1986).

7. **Police powers** refer to the power of the state and local governments to provide for the comfort, safety, and health of the citizenry.

8. **Enabling legislation** "enables" local governments to do certain things they otherwise could not.

9. Kaiser, Ronald A. *Liability and Law in Recreation, Parks, and Sports* (Englewood Cliffs, NJ: Prentice-Hall, 1986): 29.

10. Weiskopf, Donald C. *Recreation and Leisure: Improving the Quality of Life.* (Boston: Allyn and Bacon, Inc. 1982): 200.

11. Many governmental agencies have a primary purpose other than recreation, but still provide recreational opportunities.

12. Adapted from Richard Kraus. *Recreation and Leisure in Modern Society.* (Menlo Park: Benjamn Cummings, 1998): 244–276.

13. This information reflects the content of the official State Department website.

14. This information reflects the content of the official Department of Agriculture website.

15. This information reflects the content of the official Department of Commerce website.

16. All of the information regarding programs offered by the Department of Defense was drawn from the official DOD website.

17. Military recreation is multifaceted and for dependents too.

18. Reynolds, Edgar C., Janet R. Maclean, Theodore R. Deppe, and James A. Peterson. *Recreation and Leisure: The Changing Scene.* (Belmont, CA: Wadsworth Publishing Company, Inc. 1979): 134.

19. This information reflects the content of the official Department of Energy website.

20. This information reflects the content of the official Department of HHS website.

21. This information reflects the content of the official Administration for Children and Families website.

22. This information reflects the content of the official Administration on Aging website.

23. This information reflects the content of the official President's Council on Physical Fitness and Sports web-site.

24. Health and wellness is a vital concern of the recreation profession.

25. http://www.doi.gov/ (September 28, 1999).

26. All of the information regarding the DOI was obtained from the official DOI website.

27. *National Park Service Organic Act, 16 U.S.C.1.*

28. NPS contributed to a worldwide national park movement.

29. *Many of the natural wonders of the east and midwest led been lost to private interests.*

30. In 1933, 63 national monuments and sites were transferred to NPS.

31. This information was taken from the official BLM Website.

32. This information reflects the content of the official Bureau of Indian Affairs website.

33. This information reflects the content of the official Department of Justice website.

34. This information reflects the content of the official website for the Department of Transportation.

35. This information reflects the content of the official Department of Transportation website.

36. This information reflects the content of the official Veteran's Administration website.

37. This information reflects the content of the official National Endowment of the Arts.

38. The LWCF provides for the purchase of outdoor resources and aid to the states.

39. This information reflects the content of the official LWCF website.

40. This information reflects the content of the official Federal Trade Commission.

41. This information reflects the content of the official Tennessee Valley Authority website.

42. This information reflects the content of the official Land Between the Lakes website.

43. This information reflects the content of the official Advisory Council on Historic Preservation website.

44. This information reflects the content of the official CPSC website.

45. This information reflects the content of the official The National Park Foundation website.

REFERENCES

Edginton, C. R., et al. *Leisure and Life Satisfaction.* Chicago: Brown & Benchmark, 1995.

Bureau of Land Management, Communication Directorate. "U.S. Department of the Interior Bureau of Land Management." *http://www.BLM.gov.* (13 Jan. 1999).

U.S. Bureau of Land Management, Communications Directoriate. "U.S. Department of the Interior Bureau of Land Management." (13 Jan. 1999).

"Bureau of Reclamation." *http://wwww.usbr.gov/main/index.html.* (13 Jan. 1999).

"American Forces Information Service Defense View Point." *http://www.defenselink.mil/speeches.*

Wanda Jones, Director, HHS Office on Women's Health. "OPHS Office of Public Health and Science." *http://www.dhhs.gov/progorg/ophs/pcpfs.html.* (12 Jan. 1999).

Stanton, Robert. "The National Part System Caring for the American Legacy." *http:///www.nps.gov/legacy/mission. html.* (13 Jan. 1999).

"4-H History." *http://www.4h-usa.org/4h/4h_history.htm.* (13 Jan. 1999).

"Utah Gets Out MSLF Stays In." *http://www.mslf.net/html/ utah_g.* (10 Mar. 1999).

"The Cooperative State Research, Education, and Extension Service." *http://www.reeusda.gov/.* (12 Mar. 1999).

Kraus, R. *Recreation and Leisure in Modern Society.* Santa Monica: Goodyear Publishing Co., Inc., 1978.

Lader, Curt. *How to Prepare for the AP U.S. Government and Politics.* New York: Barron's Educational Series, Inc., 1996.

Maddox, Russell W., and Robert F. Fuquay. *State and Local Government.* (Fourth Edition). Toronto: Litton Educational Publishing, Inc., 1981.

Phillips, Jewell C. *State and Local Government in America.* New York: American Book Company, 1954.

Russell. R. V. *Pastimes the Context of Contemporary Leisure.* Chicago: Brown and Benchmark Publishers, 1996.

Wasserman, Gary. *The Basics of American Politics.* Reading, Massachusetts: Wesley Longman, Inc., 1997.

Wolfinger, Raymond E., et al., eds. *Dynamics of American Politics.* New Jersey: Prentice Hall, Inc., 1980.

CHAPTER 13

The Private, Not-for-Profit Sector

Nelson Cooper and Karla Henderson

Numerous voluntary and not-for-profit agencies serve the leisure and recreational needs of Missouri citizens. Not-for-profit agencies work cooperatively with tax supported parks and recreation departments and with commercial recreation businesses to provide a diversity of leisure services to residents in many communities. An essential characteristic of private not-for-profit agencies is a public service mission. They contribute to the common good through the promotion of altruistic, ethical, moral, or social values. These agencies were usually established by community members to meet significant social needs, and many predate public parks and recreation services in some communities. Programs and services offered by not-for-profit agencies are modified to meet the changing needs of society and clientele.

This chapter is concerned with not-for-profit agencies in Missouri. Private not-for-profit agencies are distinguished from public or for-profit agencies generally due to their funding sources and their heavy reliance on volunteers for leadership. They are subsidized by a variety of sources such as voluntary contributions, the United Way, state and federal grants, fund-raising drives, membership fees, and foundation grants. Generally they are called "private" because they do not typically rely on any type of tax base funding or support. Additionally, not-for-profit leisure service agencies have definable memberships and many provide services exclusively for their members. Others offer services to the public in general. Not-for-profit agencies that are open to membership from the public are sometimes called quasi-public, semi-public, voluntary, or semi-private; and many of them have a strong youth service focus. Churches may also fall into the category of not-for-profit organizations. Legally, many not-for-profit agencies are tax exempt and subsequently have open membership policies. Participation is generally made available to all without regard to race, ethnic origin, or income level. Many of these agencies view recreation as a major component of the service they provide, rather than as an incidental activity.

Opportunities are abundant for employment in Missouri through not-for-profit agencies. Some examples include Special Olympics, Boy Scouts, Girl Scouts, Young Men's Christian Association (YMCA), Young Women's Christian Association (YWCA), Muscular Dystrophy Association (MDA), American Red Cross, Children's Miracle Network, Arthritis Foundation, Easter Seals, Save the Earth, Ronald McDonald House Charities, United Cerebral Palsy,

Adapted from contributors Nelson Cooper and Karla Henderson. © Kendall Hunt Publishing Company.

Missouri Rails-to-Trails, Sierra Club, Leukemia Society, the American Heart Association, and individual churches or communities of faith.

A discussion of the entire spectrum of not-for-profit agencies in Missouri cannot be undertaken in this brief accounting. Therefore, we are selecting some common not-for-profit agencies that we label as voluntary special interest organizations that focus on serving youth, the environment, health, and sports.

Youth-Serving Agencies

Youth are one of the most highly served populations among not-for-profit agencies throughout Missouri. Youth-serving agencies that have had a long tradition in Missouri include the YMCA, YWCA, Boy Scouts of America, Girl Scouts of the USA, 4-H Clubs, Boys and Girls Clubs, Not-for Profit Camp Programs, and Special Olympics.

Young Men's Christian Association (YMCA)

The Young Men's Christian Association was founded in London, England in 1844. A group of workers in a London draper's shop, led by a young sales assistant named George Williams, organized the first YMCA to address the need for Bible study and prayer for people living in the unhealthy social conditions caused by the Industrial Revolution. Williams was a farm boy who had come to London after getting his start in the drapery trade in Bridgewater.

In England during the 1800s, the Industrial Revolution was bringing vice and corruption along with wealth and power to the cities. Hours were long and wages were low. Young clerks worked as many as seventeen hours a day. With no motion picture houses, swimming pools, football fields, lecture halls, or other constructive recreational facilities available during leisure hours, young men often turned to gambling, drinking, and immoral living. The YMCA began in these desperate conditions. The movement grew rapidly and established itself on a worldwide basis.

Today, 972 corporate YMCAs exist in the United States, operating 1,568 branches, units, and camps, and serving over 18 million YMCA members, including many youth. Over 100,000 full and part-time employees work for the YMCA, with 54,000 volunteer policymakers serving on YMCA boards and committees and more than 600,000 volunteer program leaders. Collectively, the YMCA is the largest not-for-profit community service organization in America.

The YMCA is for people of all faiths, races, abilities, ages, and incomes. No one is turned away for inability to pay. Although best known for health and fitness, YMCAs provide a variety of services, including swimming lessons, youth sports programs, massage therapy, residential and day camping, aerobics, child care, programs for people with disabilities, teen clubs, environmental programs, substance abuse programs, family nights, and international exchanges.

The organizational structure of a typical community YMCA relies heavily on a Board of Directors, an executive director, an operations director, and a financial manager. Because the YMCA is a "membership organization," a membership responsibility is identified within the traditional organizational structure. The YMCA recognizes that its quality is directly related to the training and experience of its employees; therefore, it uses a career ladder for employees. Professional Directors within the YMCA organization are members of an association and can transfer their employment from one YMCA to another.

Young Women's Christian Association (YWCA)

The Young Women's Christian Association began in London in 1855 as a Prayer Union. In 1858 the "Ladies" Christian Association was organized in New York City. The YWCA units joined together in 1906 and formalized a national movement. Many cities were faced with the need to provide low-cost housing, good nutrition, educational opportunities, and spiritual care for young women who came to the cities to work in factories spawned by the Industrial Revolution.

Today, YWCAs are located in 300 communities throughout the United States, operating at 1,778 different sites, and serving over 2 million YWCA members, including many youth. Over 18,000 full- and part-time employees work for the YWCA, along with more than 244,000 volunteers.

The YWCA's purpose is based on its creation as a women's membership movement nourished by roots in the Christian faith and sustained by the richness of many beliefs and values. Strengthened by diversity, the Association draws together members who strive to create opportunities for women's growth, leadership, and power to attain a common vision of peace, justice, freedom, and dignity for all people. The YWCA's one imperative is to use its collective power toward the elimination of racism where it exists and by any means possible. Core program themes address empowerment for women and their families by focusing on family life, youth development, health and wellness, and empowerment and community leadership.

Boy Scouts of America (BSA)

The Boy Scouts of America is the nation's largest organization for boys. Its roots are found in England in the life and work of Lt. General Robert Stephenson Smyth Baden-Powell, the founder of the worldwide scouting movement. Baden-Powell served a distinguished career in the British Army and was known for his courage, scouting skills, and tracking abilities. The Boy Scout movement came to America in 1910 with immediate success. The national program is disseminated through groups of states called regions and to local communities through councils and units (e.g., troops, packs, and posts).

Currently, the BSA provides four types of scouting programs designed to prepare young people to make ethical and moral choices over their lifetimes. Cub Scouting is a family- and home-centered program for first- through fifth-grade boys. Boy Scouting is a vigorous outdoor and peer group leadership program for sixth- through twelfth-grade boys. Varsity Scouting is an active, high adventure program for ninth- through twelfth-grade boys. Venturing is a high-adventure activities, sports, and hobbies program for boys and girls ages 14 through 20 years.

The purpose of the BSA is to build desirable qualities of character, train youth for responsible citizenship, and develop personal fitness. The Boy Scout program centers on local units (i.e., troops and packs) and subgroups (i.e., patrols and dens) within each local unit. Sponsoring organizations, such as community clubs or churches, provide trained adult leadership and facilities for weekly meetings. Skill development and leadership training are at the core of the program. Through an advancement program, boys progress through ranks and merit badge attainment while learning outdoor and life skills. In each community, the BSA is funded by the United Way, project sales, special events, registration fees, or various program and activity fees. Because outdoor experiences are at the core of its program, the BSA uses camping as a primary method of achieving its goals. Periodically, international jamborees are held throughout the world. Every four years, a national jamboree is held at Fort A.P. Hill in Virginia.

Career opportunities in the BSA exist in the career development program for entry-level district executives within council structures. In addition, employment opportunities are available in regional offices, camps, adventure base units, and in the national office.

Girl Scouts of the United States of America (GSUSA)

Girl Guides were established in 1910 in England as a result of the popularity of Boy Scouts. Agnes Baden-Powell, sister of the founder of Boy Scouts, spearheaded the movement. Within two years, Girl Guide or Girl Scout organizations were established in Australia, South Africa, Finland, Sweden, Denmark, Poland, Canada, and the United States. Girl Scouts spread to the US through the efforts of Juliette Gordon Low, a native of Savannah, Georgia. Low had become involved with Girl Scouts through her friendship with Agnes and Robert Baden-Powell while she was living in Europe. Although Girl Scouts has changed over the years, the emphasis on ecology and physical fitness has remained central to the movement.

The goals of GSUSA are to help girls develop to their full potential, relate to others with increasing understanding and respect, develop values to guide their actions, and contribute to the improvement of society. The Girl Scout program is offered to girl members through four program categories based upon age group: Daisies (grades K–1), Brownies (grades 2–3), Juniors (grades 4–5), Cadets (grades 6–8), and Ambassadors (grades 11–12).

Boys and Girls Clubs of America

In 1860, several women in Hartford, Connecticut organized a club for boys to provide them with a positive alternative to roaming the streets. Other, similar clubs were formed throughout the United States, and eventually organized into the Boys Club Federation of America. In 1931 the name was changed to Boys Clubs of America. During the remainder of the twentieth century, the number of girl participants and members grew and became a significant part of the cause. In 1990 the organization's name was changed to Boys and Girls Clubs of America. Currently, more than 4.4 million boys and girls are served in 3,700 locations in the United States. More than 40,000 trained, professional staff are employed by the Boys and Girls Clubs of America.

The Boys and Girls Clubs provide young people with a means to develop everyday leadership and guidance. Participants receive information on health and develop physical fitness through a variety of programs.

Sierra Club

The Sierra Club is the oldest and largest grassroots environmental organization in the United States. The mission of the Sierra Club is to explore, enjoy, and protect the planet. The Sierra Club was founded in 1892 by John Muir, who believed, "Everybody needs beauty as well as bread—places to play in and pray in, where nature may heal and give strength to body and soul."

Special Olympics

Special Olympics is an international program of year-round sports training and competition for children and adults with mental retardation. In 1963 Eunice Kennedy Shriver started a day camp for people with mental retardation. Her experiences with her mentally retarded sister helped her to recognize that individuals with mental retardation were virtually ignored by society. She saw that people with mental retardation were far more capable in sports and physical activities than many experts thought. This day camp program demonstrated that individuals with mental retardation not only received benefits from participating in physical activity, but that they learned from participating in organized sports.

The first International Summer Special Olympics Games were held in Chicago in 1968 and attracted 1,000 participants from twenty six states and Canada. Today over 1 million participants and over 500,000 volunteers from 143 countries are involved in Special Olympics. The mission of Special Olympics is to provide year-round training and competition in a variety of sports for children and adults with mental retardation. In addition, Special Olympics creates continuing opportunities for them to develop physical fitness, demonstrate courage, experience the joy of achievement, be included in the community, build skills, and make friends. Families of persons with mental retardation become stronger through Special Olympics.

Volunteer opportunities in Special Olympics include serving as coaches, chaperones, and fund-raisers. The major sources of funding for Special Olympics North Carolina are corporate foundations, contributions from individuals, and special events. Athletes are not charged any fees for their participation.

Other Not-for-Profit Recreation Opportunities

Other hobby organizations, special-interest groups, and club membership organizations are plentiful in Missouri. Their primary purpose is to provide their members with opportunities for socializing and recreation. A wide variety of leisure interests are collectively represented in these types of organizations, such as running clubs, quilting groups, and community service organizations like Kiwanis or Lions. These organizations often provide extensive facilities, services, and programs for their membership and are often labeled as club, society, or civic associations. Usually members pay an initial membership fee and annual maintenance fee. Membership may be restricted, depending on the philosophy and purpose of the organization.

Additional examples of not-for-profit membership organizations in Missouri beyond those previously mentioned (i.e., youth, environment, health, and sports) fall into categories such as social clubs, outdoor sport clubs, boat and vehicle clubs, biking and trail clubs, cultural and hobby clubs, and residential recreation associations. Your local Chamber of Commerce or Recreation and Parks Department may have a list of the clubs and organizations that are available in your area.

Hundreds of private clubs and institutions operate tennis, golf, and swimming facilities for their members and families. Many of these organizations employ part-time help in their seasonal programs. Others have extensive facilities and employ a full-time staff. Many have dining facilities as well as activity centers. Career opportunities in management and professional instruction (e.g., tennis, golf) are available for those interested in this facet of leisure services.

Learning Exercises

1. Investigate a not-for-profit, youth-serving or membership organization in your hometown.

   a. Focus on the following factors: history/origin, organizational structure, facility/resources utilized, capital required for development, operating budget and sources of operating capital, membership fee structure, program/services provided, number of members served, and impact on local economy.

   b. After collecting this information, present an oral report/prepare a written report for in-class discussion.

   c. Compile a list of various special interest organizations in Missouri that represent a specific leisure activity, and report your findings back to the class.

2. Visit a local YMCA/YWCA or other facility-based organization. Interview the executive director. Focus on changing needs of Y members and ways in which the Y attempts to respond within its mission and purposes. In your interview, include questions related to the Y's fund-raising methods, its impact on the local community, and its short- and long-range goals.

3. Write a paper that compares and contrasts the organizational structure and operating philosophy of a not-for-profit organization described in this chapter to those of a municipal parks and recreation agency.

4. Arrange to visit a cub pack, Boy Scout troop, or explorer post in your community or go to a girl scout meeting. You can contact your local Boy Scout Council or Girl Scout Council Office. As a result of your visit, prepare a report of your observations about the meeting, including how volunteers and youth interacted and the kinds of activities they undertook.

5. Interview a Boy Scout, Girl Scout, 4-H, or Boys and Girls Club professional. Ascertain the person's background and motivation for seeking a career in a youth-serving organization. What are the individual's long-term career development plans? What strategies will the individual employ to reach these goals?

REFERENCES AND WEBSITES

Encyclopedia of Associations: Regional, State, and Local Organizations. (2005). Detroit: Thomson Gale.

American Camp Association. http://www.acacamps.org/

Boy Scouts of America National Council. http://www.scouting.org

Girl Scouts. *Official Web site of the girl Scouts of the USA.* http://www.girlscouts.org

The Salvation Army International Home Page. http://www.SalvationArmy.org/

United Way of America: http://www.national.unitedway.org

YMCA: http://www.ymca.net

YWCA: http://www.ywca.org

CHAPTER 14

FACILITATION AND DEBRIEFING

Overview of Facilitation

Facilitation is one of the basic building blocks of relationships in our society. The manner in which we connect to people often determines how people perceive us and how they connect to us. Facilitation is the lost art of human society because of a variety of pressures people feel from all sides. People perceive they have less time than ever before and technology has removed us from one on one interactions on a consistent basis. More now than ever, we are losing the simple techniques needed to relate to others at an alarming rate. This is why one should focus on facilitation. These techniques are as old as humankind; however, they are not being used in or on a consistent format. This is not an academic book telling the studies or the exact history of facilitation but rather a guide of simple to use techniques that have been used in actual settings. These concepts are the result of years of experience of interacting with individuals and groups on a daily basis.

Overview Diagram
Source: Hugh Gibson

Defining Facilitation, Processing, and Debriefing

Throughout all fields which deal with facilitation, people describe it and define it differently; this can be both a strength and a weakness. Furthermore, facilitation, processing, and debriefing have been used interchangeably. The following sections should assist in clarifying those differences. Facilitation should be viewed as the overall umbrella term while processing and debriefing should be critical components. Facilitation should be viewed as a high form of communication while having elements of leadership intervened which are used to assist people to deeper meaning of the activities that they participate in through a variety of experiences.

Facilitation

"A process that covers everything in the adventure program a leader does before, during, and after the adventure experience to enhance the client's reflection, integration, and continuation of lasting change" (Prouty, Panicucci, & Collinson, 2007).

"Facilitation—the process of moving a group or individual toward a desired outcome" (Martin, Breunig, Wagstaff, & Goldenberg, 2017).

Processing

Processing is "an identifiable sequence of events taking place over time" (Johnson & Johnson, p. 202, 1991).

"Processing is a tool for facilitating reflection, dialogue, and individual change . . . " (Dattilo, 2008).

Debriefing

Debriefing—to evaluate. Everyone gets his/her chance to have input. Some debriefs need to be directive, where the instructor talks and the student listens. However, most debriefings operate on the group process model, using the activity as the central focus of the discussion. (Schoel, Prouty, & Radcliffe, 1988).

Debriefing—an experience is relived with all of its emotion and dynamism. Learning comes from doing and making sense of the experience (Martin et al., 2017).

There has been much discussion and disconnect about facilitation as how it relates to other aspects of human interaction such as leadership, communication, or therapy. When do you leave one and enter another? Facilitation is both a noun and a verb (Ewert, 2009).

The Evolution of Experiential Education to Facilitation in American Recreation

The beginnings of facilitation are deeply rooted in the field of experiential education. There have been numerous historical figures which have enhanced facilitation techniques through the field of experiential education. John Dewey, Kurt Hahn, Josh Miner, and Paul Petzoldt all added the techniques we now refer to as facilitation. Experiential learning or education has been widely written about and discussed in the 20th and 21st centuries. To be able to become a better facilitator one must understand the past to improve their future.

Facilitation has received much attention the past couple of decades. Facilitation has evolved within this time of inquiry from Kolb's basic model of facilitation (see page 166) and the more advance model of Priest and Gass (see page 166). Throughout this chapter further inquiry into the different levels of facilitation will be examined. Additionally, a variety of different professions will be identified which could benefit from this resource.

John Dewey is considered by most in the field to be the father of modern experiential education; although, learning by doing is as old as humankind itself. During the 1920s and '30s he fought with the educational system to prove that learning can occur outside of the classroom. This may seem like common sense; however, it was quite controversial at the time (Martin et al., 2017).

This led to Kurt Hahn (1886–1974) developing his own school in Wales which focused on the natural environment as classroom and teacher all in one during the early '40s. Hahn was able to assist people in building character and internal strength where others dare not have gone. Hahn's school later transformed into what we now know as Outward

Bound (OB). The concept was brought to America via Colorado by Josh Miner in 1964 (Ringholz, 1997).

Experiential education got a huge boost in America through OB and the people they were connected to in the field. The first Chief Instructor at Colorado OB was Paul Petzoldt, a man who brought a host of individual and group wilderness setting experiences to experiential education. One of OB's main focuses for individual development to occur was through self-examination, usually after some type of wilderness experience. In the late 1960s Petzoldt wanted to develop a leadership school for the leaders at OB. However, the administrative organization did not really want to go this direction.

This led to Petzoldt using his own finances and those of others to found the National Outdoor Leadership School (NOLS). The focus of NOLS was on the technical skills of being outdoor leaders, such as climbing, rappelling, site setup, risk management, and so forth. Petzoldt once again became at odds with NOLS leadership and went on his own way again. Petzoldt has been noted as a stellar educator, but never the best businessman (Ringholz, 1997).

Another organization to appear on the scene was the Wilderness Education Association (WEA). This organization was created in 1976 and was established with affiliates beginning in the higher education arena. Through these affiliates Petzoldt hoped to teach outdoor leadership skills directly to the people who would be in contact with participants. He designed the 18-point curriculum which emphasized judgment and decision-making (Drury & Bonney, 1992).

This led to different organizations starting in the 1970s that had roots in both OB and NOLS. The first was Project Adventure (PA), which started in the early 1970s, to provide people with the same type of challenge as a wilderness related experience without really going into the wilderness. Through the use of adventure and perceived risk during ropes course or challenge course experiences, games, and initiatives, facilitators were able to simulate some outdoor experiences. PA has been the cornerstone in experiential education with these types of activities. They were also writing and publishing materials anyone and everyone in the field was reading such as *Silver Bullets, Cowstails II, and Cobras* both by Karl Rohnke, in addition *Islands of Healing* was another standard for Adventure Education and facilitation.

Furthermore, Project Adventure developed in response to the popularity of these wilderness type experiences in the 1970s. However, the approach they took was to facilitate experiences that represented the concepts experienced in a wilderness type setting and making it available in a controlled setting. This is where experiential education, challenge courses, and facilitation all intersected because of active facilitation and the use of perceived risk through adventure activities.

Experiential Learning Cycle to Facilitation

The forerunner of facilitation can be traced back to the Experiential Learning Cycle. Kolb's Experiential Learning Cycle model had a great impact upon those who assisted people who were learning by participating in a particular activity. The broad application of Kolb's model is one of the areas that gave it such strength. Kolb's learning cycle consisted of the following: experience, reflection, conceptualization, and experimentation. Once again, the experience is the actual activity being participated in by the individual. The reflection is where the person looks back at what has happened, the conceptualization is where the individual is starting to think about the experience critically also known as the "so what." The experimentation is the time and place the individual is thinking about how this can influence their life or future decisions.

It is suggested by the authors that experiential learning is a direct descendant of facilitation. The early work by Kolb's model of experiential learning allowed for the development of facilitation as its own unique entity. The more experiential learning progressed the more it became facilitation. Now facilitation itself is more than just the result of experiential learning or "learning by doing." Facilitation offers much more insight than just what you observed or what you learned going through the process. Facilitation is the active participation of the facilitator on the experiences of the participant. The facilitator is guiding, shaping, and reshaping what the participant is experiencing or not experiencing. Facilitation is developed on an individual level; what works for one facilitator and one participant may not work for another. Facilitation is individualistic in nature.

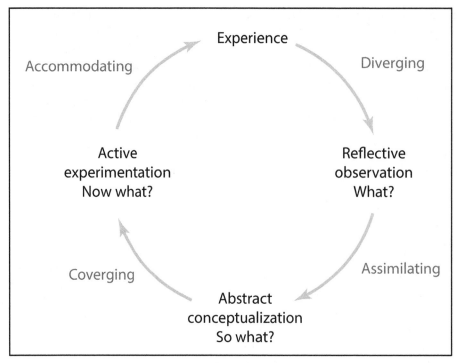

Learning Cycle

Source: D. A. Kolb, 1984, *Experiential learning: Experience as the source of learning and development* (New Jersey: Prentice-Hall, Inc.

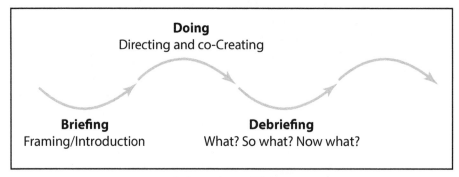

Adventure Wave

Source: Prouty, D., Panicucci, J., & Collinson, R. (2007). Adventure Education: Theory and Applications. Champaign: Project Adventure.

The Adventure Wave

The adventure wave was the predecessor to the five facilitation phases developed first by Gass and Priest. The adventure wave consists of the following: briefing, doing, and debriefing. Briefing is the base information which is needed to participate in the activity that has been selected. This helps guide what the people are not only doing physically, but mentally as well. Briefing has been called the "framing" of the experience. Doing, well that speaks for itself. It is the actual participation in a certain activity. It is

the action of the actual experience. The final step is debriefing. This is when the individual or group looks back and reflects on their experience (Schoel et al., 1988).

Five Phase Facilitation

The five phase model of facilitation includes the following: the briefing, the experience, reflection, the debriefing, and the application. Briefing is usually providing the individuals or group with the most basic information in which to undertake a particular activity. The experience is the actual involvement of the group or individual in a certain activity, usually designed to meet the predetermined goals. The reflection is the prearranged opportunity for an individual to look back on what occurred during the experience. Debriefing is the facilitated dialogue that is intended to assist individuals in garnering information about him/herself and the experience and how this information may affect future decisions or actions. The application is the internalization of the information from the entire process into future experiences in one's life.

Joplin's Five Stage Model

Joplin's five stage model was based in experiential education and Dewey's early work as well. It includes the following: focus, challenging action, support, feedback, and debrief. The focus phase is prepping the participants for what is about to happen. The challenging action is the crux of this model. It has the participants participating in a difficult situation. The support is where the group provides support to each other throughout their difficult task. The feedback comes from each other as well as any outside observers. The debrief phase is when learning is made conscious to the participants. The debriefing must have an element of non-privacy, so the participants are forced to examine things internally (O'Connell & Cuthbertson, 2009).

Eight Phase Facilitation (Priest and Gass)

The concept of facilitation has grown immensely since the early '90s. There were only five areas of facilitation; these five areas of facilitation have grown into eight areas of facilitation which include the following: (1) letting the experience speak for itself, (2) speaking on the behalf of the experience, (3) debriefing the experience, (4) directly front-loading the experience, (5) isomorphically framing the experience, (6) indirectly frontloading the experience, (7) flagging the experience, and (8) empowering people to self-facilitate (Gass & Stevens, 2007). Even though these eight areas allow for more explanation of facilitation and give facilitation more attention which is dually needed, these eight areas feel too cumbersome for the average facilitator to use on a daily basis. For academic discussions all eight have merit; however, in practical application these are not user-friendly.

Most facilitators focus on the facilitation area of letting the experience speak for itself. This leaves a variety of facilitation areas untapped and lacks depth of the activity. This type of facilitation allows the person involved in the experience to interpret the leisure experience, instead of receiving assistance from professional insight. Leisure and recreation are socially devalued; therefore, when you rely on letting the experience speak for itself participants often miss opportunities for growth. Traditionally, people have a limited understanding, or a negative view, of leisure and recreation. Additionally, the concept of debriefing oneself is really not the most desired outcome because people will not learn as much as they could from a possible situation without someone facilitating it for them.

Facilitation Funnel

All the previous models of experiential learning facilitation led to the development of the facilitation funnel. It was developed with the facilitator in mind, so that he/she can garner as much information from a participant as possible in an effort to help him/her. Additionally, this makes it user-friendly so facilitators in any discipline or profession can use it without much modification.

The components of the facilitation funnel include the phenomenon, internal debriefing, external debriefing, and remedy. The phenomenon consists of that event, experiences, or episode which causes the chain reaction of change. The internal debriefing is the scrutinization of the phenomenon through a crucial examination of one's self without outside influence. External debriefing is the most important part of the facilitation funnel. It is through the guidance of an outside individual that one can gain the most from any one experience. All dramatic change in one's life is facilitated by someone not currently having that experience. The remedy is simply the course of action which should follow, in order to take full advantage of what has been identified.

One of the critical differences between this model and others is that the main focus is on debriefing. Hence, why this model has stages out of the four dedicated to debriefing. People should be allowed and encouraged to make sense out of activities for themselves. However, the belief is that more is gained and/or learned when there is someone facilitating the growth. By no means is the facilitator the expert, the person is, but it is up to the both of them to pull out the most of any situation. Very often the remedy process occurs outside the facilitation process. The funnel represents how the information should flow through the system. Once again, debriefing is the crux of the process with internal and external debriefing. The majority of this book is dedicated to the development of facilitation skills which should assist the individual or group with their development through any of the facilitation processes mentioned above. Furthermore, the process has been simplified because in recent years the level of facilitation was more detailed and more cumbersome for practitioners to use on a regular basis.

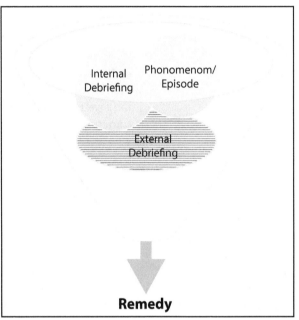

Facilitation Funnel
Source: Hugh Gibson

A comparison of the facilitation funnel and the overlap between other models **Facilitation Funnel**	Kolbs Ex Learning Cycle	Adventure Wave	5 Phase Facilitation	8 Phase Facilitation
Phenomenon	Experience	Briefing Doing	Briefing Experience	Speaking for the Experienced Direct Frontloading Indirect Frontloading Let Experience Speak for itself
Internal Debriefing	Reflection Conceptualization		Reflection	
External Debriefing		Debriefing	Debriefing	Debriefing Framing the experience Flagging the experience
Remedy	Experimentation		Application	Self-facilitation

Debriefing the Crux of Facilitating

The art of facilitation is heavily reliant upon debriefing; it has been viewed by most that one is either born with debriefing skills or not. However, the skills of debriefing can be sharpened and fine-tuned just like any other tool. There may be others with a better tool than you to start, but you can make your tools the best they can be!

Difference between Facilitation and Debriefing

Facilitation is the overall process of relating to others and assisting in working toward their goals. Debriefing is assisting people to get every drop of insight and information about themselves and others from any given situation. The following are a set of techniques to improve your debriefing skills. Through the development of these skills and a lot of debriefing practice your skills should increase.

Know Thyself

The first and most import thing a facilitator should know is, themselves! It will be very difficult to discern whether an issue may belong to a group or individual you are working with or yourself unless you are very aware of your strengths and weaknesses. Furthermore, this is complicated by the fact that you and most everyone around you will change somewhat throughout one's lifetime. It is very difficult to stay the same year after year when life is presenting us with new challenges and skills. Therefore, one of the first things a facilitator needs to know is what makes them tick inside. What are hot button issues for you? Are there things or people that just get under your skin and why? Spend time getting to know yourself so that you can use that information to become a better debriefer.

The following are some questions you need to address internally before facilitating others:

- What is your greatest strength and weakness?

- What natural abilities do you have (for example: quiet, quick thinker, funny, great smile, etc.)?

- What academic skills do you have in facilitation?

- What personal or work skills have you attained in facilitation?

- What experiences from your family (positive or negative) may distort your view about others and their issues?

- What is going on in your life right now that could affect your perception of others' issues?

- Why are you facilitating others?

- What do you need to improve in yourself?

- How do you perceive yourself?

- How do you think others perceive you?

Once those questions have been addressed internally it is generally a good idea to put these down in a format you can revisit from time to time. Your answers should and will change over time, as we all do. By having them written down or in an e-mail you can see how you are personally changing and possibly why. Often the difference between a "good" facilitator and an "excellent" one is the depth in which they know themselves.

Setting the Tone

Setting the tone is critical to working with anyone or any group. First you and the person or people you are working with need to establish a manner in which the two parties (the facilitator and the facilitates(s)) are working together to reach the desired goals. This will be dramatically different depending on the profession, the setting, number of people involved, length of time for session(s), the emotional or psychological depth, and so forth the two groups want to agree upon. The concepts mentioned are just a few of the items that need to be considered before setting the tone of your facilitation session. Setting the tone will either make or break your debriefing session. If people just want to keep it light and you go very deep, it could be emotionally damaging for people. On the other hand, if people are expecting a deep process and you stay at the surface they will be disappointed. Always think about this before you start.

Setting the Environment

Setting the environment is related to setting the tone. However, it relates more to the tangible physical surrounding. Setting the environment starts with the facilitator themselves, such as attire, appearance, language, and how one carries him/herself. Too often facilitators see themselves "above" the people they are working with, the facilitators are the expert, and the others involved are not as "good" as the facilitator. The truth is quite contrary to this point. The facilitator should act as the guide to the experience but not as the experience themselves. Further evidence for this perception is that the person or persons being facilitated are the experts in their own lives and situations and then and only then will make any future work on the issues successful or not. Set up the physical area space, such as temperature, and make sure you have enough space to do what you want. Also, control time when debriefing being way short or way long will affect how people feel about their debriefing process.

Techniques for Setting up a Debriefing Session

Ground rules: Inform everyone of your expectations, where their basic needs can be met, what you need from them, how they can be successful during the experience.

Silence: Do not be afraid of silence. Get used to silence. Most of the time the people you are debriefing will break the silence for you. The silence will usually provide deeper debriefing answers for people.

Know when to speak and when to shut up: Debriefing is a time for your group (or individual) to speak, not you! Try to keep what you say to a minimum unless redirecting or noticing something they did not. Too often new facilitators speak too much during the debriefing. If you are speaking you cannot listen and that is the most important part!

Getting to the root: During the debriefing many times people are going all around the issue without dealing with what needs to be dealt with by an individual or the group as a whole. Be sure you can get to the root of not only one issue, but all the issues needed.

Filter through information quickly: There will be a ton of information being shared. As a facilitator debriefing, you will have to go through this information thoroughly and quickly. Make notes if you need to, but make sure you keep up with highlights and do not miss any valuable nuggets. That one piece of valuable information may be the crux to the entire issue of a group.

Psychological depth: As mentioned in setting the tone, make sure not to go too deep or too shallow into the psychological depth of issues. This could sidetrack the entire debriefing process if you get into trying to solve one person's personal issues. It could also be emotionally damaging to that person as well. Make sure you discuss the depth with the group before the process and if an issue arises check in with the group letting them know when things need to go deeper or need to go shallower.

Debriefing Questions

Use these in any debriefing session. Use them all together or all alone, but please remember to use them at your discretion. The following are just examples of the 5 W's that have been used in debriefing.

- What did you learn?
- What did you get out of the experience?
- What would you change?
- What did the group's reaction mean to you?
- What would that look like?
- How did you come to that conclusion?
- How did that make you feel?
- How did or would that affect others?
- How would you do that differently?
- How would others say you or your group did?
- Why did you do that the way you did?
- Why did it succeed or fail?
- Why have others not done this?
- Where would you rather be?
- Where did things become difficult?
- When did things change?

Activities to Assist with Debriefing
Speaker-Listener Technique Rules

Rules for both people

- The speaker is the person with the floor
- Both people must share the floor throughout the exercise

Rules for the speaker

- Speaker must speak for him/herself with "I" statements
- Speaker must keep statements short
- Allow time to stop and let the listener paraphrase what you have said

Rules for the listener

- Listener has to paraphrase what you hear
- Focus on the message of the speaker, not simply on their words

(Markman, H. J., Stanley, S. M., & Blumberg, S. L., 2010)

Awards Ceremony

This can be a fun and light method for the group to bring some closure or exposure to a variety of possibilities. Each member of the group will receive an award from someone else in the group. Each person can only receive one award and every person must receive an award. If someone is left out of the awards, he/she will feel left out by the group. Make sure to keep it positive or funny to all so that everyone leaves the session feeling good about him/herself and the group.

Journaling

This debriefing technique has been proven by research to be very instrumental in participant learning. It allows you an in-depth look into how your participants are learning and perceiving the experiences around them. This can provide you with information that the person usually would not share with you. Make sure that the people are aware that you will read their information and make sure to keep their information confidential.

Writing a Letter

Very similar to the one above, have the person write a letter to him/herself or another person depending on the situation. This could be a letter that you may or may not read. This is an exercise that can allow the person to work through various issues or concerns. Another version is to have the group write a letter together to address a certain issue or problem.

Dust to Dust

Write down your biggest concern, worry, worst decision, or whatever else may be cathartic for the individual or group. You can put this information on paper, dry erase board, or write it in the dirt. Next have the people completely erase or destroy what they have made. Now let them know that this issue has been officially addressed, they can now let it go, and they are no longer required (or allowed) to address this issue or concern anymore. This allows people to let go of difficult things that may have been troubling them.

Props
Travel Bag

This debriefing prop can be used in a number of ways; however, the best way is to have people use the stuff from your bag or from their own. They need to pick one item and then tell the group why they chose it and what it represents. This is a favorite debriefing activity that will usually yield deeper results than you have ever planned. You can make your own, buy an official Track Pack, or simply use what is in your own gear.

Talking Stick

Have the group get together in a circle. Have a stick and tell them they have one minute to say anything they want or they can say nothing at all, but each person has one minute with the stick. No one is allowed to give up the stick early or keep it longer. Have someone be the official timer. The only person allowed to speak is the person with the stick. One minute never seemed so long.

Things to consider: Make sure the time is the same for everyone.

Options: May vary the allotted time and rules to suit you and your group's needs.

Dry Erase or Chalk Board/Play Dough/Clouds and Trees

This prop can be used in a variety of ways for debriefing. One main way to use this prop is to have people draw or make out their perfect trip, the hardest or best decision of the day, the ideal or perfect group, and so forth. Basically, these props can be used to decipher or explain any difficult or challenging question you wish your participants to debrief. By allowing people a creative means in which to display and discuss their feelings, emotions, or perceptions may allow you better insight to what they are thinking or feeling. Be ready to follow this session up with some deep questions about what they have created.

Rope/Webbing/Yarn

This prop can be used to demonstrate communication and commitment related to the group, following the activity. Create a closed loop with the rope (tie the ends together). Have the participants stand in a circle inside the looped rope. This creates a large hole in which everything (including the participants) is metaphorically in. Both positive and negative items should be addressed, but separately during the process. Within the "space" have all the marginal thoughts or concerns thrown outside the circle. Following the negative "throw out," have everyone step outside the circle then have them place all the good metaphorical ideas, emotions, feelings, and so forth inside the circle. When this phase of the process is completed have the participants cut the circle to allow for all parts of the good to be taken with the participants in the pieces of rope/webbing/yarn.

Things to consider: Be aware of group dynamics related to the group, as well as the "leftover baggage" that might be introduced in this process.

Group Juggling

Ask the group to make a circle. Tell them that the object must be passed around the group with it going to each person only once. Then you start it off by throwing an object to a person in the circle. After it goes around once ask how it went and did they notice any issues. Start it again with the same exact sequence. Keep it going! At this time, you can throw in more objects to pass around to increase difficulty. One of my favorites is the rubber chicken!

This is a great activity to learn people's names. It is also a quick way to assess the group and the different individuals in the group. You will see the leaders, the loudmouths, the quiet ones, the followers, and so forth. Just about anything can be passed: tennis balls, pine cones, hacky sack, pebbles, and so forth.

Things to consider: Make sure to not throw things that could be dangerous. Also, make people toss things underhanded.

Options: You can also just pass one item. Then, you can time the group and ask them if it is possible to shorten their time. Let them discuss it. Then allow them to move if they want. The only rule being, only one person can touch it at a time. There are plenty of other options as well. Have them communicate with sounds as they pass things. No communication via talking. Examine what your group needs and change the activity to suit them.

(Rohnke, 1984)

TP Shuffle

Originally designed for activities on a telephone pole (tp) lying on the ground. These activities can take place anywhere. All you need is a line of some sort (a line in the dirt or sand, tape on a floor, really close rocks, etc.).

There are a variety of activities one can do. The main rule being you must stay on the line at all times. (Also, let them know it is better to fall off the line than it is for someone to be hurt.) Another rule is deciding whether to allow them to talk or not while doing the activities. Have the group line up from youngest to oldest without talking. Line up from shortest to tallest. Have them line up alphabetically according to name, state of origin, or hometown with or without speaking. You can also divide them into two groups and have them face each other. Tell them they must switch places with the other side without leaving the line. Also, time their activity and see if they can beat their own time. Make sure to have only one person move at a time for safety.

Things to consider: As facilitators make sure you are spotting the person moving.

Options: Mentioned above

(Rohnke, 1984)

Sherpa Walk or Trust Walk

The basics of this activity is for there to be a part of the group that is blindfolded and another portion of the group being their leaders.

This can be done inside or outside. Have everyone pair up. Have one person in each group be blindfolded. Have the other person lead. Go through various obstacles as mentioned above. Then after awhile have the group switch and tell the other people to lead the way they wished they had been led. Then afterward discuss the difference of the experiences of the group plus the different kind of leading.

Things to consider: Make sure the people being led are not being teased or being made to look foolish (you will destroy trust, not build it)! Make sure the obstacles are not dangerous!

Options: You can decide to speak or not speak. Communicating only with touch is always a favorite. Then you can switch the roles as well.

Another way to do this activity is for the whole group to be blindfolded and then you pick two people to help you lead them. You can have an elaborate story to get at the meaning you are looking for the group. Explain the story then have your guides assist the blindfolded people in a manner that is safe. You can let the "seeing" decide or let the "blind" decide which way is best to lead or be led. You will see interesting differences. Once the decision has been made, lead the group through various obstacles that are difficult but not dangerous. Use whatever is handy in your setting/environment.

(Rohnke, 1989)

All Aboard

The goal of this activity is to get your group standing on a certain spot for a designated period of time without falling off of it. Once again, this activity can take place practically anywhere. You can use a wood platform, carpet, and tape on the floor, an outline in dirt or sand, a tarp, and so forth. Tell your group that they must stay on the platform with at least one foot on the platform and the other cannot touch the ground. Then inform them they must do this for a certain period of time. My favorite is to have the group sing a verse of "Row, Row, Row Your Boat." Then I usually give them a second platform that is smaller than the first and redo everything. Then I usually have a third platform that is real small and repeat everything.

Things to consider: As facilitator, make sure you are spotting.

Options: You once again can allow talking or not while the group is figuring out how to do it. A time limit is another feature that would allow for a lot of variety.

(Rohnke, 1989)

Human Knot

No props needed for this gem. Have the group gather in a circle facing each other. Have the group put out their left hand and grab someone else's left hand (preferably not the person right next to them) then have them extend their right hand and grab someone else's right hand. Then tell them without breaking their grip move themselves out of the knot into a circle. It could take forever or only 10 seconds. Once again controlling the way they communicate will change the activity greatly.

Things to consider: Some people may have a problem with being this close to other people.

Options: Use socks or ropes as extensions so that people won't have to be so close.

(Rohnke, 1989)

Two Truths & a Story

This activity is exactly like the title. Have the group get together. Tell everyone to come up with two statements about themselves that are true that most would not know. And then come up with a lie about yourself that most would not know. Then have someone in the group tell their three statements and then let the group guess which ones are true and which one is not. After everyone has guessed have the person tell which statement is a lie. Then rotate around so everyone has a chance to participate.

Things to consider: Things could get very personal and sexual quick!

Options: You can have more stories or more truths.

Two (Three) Person Trust Fall

Have two people face each other in spotting stance with arms up. Then have another person get in-between them and make their body real stiff with their arms in correctly. Then slowly "pass" that person from the spotter who is in front to the spotter who is in the back. Start with a small area of transfer and slowly work to increase the length. Make sure to not go too far or too fast for safety reasons. It will resemble a rocking motion. Also make certain to use verbal commands on this one for safety reasons. An example of commands may look like the following:

> Faller: "Are you ready?"
> Each spotter: "Ready!"
> Faller: "Falling"
> Each Spotter: "Fall On"

Things to consider: As with any falling activity be concerned with safety.

Options: Make your own!

(Rohnke, 1984)

Wind in the Willows

Have the group make a circle where everyone is standing shoulder to shoulder and real tight. Have one person volunteer to be in the middle first. Have that person get into falling stance. Everyone in the circle should be in a spotter's stance and shoulder to shoulder. Have the person in the middle make their body stiff. Have the group slowly pass the person around or from side to side. Once again make sure to go slow and start with a small area of transfer at first. Also, use the commands as you do with the two-person trust fall, only difference is that the whole group is spotting instead of just two people. Change the people in the center until everyone has had a turn. Make sure everyone is being gentle and not being rough or dangerous.

Things to consider: Make sure your group has been taught how to spot correctly. When a person's turn in the middle ends make sure to stop *slowly*, don't end their turn abruptly.

Options: Have people sit on the floor, hip to hip, spotting upward with a person in the middle.

(Rohnke, 1989)

Walk with the Angels

Divide the group into two lines that are facing each other with just enough space in-between for someone to walk down the middle. The facilitator should stand at the head of the lines. Each person will take their turn walking through the lines with their eyes closed. As the person walks down the line each person will tell the person something they appreciate about that person or like about him or her. Obviously, the more honest and more emotional and positive you are the better. If you simply state, "You have nice hair" the exercise will be a bust! This should be done with groups who know each other well or have done many things together (ropes course experience, wilderness trip, etc.). Once the person has walked the line they will get back into the line. Everyone must participate to make this go well. After everyone has gone debrief the event. This is usually a great time for some positive insight.

Things to consider: Make sure people don't get bunched up. Keep it positive and deep.

Options: Have people hug each other as they go through. Give people name tags that would allow hugging if they both wanted. The ones that did not want a hug would not have to. Simple "YES" and "NO" tags would work.

Group Hug

Have everyone grab hands. Have the person on end stay still with the line of people wrapping around them so that the first person is in the middle.

Things to consider: Some people will not like being this close.

Options: Have everyone in a circle and put their arms around the person next to them and bring them in close.

Group Lap Sit

Have the group get into a circle all facing the same direction with their side toward the middle. Have everyone move toward the center to make the circle smaller and tighter. Everyone should be very close to the person in front of them. Then have the group all sit down at the same time.

Things to consider: Make sure to spot people.

Options: Once they have done the lap sit, take some people out and then have them sit down without moving. This will emphasize how important each member of the group is.

Group Web (Dream Catcher)

Have the group get into a circle. Take one end of your yarn or rope and give it to one person and hand them the rest. Inform the group that they must hold onto one end of the rope while throwing the excess to someone else in the group; as they throw it have them make a statement. Once the rope has been used up you should have a web. Explain how the web catches all the group's dreams and desires. Then discuss how important each person is to the group. Then have one person in the group drop their rope. Have the others in the group pick up the slack. Then another and another. Then have the group examine the web again. They will see much bigger holes in their web this time. The web is not as effective as it was before.

Things to consider: Talk up the importance of group dynamics and the role it plays. Modify it to fit your group.

Options: The statements could be what they have learned, what they got out of the day, what they want to change, what they have changed, what the group means to them, and so forth. Cut the yarn where each participant is holding onto the web. This can provide a visual reminder for the participants following the activity.

Mr. Potato Head

This is my favorite communication/leadership activity. Have a Mr. Potato Head and get with your group. Make a story to go along with this activity. Make the plot to fit your group. The basics of the activity is that Mr. Potato Head is in pieces (keep the pieces in the same area) and the group is responsible for putting him back together. Ask for one volunteer from the group. Take the volunteer and blindfold them. Inform the person and the group that this person cannot talk and will do *exactly* as the group tells them. This part is crucial. The volunteer will act as a robot with no thought! They will do exactly as the group tells them. Then inform the group that each individual has 30 seconds to tell the robot (volunteer) how to put Mr. Potato Head's pieces back on. Have an official timer to keep track. Each person has a turn and only that person can speak during their turn. As facilitator you will have to enforce that rule.

Things to consider: Don't spread the parts out too far.

Options: Change the amount of time up or down. Increase the number of turns for the group. Allow other people to switch out as volunteer.

REFERENCES

Dattilo, J. *Leisure Education Programming Planning: A Systemic Approach*. 3rd ed. State College, PA: Venture Publishing, 2008.

Drury, J. K., and B. F. Bonney. *The Backcountry Classroom: Lesson Plans for Teaching in the Wilderness*. Fort Collins: The Globe Pequot Press, 1992.

Ewert, A. Wilderness Education Association Conference personal contact, 2009.

Gass, M. A., & Stevens, C. (2007). *Facilitating the adventure process*. In D. Prouty, J. Panicucci & R. Collinson (Eds.), Adventure education: Theory and applications Champaign, IL: Human Kinetics. (pp. 101–123).

Johnson, D. W., Johnson, R. T., & Smith, K. A. (1991). *Active learning: Cooperation in the college classroom*. Edina, MN: Interaction.

Markman, H. J., Stanley, S. M., and Blumberg, S. L. (2010). *Fighting for your Marriage: A deluxe revised edition of the classic best seller enhancing marriage and preventing divorce*. San Francisco, CA: Jossey-Bass.

Martin, B., M. Breunig, M. Wagstaff, and M. Goldenberg. *Outdoor Leadership: Theory and Practice*. Champaign: Human Kinetics, 2017.

O'Connell, T. S., and B. Cuthbertson. *Group Dynamics in Recreation and Leisure: Creating Conscious Groups through an Experiential Approach*. Champaign, IL: Human Kinetics, 2009.

Prouty, D., J. Panicucci, and R. Collinson. *Adventure Education: Theory and Applications*. Champaign: Project Adventure, 2007.

Ringholz, R. C. *On Belay! The Life of Legendary Mountaineer Paul Petzoldt*. Seattle, WA: The Mountaineers, 1997.

Rohnke, K. Silver Bullets: A Guide to Initiative Problems, Adventures Games and Trust Activities. Dubuque, IA: Kendall Hunt Publishing Company, 1984.

Rohnke, K. Cowstails and Cobras II: A Guide to Games, Initiatives, Ropes Courses, & Adventure Curriculum. Dubuque, IA: Kendall Hunt Publishing Company, 1989.

Schoel, J., D. Prouty, and P. Radcliffe. *Islands of Healing: A Guide to Adventure Based Counseling*. Hamiliton, MA: Project Adventure, 1988.

CPSIA information can be obtained
at www.ICGtesting.com
Printed in the USA
BVHW092310170120
569783BV00008B/101